Counseling and Pastoral Care in African and Other Cross-Cultural Contexts

Counseling and Pastoral Care in African and Other Cross-Cultural Contexts

BY TAPIWA N. MUCHERERA

WIPF & STOCK · Eugene, Oregon

COUNSELING AND PASTORAL CARE IN AFRICAN AND OTHER CROSS-
CULTURAL CONTEXTS

Wipf & Stock
An Imprint of Wipf and Stock Publishers
199 W. 8th Ave., Suite 3
Eugene, OR 97401

www.wipfandstock.com

PAPERBACK ISBN: 978-1-4982-8343-4
HARDCOVER ISBN: 978-1-4982-8345-8
EBOOK ISBN: 978-1-4982-8344-1

Manufactured in the U.S.A.   NOVEMBER 8, 2017

Table of Contents

Preface

THE AIM OF THIS book is to present an *approach to counseling and pastoral care in post-colonial indigenous* contexts with a focus on Shona Africans. It opens with a history of the impact of colonialism and Christianity. Colonization and Christianity marginalized the cultural values, religion and the humanity of the native African peoples. This book is based on research originally done for my doctoral dissertation. It has been used in different classes teaching pastoral theology, cross-cultural counseling, pastoral care and counseling, etc. When the book went out of print, the publisher continued getting request for the text, thereby advised me to re-publish the book. Every chapter has been re-worked, with a completely new chapter five. New information on cultural trauma and the fact that the DSM–V now recognizes the impact of traditional healing methods in working with people from indigenous contexts has been incorporated.

The book provides some arguments about how trauma from generations past (colonial) will have an everlasting mental impact if not handled properly or intervened. Cultural trauma from previous generations can be passed on psychologically through written and spoken word and affect present and future generations. Negative beliefs about a people (documented and spoken) can easily be internalized and passed on from old to the young. The impact of colonization and Christianity had such an impact that it has been implanted in some of the people from indigenous contexts believing that they are less human than Westerners. Some missionaries came with the "negative false news" that for an African to be a Christian they had to shade everything African, instead of the Good News that Christ died for all and you did not have to become a European first to become Christian. Even in most contemporary indigenous contexts today, many still struggle with these religio-cultural notions of being less than the Westerners. If there is no intervention, and the young people buy into these negative beliefs, they will start behaving, acting and psychologically convincing themselves that they are less than the Westerners.

Many counselors and pastoral care givers in the African and other indigenous contexts are trained in Western methods and approaches (most textbooks and other written materials) in providing care and counseling. However, the Western world has now realized the limitations of using Western approaches and methods and that "one size does not fit all." Context is everything and it matters. This is to the extend that the new DSM-V (2013) now has a "Culture Specific Syndromes" section which focuses on how certain illnesses can only be diagnosed using certain indigenous methods. For example, there is now an illness incorporated into the DSM-V, from Zimbabwe called *kufungisisa,* which means thinking too much. The translation of this diagnosis does not even do justice to the understanding of this illness for the Westerner, as compared to an ordinary native Shona African person who hears about the diagnosis. The book attempts to shade light for a Westerner who finds him/herself working with an Indigenous person more specifically a Shona African. In addition, it is one to bring attention to the Shona African other practitioners from Indigenous contexts that Western methods and approaches need contextualization in their application and in providing counseling and pastoral care.

Tapiwa N. Mucherera, PhD, Professor of Pastoral Counseling, Asbury Seminary

Acknowledgements

OVER THE YEARS, THERE are many people especially my students who I taught Advanced Cross-cultural counseling who have contributed to the revision of the contents of this text. Contents from this work was originally published in a book that went out print and my publisher encouraged me to re-work the text since there were many requests for the earlier version. I want to thank many of my colleagues in the field of counseling, pastoral care, religion and theology who also gave me feedback after having used the original text in their classes.

I will be amiss if I did not say thank you to my late grandmother who shared with me some of the stories I used as illustrations in this book. Thanks for "home schooling" me even before attending formal education. My mother and my late father, you made me who I am today: physically, you brought me into this world and nurtured me, you were my "home Sunday school teachers" and you worked hard for me to get an education. You succeeded in your two goals, which you vowed you wanted to impact on us as your children: 1). knowledge of Christ as Savior, and 2). knowledge through formal education. These gifts you blessed us with, no one will ever be able to take away from each one of us.

A big thank you to my wife Dr. Bertha Mucherera and my three children Shamiso, Anesu and Ruvimbo and my lovely niece Faro. Your questions and our wrestling with life issues together helped shape this book. Cheri Cowell, thanks for helping edit this work. Ultimately, thanks, glory and honor be to our God the Father through our Savior Jesus Christ and the power of the Holy Spirit!

CHAPTER ONE

Introduction

RELIGIO-CULTURAL REFUGEES: CHANGING, YET ROOTED IN HISTORY

> *Ziva kwawakabva is a Shona saying which translates as, "Know your history, your roots, or from where you came. Only a foolish generation forgets its history. Those who forget their history are doomed to repeat it. Worse still is that generation which not only forgets but mutilates its heritage."*[1]
>
> *You shall always remember and declare before the Lord that: A wondering Aramean was my Father (Deuteronomy 26:5).*

THE SHONAS BELIEVE THAT one's history influences who one is and who one becomes, making the above statement important for them. They believe that one's blood relations (extended family relations), as well as communal interpersonal relations and place of origin, have a great impact on one's life.

Due to arbitrary boundaries imposed by the British in the 1800s, the Shona people are mainly found in Zimbabwe, and in some of its neighboring countries; the Shona are part of the Bantu African group. Bantus are known as such because of their similar history of origin and some common meanings of words in the Bantu languages. Zimbabwe is located on the southern central part of the African continent. Its independence was gained from White (British) minority rule in 1980. Zimbabwe, colonized by the British in 1890, was formerly named after Cecil John Rhodes, and was known as Rhodesia.

---

1. Chidyausiku, *Broken Roots: A Biographical Narrative on the Culture*, p. vii.

This book addresses issues within counseling, care and pastoral theology in the African context, specifically in the urban Shona context. The main argument of this book is that: in order for counseling, pastoral care and pastoral theology to be relevant in the contemporary Shona Christian context, counselors and pastoral caregivers serving in this context must be equipped with a psychodynamic and pastoral theological understanding of integrative consciousness.

The focus is on the contemporary African people, particularly on the upper middle class Shona. The contemporary Shona context requires new and relevant paradigms in counseling and pastoral theology of care to address problems experienced by those living in such a context. One of the main tasks of a counselor or pastoral caregiver is to help people self-define and claim an identity, partially marred by colonization and urbanization.

INTERGENERATIONAL CULTURAL TRAUMA: THE WORKS OF COLONIZATION

From the time when Zimbabwe was colonized as Rhodesia (1890), fears arose among the Shona people concerning the impact of colonization on their freedom, culture, and religious tradition. The British colonization of Zimbabwe was not achieved without resistance. Native indignation (from both Shona and Ndebele people) at the colonization of Zimbabwe resulted in rebellions in 1896 to 1897, formation of political parties, and ultimately a war of liberation (1965-1979), which led to independence in 1980. Mungazi, a Shona historian, notes:

> The first two administrators of colonial Zimbabwe [Rhodesia], Leander Starr Jameson (from September 10, 1890 to April, 1896), and Earl Grey (from April 2, 1896 to December 4, 1898), shared the views of their mentor and financier Cecil John Rhodes (1853-1901), who expressed his belief in the first stage of colonizing all of Africa and bringing it under British rule for at least a thousand years. But it was the rest of the colonial officials . . . from William Milton, who served from December 5, 1898 to October 31, 1914, to Ian Smith, who served from April 1,1964 to March 3, 1979 . . . who lived and functioned by the Victorian views of the Africans and thereby set the two racial groups on a collision course.[2]

2. Mungazi, *Colonial Policy and Conflict in Zimbabwe*, p. xx.

The Victorian view or belief held that Europeans were superior to Africans and Africans were less human than the Europeans. The Europeans were to be lords over the Africans.[3] Wherever colonization appeared, it had an ugly side to its face. Martin Brokenleg, writing for the North American context, says:

> At first glance, colonization might seem like a positive process for creating common interests, fostering cooperation, and harmonizing the diverse populations that have come together . . . Colonization could seem like a laudatory dynamic, but the law of unintended consequences mutates this simple idea into a big mess. Colonization by the dominant culture was a central goal of school, church, and government. These social institutions gave us an interpretation about what has happened to us, why we are the way we are, and what we should become.[4]

In other words, as much as the initial appearance of colonization seemed positive, it resulted in oppression and dehumanization of the Native peoples. Brokenleg goes further to say that the impact of colonization on the Natives in North America (similar to colonization in Africa), has caused intergenerational cultural trauma. He says:

> Traumatic experiences are cumulative. If one generation does not heal, problems are transmitted to subsequent generations. In some form, this cultural trauma affects every Native person. It sculpts how we think, how we respond emotionally. It affects our social dynamics and, at the deepest level, impacts our spirituality. Intergenerational trauma has wounded us deeply. Not a day that goes by in which I do not think about some dynamic related to intergenerational trauma. There were times in my life that I wondered, "Is there something wrong with me? Is there something wrong with us? What did we do to cause all of this to happen?" The truth is there is nothing wrong with Native people; we are perfectly normal people responding to an abnormal history . . . Because trauma has shaped society, there is no escape. It has been hanging around just outside my normal range of vision all my life. Only if I am aware of the deep dynamics of trauma can I cope.[5]

---

3. Ibid., p. 27.
4. Brokenleg, Reclaiming Children and Youth, p. 10.
5. Ibid, p. 10

Lambo, a former Deputy Director-General of the World Health Organization in Geneva, stated that the general African social emotional and economic situation exacerbates the problem of personal identity conflict:

> Within our societies there are presently the following symptoms: collision (and fusion in some cases) of two or more cultures; the disrupting effects of industrialization; the emotional and social insecurity and isolation of the individual who is transplanted from the rural to the urban environment; the assumption of new roles, for example by young politicians, with consequent erosion of authority of the traditional elders. All this is coupled with the accompanying switch in moral and social values in the process of shedding off tribal life, thereby creating what may be termed existential frustration and existential vacuum. But there can be little doubt, unfortunately, that the cultural mingling and imposed or forced acceptance found in Africa now and in the past can often be adverse to painless evolution and have brought in their train psychopathological upheavals and severe conflicts, only too familiar to some of us.[6]

Although Lambo is addressing the general African situation, this is also true of the Zimbabwean context. In the contemporary urban Shona Christian context, the younger and middle aged generations struggle, caught between the Western and the traditional cultures. The "upheavals and severe conflicts," to which Lambo refers, result in personal identity conflicts brought about by the clash between Westernization and the traditional African cultures. Further, as Lambo notes, the problem of living in two or more cultures creates an "existential frustration" and "existential vacuum" in the lives of the Shonas. This generation has become that which I would call "*a generation of religio-cultural refugees.*" What this means is that the Shona African vacillates between two religio-cultures day in and out, and has no roots in any one of the particular religio-cultures. It is a "salad generation," a mixing cultures and/or with no specific culture.

Muphree, a Methodist missionary and scholar who taught at what was known as the University of Rhodesia, quotes an anonymous statement he says was made in London on February, 17, 1962, by someone who was then the leader of the largest nationalist party from Zimbabwe:

> "We do not want to be Europeans; we want to be Africans. The Whites thought that they could destroy our African culture, but

6. Lambo, "Mental Health of Man in Africa," p. 278.

4

they failed; it has only gone underground. It is still there, and we shall resurrect it. We shall take from the European culture that which can help us, but we shall blend it with African culture, and the end result will be *African*."[7]

In today's urban Shona context, it appears that the indigenous culture has not been fully "resurrected," but is going deeper "underground," as the present generations are becoming more and more Westernized. Among scholars of African literature, African cultural studies, and some of the older generations, there was a fear that the Shona culture was disappearing. The expressed fear by the leaders in 1962 is increasingly becoming a reality; the blending for which the older generation had hoped seems to be occurring at the expense of the Shona culture. The younger generation is taking more from the European foreign culture than from the indigenous Shona culture. As will be expounded later, becoming caught between the Western and Shona traditional cultures creates confusion for the younger generation with regard to what it means to be a Shona, resulting in lack of clarity in terms of personal identity.

Gelfand, a medical doctor and professor from the former University of Rhodesia, illustrated this confusion as he researched and wrote extensively on the culture and religion of the Shona people. In a chapter entitled, "The Urban Shona and the Degree of Change," based on a survey conducted in 1970 in the capital city of then Salisbury (now Harare), Gelfand focused on questions related to blood relations, and how modernization impacted such relations. Gelfand asked his respondents about the general impact of modernization on traditional life and culture, especially with regard to those who had moved from rural areas and who were now living in the cities. After receiving feedback from colleagues about some of the weaknesses of his survey, Gelfand reworked the questions and repeated the survey. The following is Gelfand's conclusion from his 1971 survey:

> There is no denying that Western culture has changed the lives of the Shona people . . . There is probably no phase of their lives that has not been affected by the advent of the European. It is often said that they are fast losing their cultural habits and that in the not too distant future, perhaps in a few decades, they will become like the American Negroes [African-Americans] who have long forgotten most of their African forbears . . . If an observer were to enter the

---

7. Muphree, *Christianity and the Shona*, p. 13.

home of a married family and look around he might easily come to the conclusion that the people are fast becoming Westernized.[8]

Gelfand, whose survey occurred decades ago, found that the impact of the Western influence was apparent in the lives of the Shona people. These changes are taking place all over the country, but the greatest impact is readily evident in the cities. One of the main foci then is to address the changes brought about by Westernization to Zimbabwe, more specifically to the contemporary urban Shona context and how its impact is still felt today.

The tension from changes taking place in the lives of the Shona seems to be increasing, particularly in the urban areas. A Zimbabwean daily newspaper, *The Herald*, published the following article illustrating the problems some contemporary urban Shonas are facing:

> Children of some indigenous Black people in Zimbabwe are in danger of losing their mother language and culture. The crisis has reached a point where some school authorities discourage their students from speaking vernacular languages such as Shona and Ndebele, insisting on English, the language of British settlers who colonized Zimbabwe in 1890.
>
> Some parents also forbid their children from using the vernacular language in their homes, demanding English as the household language, 16 years into independence and Black majority rule. According to Dr. John Rwambiwa, a University Zimbabwean Lecturer in Education, some Zimbabweans wrongly equate intelligence with the ability to speak English well . . . To reverse the disturbing trend, a Shona Language committee was launched recently to spearhead the cultural value of Shona . . . The original committee lapsed in 1985, paving the way for Shona to fade mainly among the youths while the use of too much English crept in.[9]

This statement's content and tone clearly show that the changes affecting the young generation are detrimental to the traditional knowledge and understanding of the indigenous culture. The same newspaper, in its Sunday edition, had an article quoting opinions of local Shona writers and other scholars on issues of identity and culture in contemporary Zimbabwe:

> There are fears that Zimbabwean culture is dying and not much is being done to preserve it . . . "Modernity, progress, comfort are good but what becomes of our identity?" asks Chimanikire . . . And

8. Gelfand, *The Genuine Shona*, p. 180-182.
9. Mafuba, "Children Risk Losing Mother Tongue," .

as long as English remains the gateway to anything in Zimbabwe, parents are justified for not encouraging their children to speak or learn local languages . . . When the kids go to school or creche [pre- school], the requirements topping the selection criteria is *kune varungu here /kuno taurwa chirungu here?* (Are there Whites and is English the medium of communication?). "It is enough that Shona is forbidden at the school or creche." Munjeri says local languages are on the verge of extinction . . . Chenjerai also asked why local writers were read more outside the borders, and why Zimbabwe's education system remained colonially biased with teachings of Shakespeare. "Who, among our learned people, can quote my works or Charles Mungoshi's off the cuff, over dinner or drink? But how many lines of Shakespeare are floating in our minds right now? Does that give us a hint as to the faulty nature of our education system? A system which approximates to teaching us self-hate," said Hove.[10]

Self-depreciation, personal and cultural identity confusion, and loss of the traditional language of self-expression are problems and key themes to which the above articles point and with which the contemporary Zimbabwean Shona urban population must contend. Because language and culture are so intimately connected, with the extinction of a language comes the extinction of a culture and a people's identity. Identity and culture are passed on mainly through communication and/or language. This argument about how language, culture, and identity influence one another will be elucidated later.

Shona adults who live in the cities may hold the values of the traditional culture, while at the same time find themselves having to exist at work as a Westerner eight hours of the day. The result is internal incongruence. The same applies to many school children in that they spend close to the same amount of time within an educational system, which is European or Western oriented in its teaching and modeling. The children then return to homes, which may be divided on whether or not to enforce traditional value systems. At home, both adults and children are exposed to Western culture through the medium of television and radio, further blurring the cultural values. It is general knowledge in Zimbabwe that the younger generation listen mostly to popular radio stations, for example, (ZiFM, Star FM & Power FM), which play mostly western music or lots of English songs by Zimbabwean musicians. Their production is mainly in English language, predominately-playing music such as "Pop, Rap, R & B, etc." from

10. Phiri, "Much has to be Done to Save our Culture," p. C1.

7

the West. This young generation has been nicknamed "*masalala*" meaning a salad generation. They have a little of both Western and Shona cultures but can't fully embrace any one of them, meaning they have become *cultural refugees*, not rooted in any of the cultures.

HYBRIDITY AND CONSCIOUSNESS

Young, an author and professor from England, asserts that existence in a context of living between two opposing cultures produces "hybridity" in terms of culture and identity.[11] Young traces the use of the word hybridity from a cultural theorist perspective. He begins with a study of the term, noting it was originally used in biology to discuss the cross-breeding of animals. Later, the word was used in reference to the creation of a new language by mixing two distinct languages. Today, it is being appropriated to describe cultural contexts where two different cultural systems, a traditional and a foreign system, exist without either of the cultures eradicating the other, thereby producing a hybrid culture. In other words, a hybrid is one, which is a "half-breed" of the two opposing cultures or religious values.

Mwikamba, a Catholic priest and lecturer in the Department of Religious Studies at Nairobi University, definition of the modern African person parallels the concept of hybridity, especially among the upper middle class urban Shona Christians:

> The African of today is a 'modern person' and feels the full impact, if not the blast, of 'modern civilization,' and its consequences.
> Many Africans are torn apart: in some sense, they are 'falling apart.' The sense of being 'double,' 'a split personality,' of being 'half,' is felt by many Africans, who are influenced by dualities: 'two cultures,' 'two morals,' 'two value-systems' and 'two world-views': the African and the Western.[12]

What Mwikamba is describing above is similar to hybridity (in the form of naive consciousness, explained later), which becomes dangerous in terms of one's identity when one is caught between two opposing cultural value systems.

Hybridity impacts people differently, creating at least two different levels of consciousness. Both the upper middle class urban Shona people

---

11. Young, *Colonial Desire*, p. 44ff.

12. Mwikamba, "A Search for an African Identity," *AFER–African Ecclesial Review* p. 31, 92.

and the counselor and pastoral caregivers experience hybridity in their everyday lives. However, the counselor or pastoral caregiver, in this urban context, must be a different type of hybrid from the counselee or parishioner, in that they have to possess a different level of consciousness from that of the counselee or parishioner, to be effective. The word consciousness is used in terms of an awareness.[13]

Dooyeweerd, who was Professor of Philosophy of Law at Free University of Amsterdam, wrote about two levels of consciousness, calling them "naive consciousness" and "critical consciousness." He notes that naive consciousness is similar to naive experience:

> ... naive experience is exclusively concerned with the typical total structures of individuality and does not explicitly distinguish aspects, ... this datum [of naive experience] must be converted by philosophy into fundamental problem; it should analyze the typical structures of individuality which also constitute a philosophic problem; modern science breaks up the naive concept of a thing in order to gain knowledge of the functional coherence of the phenomena within special modal aspect ... [14]

Even though Dooyeweerd is writing about philosophical theories and natural sciences, what he is addressing could be applied to everyday life. His above-cited "naive consciousness" is observed when people approach situations uncritically or without any analysis or objectivity.

The second approach, a different level of consciousness, uses critical consciousness or analysis. Dooyeweerd notes:

> ... common experience is called naive and at the same time rooted in an epistemological theory to be refuted by the "critical" analysis of knowledge, our consciousness in the naive attitude is systaltic; the refutation of naive experience is based on the unreliability of sensory perception as to "objective" reality ... [15]

---

13. The word consciousness in this book means a mental or cognitive awareness, being knowledgeable, informed or enlightened about something or processes. Consciousness is similar to the notion of conscientization by Freire, which is the ability to perceive and clarify oppressive situations critically, Paulo Freire, *Pedagogy of the Oppressed*, trans. Myra Bergman Ramos (New York: Continuum, 1983), p. 20. This is different from the psychodynamic use of the word, which refers to emotional processes where something needs to move from the repressed subconscious to consciousness.

14. Dooyeweerd, *A New Critique of Theoretical Thought*, vol. iv., p.164.

15   Ibid., p. 165.

In other words, what Dooyeweerd is saying above is that naive consciousness is not always reliable, and that life situations have to be approached at a level of critical consciousness. The argument is that even in everyday practical situations, critical consciousness is required to work with people in any counseling and/or pastoral care situations among the urban Shona. This hybrid (based in critical consciousness) way of functioning allows the counselor or caregiver the ability to respond to counselees or parishioners from an integrative perspective. Such a perspective allows the trained counselor or pastoral caregiver the ability to critically analyze situations of counseling and care brought to their attention and flexibility in approach, method and world-view.

There is also the question of the difference between an integrative consciousness (critical consciousness) and a hybrid consciousness of the form of naive consciousness. A hybrid of the naive consciousness type refers to the consciousness of one who does not really know who one is, in terms of religious or cultural identity. In other words, a hybrid with a naive consciousness is a person who is in a state of flux. A person with a naive consciousness often has identity confusion, and is not sure about his/her personal identity. The same person may also question whether he/she is Christian or an African traditionalist in his/her religious values and practices.

On the other hand, a person with an integrative consciousness (critical consciousness) is aware of the struggles involved in the process of this identity confusion. A person with critical consciousness uses critical thinking in his/her approach to situations or problems. Paul and Elder define critical thinking as:

> . . . the kind of thinking–about any subject, content, or domain–that improves itself through disciplined analysis and assessment. Analysis requires knowledge of the elements of thought; assessment requires knowledge of standard for thought.[16]

The counselor or pastoral caregiver with an integrative consciousness is trained and educated in a method of analysis that utilizes a critical approach. Such a counselor or pastoral person has the ability to analyze situations beyond the presenting problem. In this book integrative consciousness and critical consciousness will be used interchangeably to refer to the same phenomenon. Critical consciousness requires hermeneutical skills with which to analyze situations that are influenced by two cultures

16. Paul and Elder, *How to Study and Learn a Discipline*, p. 6.

and two religious world-views, and to avoid naive value judgments, which can impede providing adequate counseling and/or care.

In addition, a counselor or caregiver with a critical consciousness has been trained to understand the identity confusion, and may have experienced the identity confusion, and/or has resolved it for one's personal self or identity. To give a simple example, each person who is a counselor or pastoral caregiver is not free of problems in his/her life. Counselors or pastoral caregivers experience life in many similar ways as those to whom they provide counseling or care. It is, however, hoped that the counselor or pastoral caregivers' training enhances their problem solving skills to enable them to help others. The proposition here is that a counselor or pastoral caregiver who has gone through training, has acquired skills to help those still going through the crisis of hybridity and, as a result, has developed an integrative consciousness. The counselor or pastoral caregiver with an integrative consciousness becomes a "bridge to understanding" the cultural, personal, and religious identity confusions of the counselee or care-seekers. A counselor with an integrative consciousness in the Shona African context would need to develop a consciousness and abilities similar to what Sue and Sue say need to be acquired in multi-cultural counseling:

> ... defined as both a helping role and a process that uses modalities and defines goals consistent with the life experiences and cultural values of clients; recognizes client identities to include individual, group, and universal dimensions; advocates the universal and culture-specific strategies and roles in the healing process; and balances the importance of individualism and collectivism in the assessment, diagnosis, and treatment of client and client systems. [17]

In the urban Shona context, many of the upper middle class Christian people may live at the level of naive consciousness due to urban pressures, that is the impact of bi-culturalism, bi-religiousness, or the need to succeed economically at the expense of one's relationships.[18] Those experiencing such identity confusion are experiencing naive consciousness. The trained

---

17. David and Derald, *Counseling the Culturally Diverse*, p. 46.

18. Bi-culturalism means one finds himself or herself caught between the tension of two opposing cultures. There are times the person may culturally move back and forth in utilizing the cultural values, and other times they may simultaneously mix the cultural values. Bi-religiousness, however, is a bit more restrictive, since the traditional Shona religion was condemned as paganistic. Bi-religiouness means one is caught between the tensions of two contradictory religions. There is no room given to move back and forth freely in utilizing the religious values.

counselor or pastoral caregiver practices at a level of critical consciousness enabling him/her to help counselees and care-seekers operating religiously at a hybrid of naive consciousness. The level of consciousness of some of the upper middle class urban Shona people, who seek help from counselors and pastoral caregivers because of identity confusion, is problematic because it's of naive consciousness. As a result of hybridity of the naive consciousness type, one's way of existence is sometimes compromised in a struggle for one's survival. The Shona traditional culture is communal, while the Western culture is individualistic. For example, with the pressure of the colonizing culture to succeed economically, one may choose to sever one's extended family relationships in order to become successful (as defined by the foreign culture). And yet, one may sub-consciously be aware and torn about the importance of maintaining one's extended family relationships. This choice presents a conflict between the western individualistic life style as opposed to the communal way the Shonas live their lives. Ignoring traditional family and community cultural values causes great anxiety. The anxiety is an outgrowth of guilt about purposely ignoring communal values traditionally held dear (e.g., devaluing extended family relations in favor of material gains). In the Shona context, one's relationships are valued over material things; to do otherwise is a source of immense internal conflict, only correctable by righting and reconciling the severed relationships.

Hybridity of the naive consciousness type can also result in one believing in, and placing more worth on, Western values than the traditional Shona cultural values. Many members of the young urban generation may view the Shona traditional values as "an ancient and uncivilized" way of life, while the modern Western way of life is seen as "the civilized way of life." Mwikamba notes:

> Some of the Africans are running from themselves and from their traditional past. This has been caused by the rapid internalization of some aspects of Western culture. Many Africans today believe that the Western value system and world-view are of universal validity, which, as such, must be applicable also to Africa. Many believe that Africans can 'catch up,' and be like people of the 'developed' countries. Such mental enslavement is the worst side-effect of colonialism and of the uncultured missionary activity.[19]

When the modern Western ways fail to provide answers, internal conflict erupts. A person who embraces solely modern values can no longer

19. Mwikamba, "A Search for an African Identity," p. 95.

find answers through the so-called "uncivilized" means, due to pride in an internalized colonial mentality which promotes the attitude that Western values are always superior to those of the traditional Shona values.

HYBRIDITY AND RELIGIOUS PERSPECTIVE

Naive consciousness is also a problem when viewed from a religious perspective. Along with personal identity confusion comes confusion about religious identity. Religiously, the contemporary urban Shona find themselves struggling with issues of Christianity versus the African (Shona) Traditional Religion. There are many religious denominations from which the urban Shona Christians can choose. The religious aspect of this book focuses mainly on those contemporary urban Shona Christians who belong to the "mainline" and the "prophetic/deliverance ministry" churches in Zimbabwe. In Africa, the term "mainline churches" refers to the Catholic and Protestant denominations and the "prophetic/deliverance" churches are the charismatic and modern Pentecostal churches started in the early to mid 2000s. Many of the deliverance/prophetic churches preach the gospel of prosperity.

The other churches in Zimbabwe are African Independent churches. These are often indigenous churches founded and led by the local African people and many are breakaway from the mainline churches. I am of the opinion that Independent churches have done and are trying to do a better job of blending the African traditional religion with Christianity without creating a dilemma or conflict for their members.[20] Bishop Hatendi, a Shona former bishop of the Anglican church in Zimbabwe, supports the idea that most Independent churches are doing a better job of blending traditional and Western religions:

> . . . Shona indigenous Churches are sympathetic and accommodating. They do not regard being a Shona or marrying like a Shona as contrary to the known will of God. While the white-led churches would like to see the Shona 'apologize' for being what he is, the black-led Churches teach that he has no apology to make as regards his culture but to believe in the saving grace of Christ.[21]

20. There are a variety of these churches; some are very fundamentalistic in their practices of Christianity and the others are very accommodative of the traditional Shona religion and culture. This author's reference here to Independent churches refers to those that are accommodative of, and those that try to blend Western Christianity with the traditional Shona religion and culture.

21. Hatendi, "Shona Marriage and the Christian Churches," p. 147. This notion of

Even though Hatendi (who is from the mainline churches) states the above, arguments such as his have not protected the African Independent churches from being criticized as not truly Christian. Daneel, a scholar who has researched and written extensively on Independent churches in Zimbabwe and in Africa in general, says the following about the attitude of mainline churches toward Independent churches in Zimbabwe: "They are often referred to as sectarian, separatist, heretical or nativistic movements. Many of them undoubtedly reveal strong syncretistic tendencies . . ."[22] The term "syncretistic tendencies" refers to the efforts by the African Independent churches to blend Western Christianity with traditional Shona religious values. I am not opposed to the efforts of the Independent churches in blending Western Christianity and traditional Shona religion, but do not advocate reclaiming all of the African traditional religious values without applying a critical analysis of the contemplated necessity of blending each particular ritual. I advocate an effort to reclaim and integrate those rituals and values not contrary to Christian teachings, which can be utilized in the urban Shona churches today. Scholars such as Hatendi and Daneel have already written extensively on the subject of the work of Independent churches in Africa. This is not to say that all Indigenous churches practices are without their own flaws. There is need for a critical analysis to some of their practices since some of the Indigenous churches are being influenced by the new Pentecostal churches in competition for members and in preaching the prosperity gospel. This book will not pursue that debate.

One of the main causes of religious identity conflict occurs when people feel caught between traditional Shona religious practices (condemned as paganistic by the missionaries) and Western Christian religious values. Whidborne, who has written on religion in Southern Africa, and more specifically on Zimbabwe, says this about the Shona's experience of religious conflict:

> . . . the difficulties facing the Shona Christians of balancing the beliefs and practices preached by the missionaries against the more traditional Shona values are often chronic. When a man has an essential function in a traditional ritual he is expected to fulfill it regardless of whether he belongs to some Christian church. The influence of the Shona community has seen many Christians

mainline churches degrading the Independent churches is a topic that warrants its own attention altogether.

22. Daneel, "The Growth and Significance of Shona Independent Churches," p. 177.

surreptitiously accede to the demands of the society against the regulations of the Church . . . converts carried their traditional beliefs to their new faith so that 'the juxtaposition of the two religious systems has not resulted in, nor necessitated, a categorical rejection of either in its totality.'[23]

Whidborne is suggesting that the missionaries created this "chronic" situation for the Shonas by never taking time to examine the similarities between the two religions. Instead, the traditional religion was labeled paganistic by missionaries, thereby creating problems for those who converted to Christianity, yet still honored Shona traditional rituals and practices. Bishop Hatendi affirms this missionary attitude toward Shona religion and customs:

> The missionary's attitude to Shona customs and tradition is often determined by his preconceived image of the Shona. The attitude generally adopted may be to label everything Shona 'heathen' or 'pagan.' Since heathendom and Christendom are ruled by the Devil and Christ respectively, they are incompatible. It is the missionary's objective to substitute heathen faith and practice with Christian faith and practice. It means declaring war on Shona culture. For the missionary 'conversion' means turning away from the Shona culture and accepting the Western way of life. Faith in Jesus as Savior comes last.[24]

This negative missionary attitude toward the Shona culture, religion, and customs, planted in most converts' minds in the mainline churches, has not died away; in fact, it is the basis of the religious values of most of the mainline Christian churches today in Africa, and specifically in the United Methodist church in Zimbabwe.

In the traditional Shona way of life, religion is closely intertwined with culture. Inadequate knowledge of the indigenous language, culture, and religion of the Shonas develops a breeding ground for personal and religious identity confusion among the urban Shona people. The problem of hybridity in culture and religion surfaces clearly in the contemporary urban Shona context when Christians seek counseling or pastoral care on issues which make them feel they must choose between the traditional Shona and the Western culture and between Christianity and traditional Shona religion.

---

23. Whidborne, "Africanization of Christianity in Zimbabwe," p. 33.

24. Hatendi, "Shona Marriage and the Christian Churches," p. 145-146.

PASTORAL THEOLOGY, COUNSELING AND CARE IN INDIGENOUS CONTEXTS

This book, in the field of counseling, pastoral care and theology focuses on counseling and pastoral care in Indigenous contexts, specifically the urban African contemporary Christian context. Traditionally, counseling, care and pastoral theology as practiced in the West, has given scant attention to the historical, traditional religious, and cultural contexts of Indigenous settings. Attention has now turned toward cross-cultural issues in counseling, care and pastoral theology. Clinebell, a North American pastoral counselor, recognizes this when he says:

> Pastoral care (and counseling) must liberate itself from its dominant middle class, white, male orientation and become more inclusive in its understanding, concerns and methods. It must become transcultural in its perspective, open to learning new ways of caring from and for the poor and powerless, ethnic minorities, women and those in non-Western cultures. On a shrinking planet, our circle of consciousness, conscience, and caring must become global.[25]

Augsburger, another North American pastoral theologian, makes a comparable argument about counseling and pastoral care in Indigenous contexts when he argues that people of non-Western cultures encounter pastoral care problems which are sometimes similar to those in the West, but the needs have to be solved in culturally appropriate ways.[26] Direct transference of Western theories to Indigenous peoples, without consideration of the indigenous cultural and religious context, is inappropriate and harmful. For counselors and pastors who will serve in the Shona context, education and training in counseling, care and pastoral theology must incorporate the totality of life, culture, and world-views of the people who are served.

Similarly, a compilation of papers from the Pan-African Conference of Third World Theologians emphasized that, in order to speak to the needs and daily struggles of the African people, there is a need for a new theology, along with a new theological method applied by Africans in the African context.[27] This theology must not get its definition solely from Western theologies, but must be created out of the African people's conditions. Those who have writ-

25. Clinebell, *Basic Types of Pastoral Care and Counseling*, p. 27.
26. Augsburger, *Pastoral Counseling Across Cultures*.
27. Appiah-Kubi & Torres, eds., *African Theology En Route*.

ten from the Congolese, Ghanaian, Kenyan, South African, Zimbabwean and other African contexts have aired the same sentiments about the importance of cultural, historical, traditional religious values for non-Western contexts in dealing with issues of pastoral theology and care.[28] An important component of such a theological development must address how colonization and Westernization changed—or continues to change—communal interpersonal relations, social structures, and personal identity due to the differences in world-views between traditional Shona religio-culture and Western Christianity and culture.[29] This book looks specifically at how colonization impacts counseling, care and pastoral theology of care. While there is literature about education and counseling psychology, there is none that specifically addresses a pastoral theology of counseling and care for the Shona context.[30] The transition taking place in the culture and religion of the African, requires new literature to address the urban African context.

One's historical (and at times geographical) context influences theology, understanding, and internalization of God images, and religious understanding of self in relationship to others, in addition to ways with which to relate to the external world. It is essential for a pastor to understand the changes which have affected the African people before attempting to address any issues pertaining to counseling, pastoral theology and care; since one's history influences one's theological standpoint, self-understanding, and one's approach to pastoral theology, counseling and care.

Indigenous counselors, pastoral caregivers must take caution not to impose their own internalized colonial bondage or the mistaken notion that Western individualistic theories are superior to traditional ones found in Indigenous contexts. Relatedly, counselors and caregivers must not impose solely traditional methods of providing counseling and care, since the African Shona context (having been under the influence of other external forces such as Western Christianity) has changed in and of itself.

Pastoral caregivers and counselors must recognize that they work in an urban African Shona context in which religious, personal, and cultural identity are fragmented due to bi-religious and bi-cultural experiences of

28. See authors such as Hawkes, "'The Relationship Between Theology and Practice; Lartey, *Pastoral Counselling in Inter-cultural*; Mpolo, ed., *The Risk of Growth*; Waruta, ed., *Caring and Sharing.*

29. Communal interpersonal relations implies one gets a sense of belonging and self from existing in good relationship with other humans, creatures, God, Spirit world, living dead-ancestors, and the yet unborn.

30. Chikara and Manley, "Psychiatry in Zimbabwe," p. 341-354.

the urban contemporary African Shona Christians.[31] The contemporary urban Africans find themselves existing in a bi-cultural and bi-religious context: living in tension between African Shona and Western cultures, as well as between African traditional religion and Christianity. In urban settings, the force of economics and urban planning results in encouraging the African Shonas, who are usually communally oriented people, to live individualistic lives which are contrary to their traditional religio-culture.

Living in a bi-cultural and bi-religious context predisposes one to conflictual identities. How did colonization, Christianity and Westernization greatly impact traditional counseling and pastoral care by changing communal interpersonal relations? How can counseling and pastoral care be made effective and relevant to the contemporary urban Shona who have such bi-cultural and bi-religious experiences?

The focus here is on the African Shona people, with a goal to elucidate missing pieces from traditional Shona religious culture in order to develop a Shona counseling and practice of care that is African based. An African Shona pastoral theology of care and counseling refers to a pastoral theology coming out of a Shona context; it is informed by the practical situations Shona pastors must address. As a pastoral theology, it is interdisciplinary as it integrates African traditional religion, culture, African theology, Christianity, and psychology.[32] A pastoral theology of counseling and care is one, which informs, directs, and influences how one provides counseling and pastoral care. As such, pastoral theology is concerned with providing a theory, which informs the practice of pastoral care.[33] Prior to colonization, counseling, care and pastoral theology were present in the traditional Shona context, even though they were not articulated or denoted as such.[34] ma Mpolo notes, from a historical perspective, the direction of pastoral care in Africa:

31. The urban Shona Christians are those who have made the city their home and may occasionally go to the rural areas (villages) to visit. The older people (urban) are often knowledgeable about the traditional religion and culture, while the youth in this urban context may not be well informed about the traditional Shona religion and culture.

32. As much as I agree with Martin that African cultural and religious contexts are diverse and plural, when the word "African" is used it is encompassing of the Shona. Martin, "Out of Africa" p. 47-48.

33. Jennings, "Pastoral Theological Methodology," p. 862-864.

34. ma Mpolo argues that pastoral care, counseling, and psychiatry systems in the Western sense are new in the African context, but these systems have always been aspects of the indigenous African religion and medical system. ma Mpolo, "Perspectives on African Pastoral Counseling," 1.

The African pastoral care movement has been developing three major orientations: the first is rooted in Western theories, seeking to describe pastoral care in European patterns of pastoral theology (Tjega, 1971; Nomenyo, 1971). The second is purely descriptive and academic interpretation of health and healing using African patterns of thought and traditional therapies (Mwene-Batende, 1981). The third approach attempts to integrate both systems and uses African cultures, biblical theology, and Western psychodynamically oriented psychotherapy and proposes pastoral implications for the churches.[35]

I find myself in the third category of integration, in terms of both theories and approaches in providing pastoral care in the urban Shona Christian context. In addition to the above approaches, ma Mpolo recommends "further theoretical and practical research," for the development of a pastoral care that is contextual to Africa, utilizing three dynamics:

(1) the importance of understanding the parishioner's or client's world-view; (2) the importance of incorporating cultural concepts of illness and health into the therapeutic process; (3) the necessity of inserting insight-oriented approaches into the pastoral care and therapeutic process in order to promote emotional release or catharsis, personality growth, and an awareness of one's identity in relation to that of the group.[36]

ma Mpolo's recommendation for further research and development of theories relevant for Africa, and in this case for the urban Shona context, is the goal of this book. Central to this book are the recommendations stated earlier by ma Mpolo to: "understand the parishioner's world-view . . . ," "incorporating the cultural concepts of illness and health," and "to promote . . . personality growth and an awareness of one's identity in relation to that of the group."

Given some of the negative impact which colonization, Christianity, and Westernization had on the Shonas, it is of great importance that counselors and caregivers evaluate their theories and pastoral theological standpoints in light of the contemporary urban Shona context before trying to provide effective pastoral care to seekers of such care. This requires that counselors and pastors be equipped with a new pastoral theological and psychodynamic understanding of integrative consciousness. "Integrative

35. ma Mpolo, "African Pastoral Care Movement," 12.
36. Ibid.

consciousness" means that a counselor or pastor must possess an awareness and knowledge of, or easily comprehend both the Shona and the Western world-views, as well as the blending and/or integration of aspects of Shona and Western world-views in personal or religious identity formation and/or in providing counseling and care.

The urban setting of bi-cultural and bi-religious lives predisposes African Shona Christians to experience anxiety, which tends to intensify in times of crisis. This anxiety forces some of the Shonas to seek the help of the counselor or pastor, since in urban areas the village setting of living in proximity to aunts, uncles, and grandparents from whom to seek counsel no longer exists. With an integrative consciousness, the counselor or caregiver can better assist those with dysfunctional personal and religious interpersonal relations, which result from life in bi-religious and bi-cultural contexts. As aforementioned, integrative consciousness is equated with the critical consciousness, while those experiencing identity confusion are experiencing naive consciousness. The trained counselors or pastoral caregiver practices at a level of critical consciousness, enabling him/her to help parishioners operating at a hybrid level of naive consciousness.

The focus of this book is also on identity conflict caused by changes due to historic events, which took place in the Shona context, mainly the advent of colonization and the approach by which Christianity was introduced by some missionaries. It has implications for the general African population. Chapter Two presents a synopsis of traditional Shona religio-culture and a brief history of the coming of Christianity, colonization, and its impact on contemporary Zimbabwe. Chapter Three presents some of Sullivan's theory of personal identity, interpersonal relations, and anxiety. From the psychodynamic perspective, the work of Sullivan provides insights into personal identity formation. Sullivan is not the only Western theorist who addresses the importance of community in one's identity formation; Erikson and Mead, for example, argue in similar ways.[37] However, Sullivan uses clinical work to show how dysfunctional interpersonal relations are related to anxiety. Sullivan's theory will help a Western counselor or pastoral care-giver to easily connect with the Shona's experiences of community. In his theory Sullivan postulates that anxiety is a result of dysfunctional interpersonal relations, which this gives insight to a Westerner to understand anxiety in the Shona context. In addition, the third chapter briefly outlines Shona

---

37. Erikson, *Identity and The life Cycle*, and Mead, *Mind, Self and Society*, and Sullivan, *Interpersonal Theory of Psychiatry*.

traditional personal identity development and discusses how colonization and Westernization have changed the personal identity development for the contemporary urban Shona person.

Chapter Four presents examples of traditional Shona relational theology and changes, which have taken place due to the advent of Christianity. The goal of the chapter is an attempt to demonstrate that communal interpersonal relations between God, humans, and nature, in the traditional Shona society, are predicated on religion. This chapter highlights aspects of relational theology based on the traditional religion, which can be utilized by the contemporary urban Shona counselor or pastoral caregiver.

Chapter Five is about marriage and family in the Shona context. Marriage processes are no longer just traditional, neither are they purely Western. It is a combination of both the traditional and western practices. Lobola (dowry) is still expected and the wedding day takes all the characteristics of a western wedding with wedding rings being exchanged and cakes, etc. There still is the influence of the African culture in the rituals even though Christian. In other words, the marriage/wedding is a blending of cultures. Chapter Five examines some of the joys and/or pillars of marriage. It also highlights some of the dangers to marriage, especially in this day and age of both couples working outside of the home, something brought about by westernization and urbanization. The chapter also wrestles with issues of polygamy as experienced by the Christian church.

Chapter Six is the conclusion. It lays out some implications for pastoral theology of care in the education and training of pastoral caregivers for the Shona context specifically, and for the field of pastoral theology and care in general. It presents some examples of rituals and religious values needed in the urban Shona Christian churches and in the training of its pastors.

CHAPTER TWO

Colonization and Christianity:
Impact on the Shona Religio-Cultural Identity

KARE HAGARI ARI KARE, which translates as, "The past will never remain the past or the same," meaning, "Change is inevitable," is a Shona saying which influences the ways in which the traditional Shona people perceive life; it addresses life's changes, an issue which permeates the Shona understanding of life and influences the ways in which the Shonas live. Their religious and theological understanding about life's changes reflects this philosophy. Life is a dynamic process, its never static. However, the type of change brought about by Christianity, colonization, and urbanization created alienation and anxiety in the contemporary urban Shona Christians. One reason for this conflict is attributable to the fact that the change was not generated from within, but rather came from outside their religion and culture. The change brought degradation, shame, dehumanization, oppression, and mental colonization. In short, the change was forced on the Shonas in a manner that was violent and imperialistic in nature. This change resulted in the psychological internalization of self-depreciation and the religious and cultural misconception by many Shonas that Western culture and Christianity were better than the alleged "paganistic" and "backward" traditional Shona religion and culture. The following points raised by Maimela make a good introduction to the problems this chapter is presenting:

> For while most African Christians have accepted the Christianity that has been taught to them by the missionaries, and find it attractive in many ways, they are puzzled by the fact that in the historic churches the reality of witchcraft is explicitly denied despite any

experience of it . . . they are prohibited to consult with diviners and medicine men and women, and that the existence of spirits, especially ancestral spirits, are called into question. The consequence is that a large number of African Christians believe that the church is not interested in their daily misfortunes, illness, encounters with evil and witchcraft, bad luck, poverty, barrenness,—in short, all their concrete social problems . . . As to be expected, most Africans often do not know what to do with their new, attractive Christian religion and yet one, which dismally fails to meet their emotional and spiritual needs [sic].[1]

The point Maimela is raising about Christianity's denigration of African traditional religious practices and the Christianity as espoused by some of the missionaries' failure to meet the spiritual and emotional needs of many African Christians is one of the main points this author is raising. Rituals integrating the traditional Shona with Western Christian rituals would better serve the urban Shona Christians. Maimela further notes:

The reluctance of Africans to break ties with the African Traditional Religions lies in the fact that they are wedded to an African world-view in which salvation is understood in terms of relief or help in terms of trouble in this life. Salvation is thus expressed in such acts as healing, driving away evil spirits, empowerment of the individual self, the promotion of fertility, success in life ventures . . . [2]

The church must find ways to better meet the psychological and spiritual needs of the urban Shona Christians by raising questions about relevant ways in which to incorporate some traditional rituals into the life of the church rather than condemning these traditional rituals. One of my basic assumptions, as will be argued throughout this book, is that counseling and pastoral care approaches and methods need to be relevant, and therefore need to incorporate and integrate material from the traditional Shona religio-culture in serving the urban contemporary African Shona Christians.

A synopsis of the traditional Shona religio-culture, showing how the advent of colonization and Christianity impacted the post-colonial urban Shona Christian's religion and cultural personal identity will be presented.[3] Answering the following questions will also help shape and focus the

1. Maimela, "Salvation in African Traditional Religions," p. 71.

2. Ibid., p. 72.

3. Religio-cultural in this book indicates the close connection that exists between the

discussion for this chapter. What is Shona traditional religion and culture? What are some of the Shona traditional beliefs and rituals? What are some of the cultural beliefs about a person's life cycle? What is the Shona traditional social system and structure?

SOCIAL SYSTEMS AND STRUCTURES

Shona family systems are comprised traditionally of the extended families living in the context of a village. The villages are mostly comprised of people who are related either by blood, totems, or marriage. A totem is an animal or something that symbolizes one's family, clan or group ties, or relations. A child has many uncles, fathers, mothers, sisters, and the like, through blood relations or marriage. In many cases, a child is expected to treat all these brothers or sisters (whether by relation, through marriage, or totem) with the same respect as blood brothers and sisters. Respect is given in proportion to age and responsibility; younger people are expected to respect their elders. In addition, people in general are to respect their chiefs, kings, and sometimes medicine people. In most cases, community needs are emphasized over individual needs, since individuals must bring benefit to the whole community. In traditional Shona society, communalism is more important than individualism.

Aunts and grandmothers train girls about womanhood, especially in terms of sex roles. The mother also takes the role of teaching the girls about housekeeping and raising children. The older sisters practice child rearing as they help their mothers with their younger siblings. The uncles and grandfathers teach the boys about manhood and about sex roles. The grandfathers, uncles, and fathers teach the boys about hunting, fishing, ploughing, building homes, and any other duties expected of men in the society. Shona traditional society was, and to a large extent remains, very patriarchal.

Interpersonal relations have a central place in the Shona religion, spiritually and socially, and in the psychological functioning of a Shona. For the traditional Shonas, disharmony in one's interpersonal relations may cause great dysfunction to one's religious, cultural, and psychological or mental stability. If any situation is suspected of bringing disharmony to the self or another, rituals are held to right the wrongs and bring harmony. However,

---

religion and the culture of the traditional Shona people. Religion is part of one's way of life; it is part of the culture.

with the coming of Christianity and colonization, there were changes in the lives of the Shonas in their personal and religious identity.

LIFE CYCLE AND RITUALS

Life cycle and rituals are considered together since the rituals are involved in every transitional stage in the life cycle in African traditional religio-culture. The life cycle of the traditional Shona world is comprised of three realms: the yet unborn, that is the spirit of those who have the potential to be born, whose spirits God has already created; the living, with both the spirit and body intact; and the living dead, whose bodies are dead but whose spirits live on. One's spirit, yet unborn, begins with God the Great Spirit in the Spirit World, is conceived and lives in this physical world, and then returns to the Spirit World after death. Metaphorically, death is seen as a bridge from physical life to the eternal spiritual life. The following diagram from another of my books illustrates this idea.

The Circle of Life

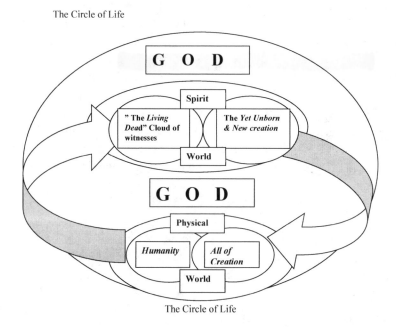

The Circle of Life

As indicated in (The Circle of Life), life starts with God (spirit world), lived out on this earth (physical world), and ends with God (spirit world).[4]

Even in situations not related directly to the life cycle, rituals play a key role in African people's lives. ma Mpolo, writing from a pastoral care perspective, notes how rituals from the African historical religio-cultural meaning can inform today's African society. He notes about ritual:

> Through ritual and its corresponding symbols, people tell and dramatize their stories. The pastoral counselor enters with them in telling and interpreting of such stories . . . . Rituals and symbols play the role of integrating the individual in the community, provided that the community and the individual impart the same meaning to them. Rituals and symbols express the experience that the human being is fully human by virtue of his or her participation in a whole which transcends his/her particular existence and existential situation.[5]

The beliefs and rituals involved are sometimes contrary to Western Christian beliefs. A pastor or counselor who works with the urban Shona Christians must be aware of these contradictions to address effectively issues of anxiety that arise from the contrasts experienced by the urban Shonas in beliefs and the rituals.

There is no idea of hell in the Shona world-view. However, there is the belief that the spirit of an evil person, such as a witch, becomes restless after death. Living human beings have the influence to grant, or not to grant, a dead person's spirit entrance to the Spirit World; if not accorded proper burial, or if a ritual, such as a cleansing ritual, is not performed, the deceased spirit will wander around. The cleansing ceremony, called *chenura*, allows the deceased spirit to join the Spirit World by the elder leading the ritual announcing to the Spirit World to accept the deceased spirit. Because the dead can influence the affairs of the living, they need to be remembered. In order for a positive influence to be experienced, Shonas must remember but not worship, the ancestor spirits as some have suggested.

Shonas believe that one cannot take away a life without having consequences. The avenging spirit, *ngozi*, is believed to hound the murderer's family if reparation and rituals of reconciliation are not performed. If these

---

4. Mucherera, *Meet me at the Palaver*, p. 85.

5. ma Mpolo and Kalu, *The Risks of Growth*, p. 116, 118. Other authors, even though writing from the West, see the functions of ritual in a similar way as ma Mpolo describes. For further discussion on ritual studies see Mitchell, *The Meaning of Ritual*, and Bell, *Ritual Theory*.

rituals are not performed, the avenging spirit (the spirit of the murdered person) will not rest and will cause misfortunes, illness, and death, even to the fourth or fifth generations, until reconciliation or restitution is given. Muphree says of the *Ngozi* spirit:

> This spirit can bring sudden retribution on those who have wronged it in life, and the procedure for placating it can involve a long and expensive process for the offender and /or his family. This process includes one of the few instances in the Budjga [a Shona sub-group] society where restitution is not made simply by the payment of cattle or other property, but requires a long public period of public penance, known as 'Kutiza botso.'[6]

The ritual to resolve issues of a *ngozi* spirit is seen as a justice issue and as a way to restore harmony, reconciliation, and fellowship between and/ or among the families. A death affects the whole community, hence the involvement of the wider community in the *ngozi* ritual of reconciliation.

The next few paragraphs give a synopsis of the life cycle from the time of conception in a traditional Shona experience. Rituals are performed with the aid of the medicine person as soon as a woman discovers she is pregnant. *Kudzinga mamhepi*, a ritual in which the woman is given certain medicines to drink and to smear on her body, bars any evil spirits from attacking the fetus. Daneel says, "Pregnant women are regarded as highly vulnerable. If there is the least indication or mere suspicion of an interfering spirit who wants to cause damage to a pregnant woman through 'gripping her womb,' all sorts of protective charms will be carried around the waist or upper parts of the body."[7]

A Shona woman does not announce freely that she is pregnant; to do so might provide greater opportunity for others to wish misfortune on and/or bewitch her. Traditional Shonas communally celebrate the birth of a child. The child belongs to the community from the point of birth. Protective charms are used since children are considered vulnerable to attack by evil spirits or by other evil powers. In some communities, adolescence is recognized by circumcision or by transitional roles assigned in acknowledgment of the move from childhood to adulthood. For example, the performance of such duties as herding or taking the family animals to the pastures is a task assigned during the transition stage for boys from childhood to adulthood.

6. Murphree, *Christianity and the Shona*, p. 57.

7. Daneel, *Old and New in Southern*, p. 154.

Another important transition in one's life is from singleness to marriage. A Shona marriage is not just between two people, but it is the uniting of two families. One marries into a family. The birth of new children in the family is seen as a sign of perpetuation of the patriarchal family name. Taboos are used to control whom one can marry. In this book, the use of the word taboo is as defined by Raddcliffe-Brown an anthropological scholar, who refers to a taboo as a "ritual avoidance" or "ritual prohibition," a ritual prohibition is a rule of behavior which is associated with a belief that an infraction will result in an undesirable change in the ritual status of the person who fails to keep the rule . . . there is the idea that it involves the likelihood of some minor or major misfortune which will befall the person concerned.[8]

For example, it is a taboo for people of the same blood relations or same totem (plant, animal, or object which is an emblem for a family) to marry. If marriage happens between related people, then a ritual *chekaukama* is performed to officially "cut" the original blood ties or the relationship.

There are no rituals marking transition into the position of "eldership" in a family. As one grows older, through leadership and life experiences, one is expected to gain wisdom with age and to attain the role of the "elder." Death is the final stage or transition from this physical life into the next world, the Spirit World. Burial, memorial, and cleansing rituals surround the death.

Other rituals not associated with the life cycle are related to the land. The rain ritual (*mukwerere*) is performed if the rains are late for the purposes of appeasing the spirits and asking God to bring the rains on time or to save the dying crops. A pre-planting ritual is also performed in which people take the seeds to be planted to the chief and the medicine person(s) in the village, praying through the ancestors to bless the seeds. The prayers in this ritual ask for the rains to fall on time. In addition, the prayers announce to "Mother Earth" that people are about to cut wounds into her with plows, but that no harm is intended. Also associated with crops are harvest thanksgivings, in which the giving of one's first produce from the fields is observed. No one is allowed to eat the first crops until the ritual of thanksgiving has been performed. The cleansing (*Chenura*, mentioned earlier) is performed for the deceased. In all rituals there is always the use of drums, shakers, and dancing. Rituals are important for the traditional Shonas as a person develops through life and for the maintenance of harmony between humans, creation, and the Spirit World.

8. Radcliffe-Brown, "Taboo," p. 73-74.

TRADITIONAL SHONA AFRICAN RELIGIO-CULTURE: A SYNOPSIS

Shona African Traditional religion, practiced by the Shonas before the coming of Christianity and Islam to the continent, is still practiced today in many Shona communities. The religion and culture of the Shonas is communally based. One would find that there are underlying similarities in the general communities of the Shonas, even though variations do exist from community to community. This book will not pay attention to particular regional nuances, rather it approaches the breadth of the general Shona religion and culture.[9] In the traditional Shona context, religion and culture are sometimes intertwined in ways that make it difficult to differentiate between them.

Religion is often compared to the air one breathes or is likened to one's skin: one can't take it off at any moment and one cannot live without it. Mbiti says about the African's religion: "Wherever the African is, there is his religion . . . to be without religion amounts to a self-excommunication from the entire life of the society, and African peoples do not know how to exist without religion."[10] Likewise, there are no known missionaries who have evangelized or propagated the Shona traditional religion. Among the Shonas, religion is part of one's personal human development, affecting who a person becomes. There are no known written Scriptures in the Shona religion. Shona traditional religion is passed on by oral tradition and through practice. As the common African saying suggests, 'You don't teach a child about religion;' rather one learns religion through practice and observation. Just as one grows up physically and mentally, one is also believed to develop spiritually or religiously. One's life is both cultural and religious.

There were prophets and medicine people who played a central role in the traditional religion. Historically, among the Shona, there are three national prophets or 'spirit mediums,' who are said to have prophesied about the coming of the colonizers and missionaries: *Nehanda* (a female), and *Kaguvi and Chaminuka* (both males). These three have attained a position of "multi-tribal" spirits. Songs sung about their prophecies during the liberation war (1965-1979) are still sung today. The three prophesied about the coming of oppression (*udzvinyiriri*), and about how the Europeans

---

9. For further discussion on the regional nuances see Bourdillon, *The Shona Peoples,* p. 16ff.

10. Mbiti, *African Religions and Philosophy,* p. 2-3.

(*vapambepfumi- land grabbers*) were going to take the land by force and move the Shonas into the more barren areas.

A woman or a man can be a medicine person. Traditionally and in contemporary rural Africa, medicine persons have played, and continue to play, a central role as counselors or doctors similar to psychiatrists in the West, while others act as the prophets and priests for the community. These skills are acquired either through training under another medicine person or by inheritance. It is also believed that there are some who get their training from mermaids (*njuzu*). In Zimbabwe today, some medicine people, the *N'angas*, have been incorporated into the health system of the country (ZINATHA- Zimbabwe National Traditional Healers Association). The ministry of health has found it necessary to incorporate some of the traditional practitioners into the medical system. On the other hand, due to the influences of Western Christianity, the church in Africa has not seen the necessity of honoring some of the traditional practices, even by herbalist. It is understandable why the church is suspicious of medicine people since some of them practice magic and others do it just to make a profit. In the Western world today, herbalist have become very popular, but in the African context they are still suspect by the church and Christians are discouraged from consulting herbalists.

THE IMPACT OF WESTERN CHRISTIANITY ON THE SHONAS' RELIGIOUS IDENTITY

This section recapitulates the advent of Western Christianity and colonization in the Shona context, focusing on some of the changes Christianity and colonization wrought in the Shona peoples. Since post-colonial issues continue to affect the formation of Shona personal and religious identity, it is important to note the impact of Western Christianity on the culture.

Daneel notes that the first missionary to make contact with the Shona people was a Portuguese named Father Goncalo da Silveira in 1561. He was also the first Christian martyr to die among the Shonas and was killed the same year he arrived. The Dominicans tried to continue the work of da Silveira without success. Other missionaries, such as Robert Moffat, concentrated on working with the Ndebele, another Bantu group found in the western and southern part of Zimbabwe. Around 1855, David Livingstone also began working with the Ndebeles. A wave of different missionary societies arrived in the area around the time of colonization, during the 1890s.[11] The impact of Christianity and its influence have been felt strongly since the time of colonization.

As they spread Christianity in non-Western worlds, most missionaries believed that the indigenous people, including the Shona people, were paganistic, heathenistic, non-religious, and animistic. This belief by most missionaries was incorrect because non-Western contexts were not without religion or religious practices before the advent of Christianity. The Shonas had a traditional religion prior to the arrival of Christianity and colonization. When Christianity was brought to Africa, missionaries did not seem to recognize that they were also bringing their Western culture. Thus, the Christianity brought to the Shona context was a Christianity heavily influenced by Westernization. Both the colonizers and the missionaries believed that Africans, which included the Shonas, were less human than missionaries. Besides being heathen, the Shonas were believed also to be savages, cannibalistic, animal-like in their behavior, and barbaric. The colonizers and missionaries believed the best thing they could do for such a people was to tame the "animal in the African." One way to accomplish this was to introduce Western civilization; i.e., to provide an educational system that would train the Shona to think as Europeans, learning European history, culture, and literature (such as Shakespeare), and Christianity.

As Whidborne, who has written on religion in Southern Africa, says about the missionary approach: "The European missionaries came to Africa to convert the heathen to Christianity, an attempt at replacing the traditional religion and culture in its entirety by Western Christianity."[12] One of the ways to "humanize" the Shonas was to teach the Shonas "good" religion, Christianity, and to have the Shonas literally abandon their "paganistic" surroundings (the village) and traditional religious practices. Zvobgo, a Shona, who writes about the common missionary attitude and beliefs, says:

> . . . missionaries did not understand, and did not bother to understand at the beginning, the African society which they came to evangelize . . . [they] assumed that Africans either had no religion at all, or that they had only a vague conception of the existence of a Supreme Being.[13]

11. Ibid., p. 26, 186-187.
12. Whidborne, "Africanization of Christianity," p. 31, 64.
13. Zvobgo, "The Influence of the Wesleyan, p. 64.

Zvobgo further quotes one of the missionaries, Shimmin, who wrote: " . . . these people with centuries of barbarism behind them, and with the bias of their moral nature so set against godliness are at first incapable of comprehending even those plain religious facts which appear so self evident to every Christian child."[14]

With missionaries using this type of approach, Christianity subverted healthy aspects of communal interpersonal relations basic to the center of Shona existence, both religiously and culturally. Illustrative of this subversiveness was a change in the understanding of salvation. The Shona traditional understanding of salvation considered it a communal event while Christianity's emphasis was on salvation as an individualistic personal concept. Murphree, a Methodist missionary and former professor at the University of Zimbabwe, notes the changes this notion of salvation had on the indigenous Shona:

> Conversion to Christianity was usually individual, and at conversion the individual frequently moved out of his tribal milieu into the society of the mission station . . . The Methodist emphasis on a subjective personal experience of conversion meant that the church did not attempt mass conversions or baptisms, rather . . . an attempt was made to lay the Methodist Gospel before the Budjga [a subgroup of the Shona] in such a way that they would accept it individually.[15]

Contrary to traditional beliefs, that an individual's salvation meant the family's salvation, individuals could now be saved while their whole family might be condemned by the wrath of God. Bhila, a Ndebele writer from Zimbabwe, arrives at the following conclusion about the activities of missionaries:

> The early missionaries paid scant attention to the complex, and often highly organized, systems of the religious cults among the African peoples. They erroneously believed that Africans "had no concepts of religion," and ascribed their slow progress in converting Africans to Christianity to what they called the "depraved habits" and the low intelligence of Africans.[16]

The problem created by the approach of the missionaries was that it placed the Shona between two conflicting religions and world-views. On

14. Ibid., p. 65.
15. Murphree, *Christianity and the Shona*, p. 9.
16. Bhila, "Trade and the Early Missionaries," p. 39.

the other hand, the Shonas may have liked the new Christian religion and wanted to convert to it, but conversion meant abandoning that which was familiar and was known, since the Shona traditional beliefs and culture were condemned by Christianity.

Several different reactions of the Shonas to Christianity were apparent: rejection of Christianity and its values; acceptance of Christianity; ambivalence towards it; or acceptance with modifications (African Independent churches). For example, most of the United Methodists who converted to Christianity fell in the category of acceptance since this was the norm set by the missionaries. The current impact of missionary Christianity on the Shona can be seen in the United Methodist members who today find themselves caught between Christianity and African Traditional Religion. For example, in *The Central Africa Book of Discipline*, the following are to be adhered to: no smoking, no drinking alcohol, and no polygamy.[17] It is common knowledge that a Shona United Methodist Christian is not allowed to participate in *zvinhu zwechivanhu* (traditional Shona religious cultural activities), such as pouring of libation, rituals of *chenura* (cleansing ritual), or honoring of or praying through ancestors. The prohibition of church members participating in such activities results from the condemnation of the traditional rituals and religio-cultural activities still considered paganistic by the Shona Christian church today.

Chavhunduka, a Shona sociologist and former Vice-Chancellor of the University of Zimbabwe who believes in traditional medicine, in addressing the impact of Christianity and Western education on the Shona Christians, notes that," . . . many people are now ashamed of revealing their connections with traditional practitioners because of the stigma attached to traditional treatment." Chavhunduka relates a story of a sick individual, who claimed to be a Christian, who vowed she would not consult traditional practitioners or medicine people because only "heathens" would do that. A few days later, Chavunduka met the woman at a medicine person's home. When he confronted her about her Christianity, she responded by saying there was nothing wrong with just consulting.[18]

Chavhunduka contends that there is awareness among Shona Christians that certain medicines of traditional practitioners are effective. Nevertheless, the church says Christians cannot use or consult traditional practitioners for such. The Shona Christians, when faced with situations

17. Patterson ed., *The Book of Discipline*, p. 44, 53.
18. Chavhunduka, "Traditional Medicine," p. 134-136.

such as life or death, find themselves in a psychological dilemma about whether to comply with Western Christian guidelines or to engage in Shona Traditional methods.

Chavhunduka gives other examples, from his personal experiences, of people who were strong Christians, and some who were leaders in the church, whom he observed in a struggle between their Western Christian values and their Shona traditional beliefs. He quotes a married couple who were leaders in a church, whom he saw consulting the traditional practitioners. After he confronted them, they responded:

> At least we are doing it publicly. There are many people in the church, including some ministers, who consult these traditional practitioners at night and condemn them in their church sermons. We know some prominent members of the church- 'educated people'-who have been to the *n'anga* but do not want people to know about it.[19]

Even though the Christian church is led by the Shona people, the approach and doctrines have not changed much from what was established by the Western missionaries. The readily noticeable changes include the incorporation of some worship songs composed by the indigenous people, the use of drums and shakers (*ngoma nehosho) respectively*, originally prohibited), clapping of hands, and dancing during worship. However, today, some of the Shona Christian maintains some of the convictions by missionaries, regarding the traditional African religious beliefs and values as heathen. This situation perpetually casts the urban Shona Christians into a dilemma about healing in times of crisis.

The above missionary approach was also used in the educational system with the backing of the church. The missionaries believed that the most effective approach to convert the Shonas was to change both their religious values and psychological awareness of themselves. Father Shropshire, who wrote extensively on missionary activities in the early part of the 1900s in Southern Africa (including Zimbabwe), says:

> Not until a truly Christian and scientific education has corrected the balance of the present Native psychological complex, and enabled the Africans to meet their phobias with a critical mind, giving them confidence in themselves and ability to control their own environment, will they come to see that the wonders of magic and sorcery are not so marvelous as wonders of a truly and

19. Ibid., p. 137.

proportionately developed personality, the more especially if that personality at the same time maintains the true 'abundant' of the fullest Christian life.[20]

Both missionaries and colonizers, as per Father Shropshire's statement, truly believed Bantus (which included the Shonas) were very primitive and were inferior to Europeans. The agenda of the missionaries was to reach and change the mind-set of the children while still young in order for effective conversion to take root. At the same time, the educational goals of the colonizers were not as beneficial for the African peoples. Instead, education contributed to bringing Shona people down to a level where they could be "used" by the colonizer as a tool, and still be reminded that they (the Africans) were inferior to the Europeans, despite the Africans' achievements in the process.

This psychological and spiritual dilemma, in part, is what this book is attempting to address. How does the counselor or pastoral caregiver help people in such a religious crisis? The Shona Christian may believe in the possibility of the medicine person's ability to cure their illness, or might have witnessed others being cured of an illness after having consulted traditional practitioners. When equipped with an integrative consciousness, counselors or pastoral caregivers address these conflictual issues, both personally and communally, for those in crisis, and can challenge the church to re-examine its doctrines and stance. The Western world has now recognized that there are culture specific issues so that the DSM-V now has a whole section dedicated to these types of problems from different cultural contexts.[21] These are known as culture bound syndromes, culture specific disorders or culture specific syndromes. One such syndrome from the Zimbabwean context now entered in the DSM-V is named *kufungisisa*. In the DSM-V it says:

> *Kufungisisa* ("thinking too much" in Shona) is an idiom of distress and cultural explanation among the Shona of Zimbabwe. As an explanation, it is considered to be causative of anxiety, depression, and somatic problems (e.g., my heart is painful because I think too much"). As an idiom of psychosocial distress, it is indicative of interpersonal and social difficulties (e.g., marital problems, having no money, to take care of children). *Kufungisisa* involves ruminating on upsetting thoughts, particularly worries. *Kufungisisa*

---

20. Shropshire, *The Church and the Primitive*, p. 421-22.
21. APA, Diagnostic and Statistical Manual (DSM-V) 5th ed, 2013.

is associated with range of psychopathology, including anxiety symptoms, excessive worry, panic attacks, depressive symptoms, irritability. In a study of a random community sample (Zimbabwe), two-thirds of the cases identified by a general psychopathology measure were of this complaint.[22]

THE IMPACT OF COLONIALISM ON SHONAS' PERSONAL IDENTITY

In this section this writer will make reference to some of the discourse taking place in present Africa, particularly in relationship to the crisis of post-colonial identity. My stand is that colonialism had an impact on the current situation in most of Africa, including the present Zimbabwe. Much debate continues on the question of what post-colonialism means, but the focus here is not on the debate about whether there is anything called post-colonial discourse or neo-colonialism.

Scholars debate about the use of the term "post-colonialism" and this author agrees with the way Shohat defines this term:

> . . . the "post-colonial" implies both going beyond anti-colonial nationalist theory as well as a movement beyond a specific point in history, that of colonialism and Third World nationalist struggles. In that sense the prefix "post" aligns the "post-colonial" with another genre of "post"-post-war, "post-cold war" . . . all of which underline a passage into a new period and a closure of certain historical event or age, officially stamped with dates.[23]

It is up to the reader to categorize this period as post-colonial or neo-colonial. I am more interested in the effects and/or impact of colonialism on Zimbabwe before and after independence. Educational social systems and cultural changes in independent Zimbabwe, caused by the effects of colonialism, are still felt today. These changes are the primary concerns of this writer.

Mungazi, a Shona historian and educator, traces the coming of colonialism to Africa in general, and to Zimbabwe in particular. He suggests that the mind-set of the colonizers or Europeans about Africans can be captured this way:

22. Ibid, p. 859.

23. Shohat, "Notes on the Post-Colonial," p. 101. For further discussion on the debate about post-colonialism or neo-colonialism see also Williams and Chrisman, eds., *Colonial Discourse.*

They equated the universal man with themselves; Europeans were synonymous with the universal man. Although emphasis on the study of man formed a philosophy known as humanism, the concept of humanity excluded the African until studies were conducted to determine whether they were actually human.[24]

Mungazi goes on to elaborate about the mind-set and beliefs of the pioneers of colonization in Zimbabwe from 1890 to the period of independence 1980.[25] He quotes Rhodes, who got a standing ovation in 1896 for saying in a parliamentary debate in Capetown:

"I say that the Natives are like children. They are just emerging from barbarism. They have a human mind, but they are like children, and we ought to do something to develop that mind ... We have to treat the Natives where they are, in a state of barbarism. We are to be lords over them. We will continue to treat them as subject race as long as they continue to be in a state of barbarism."[26]

Even in these modern days there are those who continue to reinforce such racist mentalities by publishing studies claiming that all peoples of African descent are inferior to the White race. A case in point is the publication of authors Herrnstein and Murray who claim that Black people are of inferior intelligence to the Whites.[27] The proclaimed mind set about Africans by Rhodes gave power to all the Europeans residing in then Rhodesia, including to a lot of the missionaries. In this way, Rhodes provided the Westerners with grounds to treat Africans unjustly.

Similarly Huggins, who was prime minister of colonial Zimbabwe in the 1930s to the early 1950s, is quoted as saying:

"We must unhesitatingly accept the doctrine that our superiority over the Natives rests on the color of our skin, civilization and heredity. We must appreciate that we have a paramount monopoly of these qualities and that the natives have been denied them by their primitive culture. You can call me an imperialist of the old school. True imperialism entails paternal government. It would

---

24. Mungazi, *The Mind of Black Africa*, p. 27.

25. Ibid., p. 27, Mungazi discusses the mentality of Rhodes, Huggins and finally Smith, who were Prime Ministers of Rhodesia at different time periods.

26. Ibid. p. 28.

27. Herrnstein and Murray, *The Bell Curve*.

be outrageous to give the Native a so called political partnership when he is likely to ruin himself as a result."[28]

Huggins delivered the above statement as late as 1952. This cultural chauvinistic mentality would continue beyond Huggins' era. Neither did it die with Smith's declaring independence from Britain (Unilateral Declaration of Independence) in 1964, nor Smith's appointment as Prime minister of Rhodesia until 1979. Smith's government deported bishops such as Ralph Dodge (United Methodist) who were arguing for the rights of the Africans in then Rhodesia. The Prime Minister's argument was that he did not believe that the Africans possessed an intellect and culture similar and equal to that of the Europeans.[29]

Much of this mentality and belief in the superiority of the "White man, his culture and language," is still pervasive in Zimbabwe today, even among some of the Shona people, as indicated by earlier quotations from the newspapers in 1996. This mindset is one from which a lot of the younger generation, growing up in the urban Shona context, need to be decolonized. Decolonization means freeing people from the mental oppression of believing in the superiority of the colonizer (the Western people) and the inferiority of the indigenous people in every sense or form.

One of the most noticeable signs of what this author sees as cultural colonialism in the present Zimbabwe is the use of the English language. In schools as well as in homes, children are taught to learn English rather than their mother language. Ngugi wa Thiongo, an author of African Literature from Kenya (a former British colony), correctly argues that one of the tools used by the colonizer to complete colonization was forcing European languages on the colonized. wa Thiongo states that the colonized thought, and still think, that the more articulate one becomes in speaking these colonial languages, the more intelligent one is. He also discusses how African traditional languages were used in traditional African societies to educate children, and how this has changed with the coming of the Western educational system. wa Thiongo wrote:

> Language was not a mere string of words [in traditional society]. It had a suggestive power well beyond the immediate and lexical meaning . . . The language through images and symbols, gave us a view of the world . . . And then I went to school, a colonial school, and this harmony was broken. The language of my education was

28. Mungazi, *The Mind of Black Africa*, p. 29.
29. Ibid., p. 19.

no longer the language of my culture . . . English became more than a language: it was the language, and all the others had to bow before it in deference.[30]

Thus, English became the medium for instruction in schools, even for the teaching of native languages. In Zimbabwe, for example, the Shona language is taught using English. One of the most fundamental implications for the use of English, again, as wa Thiongo observes, is that it produces self-alienation of African children, alienating them from their language of familiarity through the use of English:

> It starts with . . . dissociation of the language of conceptualisation . . . of mental development, from language of daily interaction in the home and the community. It is like separating mind from the body so that they are occupying two unrelated linguistic spheres in the same person . . . it is like producing a society of bodiless heads and headless bodies.[31]

Thus, colonization, as per wa Thiongo's statement, produces divided cultural and personal identities in the African. I concur with wa Thiongo and believe that language influences one's understanding of a culture, one's epistemology, and that it is the medium through which culture and epistemology are communicated. Because the instruction of the children is in English, the Western educational system exacerbates identity conflict for children who are not fully cognizant of their Shona language, culture, and history.

Memmi, a Tunisian Jew who wrote about anti-colonialism and the impact of colonialism on both the colonizer and the colonized, airs similar sentiments about the implications of the type of colonial education for the colonized. He notes:

> The memory, which is assigned him is certainly not of his people. The history which is taught him is not his own. He knows who Colbert or Cromwell was, but he learns nothing about Khazanadar [local hero] . . . Everything seems to have taken place out of his country . . . The books talk to him of a world which in no way reminds him of his own . . . [32]

---

30. Thiongo, *Decolonizing the Mind*, p. 11.

31. Ibid., p. 28.

32. Memmi, *The Colonizer*, p. 105.

Memmi also makes an insightful observation on the use of a second language in the education system of the colonized, and the mental or psychological effects of the second language on the same. He asserts:

> Possession of two languages is not merely a matter of having two tools, but actually means participation in two psychical and cultural realms. Here, the two worlds symbolized and conveyed by the two tongues are in conflict; they are those of the colonizer and the colonized.
>
> Furthermore, the colonized's mother tongue, that which is sustained by his feelings, emotions and dreams, that in which his tenderness and wonder are expressed, thus that which holds the greatest emotional impact, is precisely the one which is least valued. It has no stature in the country or in the concert of peoples. If he wants to obtain a job . . . exist in the community and the world, he must first bow to the language of his masters. In the linguistic conflict within the colonized, his mother tongue is that which is crushed. He himself sets about discarding this infirm language, hiding it from the sight of strangers.[33]

This above statement by Memmi appears to be a prophecy fulfilled in the Shona context as per newspaper articles from 1996 quoted earlier. Among the urban Shonas, the impact of colonization is evidenced by the use of English language in schools, businesses, and generally by the majority of the younger generation. Colonization has stripped the younger generation of the pride of using or knowing their mother tongue. Memmi further addresses the devastating psychological effects of colonization on the personal or self-identity of the colonized:

> The first attempt of the colonized is to change his condition by changing his skin . . . . The first ambition of the colonized is to become equal to that splendid model and to resemble him [colonizer] to the point of disappearing in him . . . Rejection of self and love of another are common to candidates for assimilation. Moreover, the two components of this attempt at liberation are closely tied. Love of the colonizer is subtended by a complex of feelings ranging from shame to self-hate.[34]

Memmi is saying that the colonized internalize the idea that to be fully human, they have to lose cultural identity and take the identity of the

33. Ibid., p. 107.
34. Ibid., p. 120-121.

colonizer. The colonized have to literally change, not just the skin color, but their mental or psychological functioning as well. He contends that colonization spiritually destroys, distorts, and kills even the colonized. Memmi observes:

> We have seen that colonization materially kills the colonized. It must be added that it kills him spiritually. Colonization distorts relationships, destroys or petrifies institutions, and corrupts men, both colonizer and colonized. To live the colonized needs to do away with colonization. To become a man, he must do away with the colonized being he has become . . . He must conquer himself and be free in relation to the religion of his group which he can retain or reject, but he must stop existing only through it. Finally, he must cease defining himself through the categories of colonizers.[35]

Many other writers on post-colonial discourse, such as Frantz Fanon, Aime Cesaire, and Ashis Nandi, have also written about the effects of colonialism on the colonized. Despite the different ways in which they approach this subject, they all seem to agree that people in former colonial countries need to move away from their colonial, oppressed, colonized minds to be whole again.[36]

In his writings, Fanon, a Martinique-born, black psychiatrist, social scientist and anti-colonialist has as his, main concern and focus the psychological destruction of the identity and consciousness of the colonized people by colonialism and its systems. He argues that physical domination in the colonized countries is self-evident. However, the more dangerous and pervasive domination, Fanon points out, is the psychological and mental domination. He states that physical domination can be removed by a revolution or other means, but mental and psychological oppression is too complex to remove because it is ingrained in the psyche and conscience of the colonized. Even if the colonizer was to leave, mental colonization remains in place because it outlives the physical presence of the colonizer.[37] Fanon aptly observes that colonialism creates an "inferiority complex" in the natives which results in "the so called dependency complex of the colonized people." He argues however, that the colonized were not born

35. Ibid., p. 151-152.

36. Nandi, *The Intimate Enemy*, see also Memmi, *Colonizer*, and Fanon, *The Wretched*, Cesaire, *Discourse on Colonialism*.

37. Fanon, *The Wretched*, p. 210ff.

with this complex; this is something that came as a result of the colonial system.[38] Fanon also notes the detrimental effects of colonization:

> Perhaps we have not sufficiently demonstrated that colonialism is not simply content to impose its rule upon the present and the future of a dominated country. Colonialism is not satisfied merely with hiding a people in its grip and emptying the native's brain of all form and content. By a kind of perverted logic, it turns to the past of the oppressed people, and distorts, disfigures and destroys it. This work of devaluing pre-colonial history takes on dialectical significance today . . . The effect consciously sought by colonialism was to drive into the natives' heads the idea that if the settlers were to leave, they would at once fall back into barbarism, degradation and beastiality.[39]

For Fanon, colonialism creates an empty shell mentally in the colonized. What then is replaced in this shell is the colonized's belief in the superiority of the colonizer. Part of this belief is that, if the colonizer was to leave, the colonized would not be able to function on their own. The basis for the identity of the colonized is the colonizer's history, culture, language, and religion. Colonialism creates self-alienation and identity dissonance as well as confusion about the self.

Fanon goes on to describe what the process of overcoming a colonial mentality might be. He says that the natives, especially the educated, start by trying to assimilate or emulate the European. This assimilation is even reflected by the type of writings they produce. In the process of emulating the Westerner, the indigenous people lose a lot of their cultural values but are not consciously aware that this is taking place. This initial stage described above he calls "unqualified assimilation."

When a native is disturbed by the unfulfilling processes of assimilation, s/he then tries to remember who s/he is and this marks the emergence of Fanon's stage two.

This period of creative work approximately corresponds to that immersion which we have just described. But since the native is not a part of his people, since he only has exterior relations with his people, he is content to recall their life only. Past happenings of the bygone days of his childhood will be brought up out of the depth of his memory . . . but often

---

38. Fanon, *Black Skin*, p. 83ff.
39. Fanon, "On National Culture," p. 37.

too it is symptomatic of a period of distress and difficulty, where death is experienced and disgust too. We spew ourselves up . . . [40]

What Fanon addresses is similar to what is called in this book, a person's experience of the hybridity in the form of naive consciousness. A crisis results in someone being disturbed, disgusted, and distressed ultimately eventuating in a search for identity. The third and final stage of overcoming colonization is what Fanon calls "the fighting stage."

. . . the native, after having tried to lose himself in the people and with the people, will in contrary shake the people. Instead of according the people's lethargy an honoured place in his esteem, he turns himself into an awakener of the people, hence comes a fighting literature, revolutionary literature and a national literature. [41]

This third stage is what this writer hopes a counselor or pastoral caregiver with an integrated consciousness possesses. The goal is for this individual to be fully aware of who s/he is, to be aware of the two cultures to which s/he has been exposed, and to use this integrative (critical) consciousness to help awaken and challenge the status quo.

Cesaire, the best known poet in the French Caribbean, and a writer as well as an elected politician, says the following about colonialism:

Between colonizer and colonized there is room only for forced labor, intimidation, pressure, the police, taxation, theft, rape, compulsory crops, contempt, mistrust, arrogance, self-complacency, swinishness, brainless elites, degraded masses. No human contact, but relations of domination and submission which turn the colonizing man into a classroom monitor . . . slave driver, and the indigenous man into an instrument of production.

My turn to state an equation: colonization = "thing-ification." . . . I am talking about societies drained of essence, cultures trampled underfoot, institutions undermined, lands confiscated, religions smashed and magnificent artistic creations destroyed, extraordinary possibilities wiped out. [42]

Cesaire also makes a similar argument to Fanon's that the Europeans or the colonizers believed and were convinced that the colonized people were born psychologically inferior to the colonizers. In an interview, Cesaire says that European writers such as M. Mannoni (Cesaire does not give title of the

---

40. Fanon, "On National Culture," p. 41.

41 Ibid. p. 43.

42. Cesaire, *Discourse on Colonialism*, p. 21.

book he is discussing) believe in the dependency complex of the colonized and that Mannoni's negative notion needs to be argued against. Cesaire says:

> Follow him [Mannoni] step by step through the ins and outs of his little conjuring tricks, and he will prove to you as clear as day that colonization is based on psychology, that there are in this world groups of men who, for unknown reasons, suffer from what must be called dependency complex, that these groups are pyschologi-cally made for dependence; that they need dependence, that they crave it, ask for it, demand it, that this is the case with most of the colonized peoples . . . . These Negroes can't even imagine what freedom is. They don't want it, they don't demand it. It's the white agitators who put that into their heads. And if you gave it to them, they won't know what to do with it.[43]

The beliefs stated above were not held by colonizer only, but also taught to the colonized; they still exist in the post-colonial contexts today, since these beliefs were internalized and did not vanish with the coming of independence. Thus, the need for a search for identity in the post-colonial context is a result of the above theories of the inferiority of the colonized being ingrained and lodged in the psyche of the colonized.

The above arguments show the evils of colonization and its impact on the natives. One will notice that the common thread or the central theme to colonization was/is *power*. The colonizers not only had *prejudices* against the natives wherever they went and conquered, but also had the *power* to impose. They created systems that benefited them or those who looked like them, who did not resist or felt they benefited from the oppression of the natives. As stated earlier the colonizers believed that the "natives were like children or had minds like children," were barbaric, and the colonizers were to be "lords over them." The thrust had to do with *power* and *control* of the natives. This is the same thing that we see when it comes to tribalism, eth-nocentrism, sexism and racism; they all have a common element of *power and control.* It is this author's conviction that all human beings hold some form of personal prejudice against another group of people. However, when one holds prejudice but does not have power to impose it, the prejudice is lived out as an idea that never comes to fruition, compared to one who holds *prejudice* and has the *power* to impose. For example, the oppressed may hold prejudice against their oppressor but cannot put it into practice since the oppressor usually has a system to control the oppressed. However,

43. Ibid., p. 39-41.

an oppressor who has a system, that is *the power* and *prejudice,* can easily impose or subjugate those without power. In other words, prejudice without power remains an idea or feeling that has not a means of expression.

This is always an interesting debate for individuals who belong to a group that holds power and control when they are told that by virtue of being members of the oppressive majority group they are benefiting from an unjust system, which means they themselves can be counted as tribalist, racist, ethno-centrist or sexist. If they do not advocate, voice or work against the unjust system, they automatically are a part of a tribalist, sexist or racist institution. Many usually make this personal and try to defend that s/he, as an individual is not racist but that it is the system that is to blame.

In an interview Lance Smith said that many white counselors in North America don't believe they are racist, such as card carrying KKK, but they don't realize they may be carrying some biases.

> And of course, most counselors know that they are good, moral, kind, beneficent people, so it follows that, by definition, they cannot be racist. Therefore, he explains, not only are they likely to fail to interrogate the ways in which they more subtly harm and micro-aggress their clients and students of color, but they are also likely to ignore, deny and therefore inadvertently support institutional forms of racism such as the school-to-prison pipeline and anti-affirmative action. But racism, and all isms for that matter, are more complex, . . . For most of us it is not a matter of if I am racist, but rather how much. How many racist stereotypes do I subconsciously hold? How much do I unknowingly contribute to institutional racism? What are the microaggressions that I am more to commit? How much do I ignore white dominance? How much work do I need to do to break free from my segregated social bubble in order to develop authentic and genuine relationships with folks from targeted groups.[44]

Those aligned with the oppressive structures usually don't examine the truth of how they might be benefiting from the system, since the powerful ones running the system are those from their people group. What makes a group of people to be considered as tribalist, sexist, or racist is not about whether they don't' have friends from the oppressed group. It is when the ones who belong to the oppressing group keep silent when they see injustice and they look at it as someone else's problem, and in addition, they benefit from that unjust system. Power plus prejudice equals racism, sexism,

44. Meyers, Counseling Today, Vol 59, Num. 7, Feb., 2017, p. 27.

ethnocentrism and/or tribalism. Prejudice with no power is a (DOA) dead on arrival; it may never see the light of day as long as the status quo is maintained. In some cases, or in the end, some of the oppressed may start identifying with the oppressor to lessen the pain as a way not to deal with the "psychological whiplash," or as a way to address the experiences of "cognitive dissonance" as a result of the oppression. For Cesaire, the way to recover a cultural identity lost as a result of colonization (racism) in the post-colonial context is to reclaim the past history, culture elements, and values:

> We live in an atmosphere of rejection, [colonized and black people] and we developed an inferiority complex. I have always thought that the black man was searching for his identity. And it has seemed to me that if what we want is to establish this identity, then we must have a concrete consciousness of what we are-that is, of the first fact of our lives: that we are black; that we were black and have a history, history that contains certain cultural elements of great value . . . in sum, we assert that our Negro heritage was worthy of respect, and that this heritage was not relegated to the past, that its values were values that could still make an important contribution to the world . . . R.D. [Rene Depestre]: Certainly, because the relationships between consciousness and reality are extremely complex. That's why it is equally necessary to decolonize our minds, our inner life, at the same time that we decolonize society.[45]

It is fair to conclude that, because of the impact of colonialism on some of the urban contemporary Shona people, they suffer from an inferiority complex, believing that the Western way of life is the right one and the Shona traditional way has to be relegated into the past.

Writing from the context of India, another former British colony, Nandi, a psychoanalyst, gives an example of the problem of colonization by writing about a man he calls Kipling, who is caught between cultures. In this illustration he addresses the psychological and mental impact of colonization on the colonized. He says:

> Kipling's dilemma can be stated simply: he could not be both Western and Indian; he could be either Western or Indian. It was this imposed choice which linked his self-destructiveness to the tragedy of his life: Kipling's avowed values were Western, his rejected under-socialized self Indian, and he had to choose between the two. Had it been the other way round he might have

45. Ibid., p. 76, 78.

managed as a brown sahib or as a babu at least to acknowledge his bi-cultural self and reconcile however crudely the East and the West within him.[46]

Kipling is a photographic parallel to what I see as happening in the urban contemporary Shona context. Some of the Shonas in the urban context are "under-socialized" when it comes to the Shona traditional culture. Consequently, they cannot claim to be traditional Shonas nor can they claim to be Western. Nandi suggests that people such as Kipling are caught in a psychological battle of having no identity based on culture and/or religion. Urbanization, in fact, compounded the situation where the Shona lost their culture.

Colonization also brought urbanization. Urbanization compounded the situation by the Shona losing their culture. The Westernized cities did not match the village life, thereby changing the social structures and systems of the people. In place of extended families in the villages, nuclear and individualistic family systems became prominent in the cities. This urban context runs contrary to the Shona way of life where communal existence in the village settings is central to one's sense of being or wholeness. Contemporary urban Shonas find themselves existing in a *bi-cultural* and *bi-religious* context: they live in the tension of traditional Shona and Western cultures, as well as that of Shona traditional religion and Western Christianity.

Colonization and colonial mentality were and are detrimental to one's identity, for they strip one of personal or religious identity. The best way to be rid of this mental oppression is to be decolonized of such a mind-set as suggested by Fanon above. My hope is that an integrated consciousness is one which is also decolonized, as well as free of mental oppression by the colonial ideological thinking that everything Western is superior to the traditional Shona religio-culture.

Crisis hits when the Shona people start to search for their personal identity. Having been raised in a hybrid culture (in the form of naive consciousness), with the European culture considered superior, such people are caught in an identity crisis. It is the hope of this writer that a counselor or pastor who is trained and possesses an integrative consciousness (critical consciousness) will help the parishioner in resolving this identity crisis, since the pastor is trained in the awareness of or identification of the struggles involved.

46. Nandi, *The Intimate Enemy*, p. 71.

In conclusion, in this chapter I have presented a synopsis of the Shona traditional religio-culture, a brief historical presentation of the coming of colonization and Western Christianity, and an introductory discussion of the impact of Western Christianity and colonization on the contemporary urban Shona context. My argument is not that the Shonas' religion and culture were eradicated by the coming of colonization and Christianity, but rather that they were fundamentally changed in the urban Shona context, thereby creating a hybrid Christianity and culture for the urban Shonas, to be addressed by new pastoral care paradigms possessed by those with an integrative consciousness (critical consciousness).

The bi-cultural and bi-religious context in which the urban Shonas find themselves creates anxiety. As presented in Chapter One, anxiety sends the contemporary urban Shonas to the pastoral caregiver. My theory about anxiety and pastoral theology of care in the Shona context relates to Sullivan's theory of anxiety presented in detail in the next chapter:

> . . . it is anxiety which is responsible for a great part of the inadequate, inefficient, unduly rigid, or otherwise unfortunate performances of people; that anxiety is responsible in a basic sense for a great deal of what comes to a psychiatrist for attention. Only when this is understood, can one realize that this business of whether one is getting more anxious or less is in a large sense the basic influence which determines interpersonal relations . . . it more or less directs the course of their development.[47]

Anxiety produced by dysfunctional interpersonal relationships is apparent in the Shona urban context because of the effects of bi-culturalism and bi-religiousness. As a result, most contemporary Shona Christians arrive at their pastor's door seeking care for issues of personal and religious identity confusion. The next chapter addresses the issues of personal identity confusion and anxiety experienced by the urban contemporary Shonas.

---

47. Sullivan, *Interpersonal Theory*, p. 160.

48

CHAPTER THREE

Interpersonal and Religio-Cultural Identity Conflict

MUNHU VANHU, IS A Shona saying which translates to "a person is because of other people." This saying illuminates the way Shona people define the self.[1] One's identity is defined out of one's community of "embeddedness."[2] Other common African sayings support the idea that the world-view, philosophy, and self-understanding of most Africans, including the Shonas, is community based: "I am because we are, and since we are, therefore I am;" "One tree does not make a forest;" "A charcoal or coal gets its burning energy from being in the fire of others." Out of interpersonal relations, one develops an individual identity. Humans get their vitality, their physical, social, psychological and spiritual security and their identity from being in healthy interpersonal relationships with others.

BACKGROUND PROBLEM TO PERSONAL IDENTITY IN THE URBAN SHONA CONTEXT

The introduction of alien and foreign western understandings of the self has resulted in identity conflict for some of the contemporary urban Shona.

1. Self in this book means how one sees oneself based on one's physical, mental, psychological, spiritual make-up and in one's relationship to the spirit world and all of creation.

2. Kegan, *The Evolving Self,* p. 115-6. The phrase "community of embeddedness" is appropriated in this book in a similar sense as Kegan uses it in referring to a "culture of embeddedness." He defines this as a "psychosocial environment or the holding environment." He says that it is a particular form of the world or context in which or out of which a person grows and evolves psychologically and socially.

Due to their minds being infiltrated by colonization, modernization, and Westernization, some of the contemporary urban Shonas have lost many of the traditional understandings of what it means to be a Shona person— *munhu ane unhu*. Chidyausiku, a Zimbabwean author, who has written books in both Shona and English, writes about the dangers of the fast changes taking place in contemporary Zimbabwe. As stated earlier, he is of the mind-set that the infiltration of the Western culture upon the Shona people is detrimental:

> We Shona have a culture, which is in danger of being forgotten. Nursed within a colonial context many of us have come to think that 'the nanny is better than the mother.' We are now going through a period of transformation which affects all aspects of our way of life as it was in the past and as it has persisted to this very day . . . It is very sad to witness how this heritage is now being eroded and in danger of getting lost. If we are not careful, our generation may become like a dying tree with *broken roots*.[3]

In this quote Chidyausiku refers to the effects of the Western culture and its erosion of the Shona culture, leaving people with broken roots from their culture of embeddedness. In Chidyausiku's metaphor of the mother and the nanny, the mother represents the traditional Shona culture and the nanny represents the Western culture. This book argues that the urban contemporary Shonas are at a crossroads for they do not have enough knowledge of either the "mother" or the "nanny."

One of the reasons for this identity conflict is found in the fact that the starting points of self-definition for one's personal identity in the two cultures (traditional Shona and Western) are different. The term "identity conflict" for this book means that a person is not sure who s/he is because that individual is caught between two conflicting social systems upon which their self-definition is based. The Shonas define the self-based on their community of embeddedness and the notion of "we." In the West, one's sense of self is centered in an understanding of the "I or me," with the emphasis on the individual.

Most of the Western psychological theories influencing the field of counseling and pastoral theology of care have been criticized as being very individualistic. Pastoral theologians such as Larry Graham and others argue that Western theories in pastoral theology and care are individualistic and may not always fully address problems clients bring to the table, since

---

3. Chidyausiku, *Broken Roots*, p. vii, viii.

the individualistic theories may miss the communal aspects of the presenting problem.[4] Bodian, a western psychotherapist, notes, "Some critics have
also noted that the therapeutic world-view has surreptitiously suffused
our cultural mainstream, helping to shift our values from a concern for
community and communal good to an increasing preoccupation with individual fulfillment and personal growth."[5] In the same journal, Safransky,
also a Western psychotherapist, offers a similar critique:

> Therapy has become a kind of individualistic, self-improvement
> philosophy, a romantic ideology that suggests each person can
> become fuller, better, wiser, richer, and more effective . . . There
> are many who have located the roots of the therapeutic movement
> in the individualism embraced by the 19th-century modernism, in
> which everyone is the author of his or her intentions and is re-
> sponsible for his or her own life. Own. Own is a very big word
> in therapy; you own your life, as if there's a self, an individual,
> enclosed self, within a skin. That's individualism. That's the phi-
> losophy of therapy. I question that. The self could be redefined,
> given a social definition, a communal definition.[6]

These individualistic approaches or theories apply in many instances;
especially in the urban settings and in most cases they do not apply as much
in the rural settings. This is because the contemporary urban Shona society
is still very much in transition between communal and individualistic social systems and world-views, leaving many of these people in a dilemma
about which system to use.

In this book, since I am arguing that a counselor or pastoral caregiver is someone who possesses an integrative consciousness–meaning
being cognizant/knowledgeable of both Shona traditional approaches as
well as Western, there is need to present both the Shona and the Western
approaches. This chapter will present both a Western theory of personality
development by Sullivan and a Shona traditional understanding of personality development. For the benefit of the Western audience and those being
introduced to the Shona African worldview and culture, I have chosen Sullivan's western based theory as an approach that could mirror or illuminate
some of what would be appropriate for the Shona context. Sullivan's theory

---

4. Illustrative of concerns in the field are: Couture and Hunter eds., *Pastoral Care*;
Graham, *Care of Persons*.

5. Bodian, "Is Psychotherapy a Waste of Time," p. 50.

6. Safransky, "Psychotherapy," p. 52-53.

in many respects is compatible to the traditional Shona view of being human or personal self-definition.[7] His (Sullivan's) theory together with the African Shona theoretical understandings are used in this book to help inform and provide counselors or pastoral caregivers with theories which when integrated can appropriately address issues arising from this changing communally oriented African Shona context. As a result of the pressures discussed earlier in this book (economics, conflict produced by the urban settings, the effects of hybridity, *bi-culturalism,* and *bi-religiousness),* the contemporary urban Shona may choose not to tap into the traditional communal living wisdom and philosophy. Some contemporary urban Shonas would rather hang on to modernized scientific solutions, even in situations where they acknowledge that the traditional wisdom and philosophy may provide an answer. In addition, due to the lack of availability of written Shona literature, or communally oriented theories, which suit the Shona context today, some Shona counselors or pastoral caregivers may apply individualistic theories from the West.

In this fast changing society of the Shonas in Zimbabwe, a Shona counselors or pastoral caregiver with an integrated consciousness is cognizant of the fact that he/she can still tap into Shona traditional wisdom and philosophy. At times it is more appropriate for the counselor or pastoral caregivers to use communally oriented approaches and blend them with individualistic ones. This is because, for example, the Shonas can be forced to *consciously* live individualistic lives due to urban pressures, while *subconsciously* (in their suppressed or repressed memory), they are aware that some of the communal living lifestyle is the ideal choice for them.

In short, the argument here is that being forced to live bi-cultural and bi-religious lives, is creating religious and cultural dissonance for the Shonas. A definition of dissonance is that one finds himself or herself caught between two differing attractive opinions. When one is forced to choose that which is counter to one's belief system, dissonance occurs. Dissonance is based on the idea that individuals need consistency and balance in the function of their beliefs, knowledge, and attitudes. When new information is encountered which challenges the consistency of those beliefs and attitudes it results in dissonance:

> . . . dissonance results when an individual must select one of two
> equally attractive alternatives . . . dissonance arises when persons

---

7. Sullivan, *Interpersonal Theory,* says to be human is to be in communal existence, p. 32, 37.

are forced to behave counter to their private [even public] attitudes. As a result, either the behavior or the attitude must change to bring cognitions into harmony.[8]

In the Shona context, dissonance is experienced religiously and culturally when one has to live with or choose between two contradictory, incompatible, or irreconcilable thoughts, or when one encounters inconsistency in one's beliefs or ideas. The conflict between Western religious culture and the Shona religio-culture creates dissonance at various levels for the Shona urban population. The resulting dissonance produces anxiety as one tries to deny the conflict to reconcile the differences in the beliefs or ideas. For example, in the bi-cultural contemporary urban Shona context, conflict may be found in an attempt of self-definition. A Shona may find trouble defining him/herself because their everyday way of life driven by economic pressures may be contrary to the sense of communal living found in the Shona traditional society.

BACKGROUND TO THE DEVELOPMENT OF SULLIVAN'S THEORY

Sullivan drew not only from psychology, but also from other fields of discourse. Recognizing the impact of these disciplines on his thought adds depth to understanding his theory. Sullivan is classified as a neo-Freudian. He was trained as a Freudian psychiatrist, but later modified Freud's theory saying it was inadequate in the understanding of human development and the treatment of pathology. Neo-Freudians compose a large group of analysts who adhered to the central principles of Freudian theory and premises, but expanded on and modified certain aspects of that theory.

Sullivan was also influenced by other theorists and by his personal experience as a practicing psychiatrist. As much as other theorists whose emphases were on the individual influenced Sullivan, one of his main contributions was to address the impact of communal interpersonal relations on the individual. Sullivan's theory of interpersonal relations, or his interpersonal approach in psychiatry, was influenced by the theories of Freud, Adolf Meyer, G. H. Mead, and Malinowski.

---

8. Brakensiek, "Cognitive Dissonance," p. 188.

Sullivan notes that from Freud he gained the understanding of "the individual person as the central unit of study."[9] He also learned about instinctual drives and the libido, a theory he discarded later in the development of his own thought. Yet, Sullivan was not enamored by the individual alone. Mullahy and Melinek studied and wrote on Sullivan's work and theories, and they note that " . . . it is not difficult to understand that the main unit of study for Freud is the more or less self-contained individual. For Sullivan, the unit of study is always an interpersonal situation or an ongoing series of interpersonal processes."[10] For Freud the center of study was the individual and his or her intra-psychic process.

These intra-psychic processes were mechanistic using physicalistic principles. In a "Project for Scientific Psychology," Freud's goal was to show that psychology is a natural science and that human minds operated like machines in the way they function or process. It would follow, according to Freud's theory of how the mind operates, that human behavior and personality are determined and mechanistic.[11] For Freud, there is always a cause to each human action, and human actions are always conscious or unconscious. Freud said early in his development of psychoanalytic ideas, "The intention is to furnish a psychology that shall be a natural science: that is, to present psychical processes as quantitatively determined states of specific material particles . . . "[12] As will be expounded later, for Sullivan it is not the self-contained individual's intra-psychic mechanistic functions that determine being a person; rather, it is the interpersonal relations that occur within interpersonal situations.

Sullivan also saw Freud's theory as closely connected to psychobiology. Psychobiology is the theory that there is a relationship between psychological and physical functioning of humans. Sullivan incorporated Adolf Meyer's theory of psychobiology into his theory of interpersonal relations. The following captures a few major points of Sullivan's understanding of Meyer's theory: "Psychobiology . . . is the study of man as the highest embodiment of mentally integrated life . . . Meyer stated specifically and succinctly that psychobiology is concerned with the individual human organism as a primary entity."[13] Sullivan agreed with the idea that

9. Sullivan, *Interpersonal Theory*, p. 16.

10. Mullahy and Melinek, *Interpersonal Psychiatry*, p. 2.

11. Freud, *The Standard Edition*, p. 295.

12. Ibid. p. 297.

13. Sullivan, *Interpersonal Theory*, p. 16.

to understand humans, one has to study the individual human organism. However, he believed this alone would not give us a full picture of what a human being is, unless this knowledge was gathered within a context of interpersonal relations and community.

Another theorist who influenced Sullivan was George H. Mead, a social psychologist whose theory emphasized the importance of social interactions. From Mead, Sullivan draws conclusions about how humans influence each other in becoming a self. Sullivan quotes Mead who says:

> "The capacity of the human organism to play the parts of others . . . is the basic condition of the genesis of the self. In playing the parts of others we react to our playing as well. When the organism comes to respond to its own role assumptions as it responds to others it has become a self. "[14]

In short, Mead suggests that we develop personal identities as a result of complex interactions with others. Our reactions toward other people's responses to our play and behavior, and how we in turn react to the roles we assume, play a great part in the formation of our individual identities. Individuals "internalize" the play, and from those behaviors they get positive responses from others who are within acceptable community norms and values.

From Malinowski, a cultural anthropologist, Sullivan draws upon the idea of human connection and the social rules and customs which tie human beings together:

> " . . . human beings are bound together by their connection with a definite portion of environment, by their association with a common shelter and by the fact that they carry out certain tasks in common. This concerted character of their behavior is a result of social rules, that is customs . . . "[15]

Malinoswki's cultural anthropological understanding aided Sullivan in comprehending and incorporating into his theory the influences of culture on human beings in the midst of personal identity development. Established social rules and customs assist in formulating characteristics of one's actions, and in the process aid in the establishment of one's personal identity.

As stated earlier, Sullivan recognized how much he borrowed from other fields involved in the study of humans in developing his own theory.

---

14. Ibid., p. 17.
15. Ibid., p. 18, Sullivan cites Malinowski, "Culture," p. 622.

For Sullivan, all other theories lacked the interpretation of the impact of *interpersonal relations and situations* (elaborated later) in personal identity formation. Sullivan therefore concluded:

> Thus as psychobiology seeks to study the individual human being, and as cultural anthropology, which has been a powerful tributary to social science, seeks to study the social heritage shown in the concerted behavior of people making up a group, so psychiatry—and its convergent, social psychology—seeks to study the biologically and culturally conditioned . . . interpersonal processes occurring in the interpersonal situations in which the observant psychiatrist does his work.[16]

Thus, in addition to the study of the biological and cultural influences, Sullivan argues that one has to consider how interpersonal relationships influence personal identity formation.

COMMUNAL EXISTENCE, ANXIETY AND INTERPERSONAL RELATIONS IN PERSONAL IDENTITY

Sullivan defines humans as *social beings* who cannot survive without *interpersonal relations*. He uses words such as *interactions* and *interchange* to define interpersonal relations and situations.[17] There is reciprocity or an interpersonal exchange taking place in an interpersonal situation. An interpersonal situation is the condition under which the relational exchange between persons occurs.

Sullivan gives an example of a mother feeding a baby as an interpersonal situation in which an interpersonal relationship is also taking place. There is more than feeding transpiring; there are also interactions or relational exchanges, bonding, or emotional, physical and psychological connections between the mother and the infant. Wherever there is interaction, reciprocity, or communication between humans, there is an interpersonal relationship taking place. However, the relationship may be positive or negative. The negative relationships are the ones that result in anxiety. The development of anxiety becomes an important notion and will reappear in this book.

Directly connected to interpersonal relationships, Sullivan borrows from Freud the concept of instincts. Sullivan says that human beings, like

16. Ibid., p. 20.
17. Ibid., p. 32.

other animals, are born with instincts. However, the instincts in humans are to be qualified by the word *human* because they are different from those of other animals. Sullivan calls these instincts *human instincts*. The human instincts are instincts to *relate*. The instincts to *relate* are different from Freud's *instinctual drives*. Freud notes about an instinct:

> An instinct differs from a stimulus in that it arises from sources of stimulation within the body, operates as a constant force, and is such that the subject cannot escape from it by flight as he can from an external stimulus. An instinct may be described as having a source and an aim. The source is a state of excitation within the body and its aim is to remove that excitation; in the course of its path from its source to the attainment of its aim the instinct becomes operative mentally. We picture it as a certain sum of energy forcing its way in a certain direction.[18]

The example Freud gives as a way to satisfy an instinctual stimulation is through activities such as eating, having sex, and drinking. However, Freud does not say that an instinctual drive can be permanently removed by satisfying it once, since "it arises from the sources of stimulation within the body," which are still present and can again be excited.

In his later writings, Freud also says there are two basic instincts, the life (Eros) instinct and the death (Thanatos) instinct. The life instinct is the "instinct of self-preservation and of the preservation of the species," examples being, hunger, sex, and thirst. The aim of the second instinct (death), "is to undo connections and so to destroy things," examples being, suicide, aggression, and hatred of others.[19] He further says, "We may picture an initial state of things by supposing that the whole available energy of Eros, to which we shall hence-forward give the name *libido*, is present in the as yet undifferentiated ego-id and serves to neutralize the destructive impulses which are simultaneously present."[20]

As much as Sullivan is borrowing the concept of instincts from Freud, for Sullivan the origin of the instinctual drives is not the libido. The base of the human instinct to relate is the connection between the biological being and the human environment. Sullivan does not give a direct definition of an instinct. However, he describes an instinct through its functions. Thus for example, in Sullivan's understanding, one of the main functions

18. Freud, *New Introductory Lectures*, p. 132-133.
19. Freud, *An Outline Of Psychoanalysis*, p. 20ff.
20. Ibid., p. 22.

of human instincts is to be in good interpersonal relationships, contrary to the example of Freud's instinctual drive, such as sex, which one satisfies by having sex or sometimes engaging in sexual aggression. Sullivan notes about human instincts:

> There is abundant evidence that the human animal is not able to look after himself for a long time after birth; and that the abilities that characterize him are matured serially over a term of no less than ten to twenty years. The human animal is utterly dependent at birth and, diminishingly but still greatly, dependent on the tender cooperation of the human environment . . . The idea of "human instincts" in anything like the proper rigid meaning of maturing patterns of behavior which are not labile is completely preposterous. Therefore, all discussions of 'human instincts' are apt to be very misleading and very much a block to correct thinking, unless the term *instinct*, modified by the adjective *human*, is so broadened in its meaning that there is no particular sense in using the term at all.[21]

Sullivan's use of the word instinct means general non-human tendencies which are inborn. Instincts are naturally inborn dispositions: acquired human tendencies are what make "human instincts" different from the Freudian use of the term "instinct." In other words, Sullivan is arguing that humans are interpersonal beings and cannot survive without interaction with others. The biological and psychological self interacts interpersonally with the social world. The importance of instincts to relate, as posed by Sullivan and for this book, as will be expounded, is that they play a major role in personal identity development. From a developmental point of view Sullivan notes:

> . . . before speech is learned every human being, even those in the lower imbecile class, has learned certain gross patterns of relationship with parent, or with someone who mothers him [the infant]. Those gross patterns become the utterly buried but quite firm foundations on which a great deal more is superimposed or built.[22]

Sullivan notes that the relationship of the infant to the mothering one is very important since it is the "foundation" upon which one's personality is formed. The interactions between the mother and the baby make the two

21. Sullivan, *Interpersonal Theory*, p. 20-21.
22. Ibid., p. 6.

to connect emotionally and psychologically such that they can sense each other's increase in anxiety. The relationship between the mother and the infant is a basic example of how one could come to an understanding of, what we would term, Sullivan's interpersonal relations theory. There is reciprocity between the infant and the mothering one in the form of sensing anxiety.

The term anxiety is one Sullivan also borrows from Freud.[23] In discussing the sources and functions of anxiety, Freud notes the following:

> . . . anxiety arises directly out of the libido; that is to say, there is brought about that state of helplessness of the ego in the face of excessive tension arising from ungratified need which results, as in birth, in the development of anxiety, so that there is again a possibility, which although obvious is of no great consequence, that it is precisely the excess of unutilized libido that finds its discharge in the form of anxiety.[24]

For Sullivan, the source of anxiety is tension in interpersonal relationships. Where anxiety exists, for example, between the mother and the infant, it is defined as the tension in opposition to the relationship between the mother and the baby. The root cause of anxiety for Sullivan is tension in relationships between the individuals or between the mother and the baby. Sullivan notes, " . . . anxiety in the mother induces anxiety in the infant . . . understand that the induced anxiety of the infant makes him more difficult and worrisome to care for, so that his behavior may seem to justify disparagement of the mother's work with him."[25] As it pertains to adults, anxiety is that tension which interferes with one's interpersonal relationships or threatens the *self-system*.

The *self-system* is a learned defense mechanism whose work is self-preservation. Borrowing from Freud, the functions of the *self-system* in Sullivan's theory are similar to the ego's defense mechanisms in Freud's theory. Freud notes:

> Just as the id is directed exclusively to obtaining pleasure, so the ego is governed by considerations of safety. The ego has set itself

---

23. Freud, *The Problem of Anxiety*, p. 81.

24. Ibid., p. 83.

25. Sullivan, *The Interpersonal Theory*, p. 114. Anxiety as defined by Sullivan means a "fear-like state," which causes distress or discomfort by interference with one's interpersonal relationships. The disruption of an existence of good interpersonal relations results in tension, and the tension produces distress, the "fear-like state" anxiety in the individuals involved.

the task of self-preservation, which the id appears to neglect. It makes use of sensations of anxiety as a signal to give a warning of danger threatening its integrity . . . Thus the ego is fighting on two fronts: it has to defend its existence both against an external world that threatens it with annihilation and against an internal world that makes excessive demands.[26]

Similarly, the *self-system*, as defined by Sullivan, is a learned defense system in response to the mother or others; its aim is protecting the self psychologically, emotionally and mentally (in both children and adults). In other words, the self-system is an individual emotional and psychological defense structure or process. He says, "The self-system thus is an organization of educative experience called into being by the necessity to avoid or to minimize (diminish) incidents of anxiety. The functional activity of the self-system . . . is primarily directed to avoiding and minimizing this disjunctive tension of anxiety, and thus indirectly to protecting the infant from this evil eventuality in connection with the pursuit of satisfaction."[27]

When one's security is threatened, anxiety triggers the self-system as a defense mechanism. He argues that when anxiety is constant, or when one is exposed to too much of it, then it becomes harmful, dangerous, or unhealthy. Sullivan claims that anxiety is one of the key disruptive forces in interpersonal relations. Too much anxiety or constant anxiety causes disequilibrium to the self.[28]

Since anxiety is experienced when one's sense of security is threatened, and since interpersonal relations are central to one's sense of security, anxiety arises when interpersonal relations are threatened. Sullivan says, "The point is that the self is approved by significant others, that any tendencies of the personality that are not so approved, that are in fact strongly disapproved, are dissociated from personal awareness."[29] What forces one to disconnect or disengage from choices that are disapproved by others is that these options interfere with one's interpersonal relations. In other words, Sullivan is saying the result of continued engagement in disapproved tendencies is anxiety. To avoid anxiety arising from situations that interfere with one's interpersonal relations, the inclinations are to disengage or separate from such situations, or disconnect them from personal awareness.

26. Freud, *An Outline of Psychoanalysis*, p. 110-112.
27. Sullivan, *The Interpersonal Theory*, p. 165-166.
28. Ibid., p. 160.
29. Sullivan, *Conceptions*, p. 22.

Anxiety or anxiety-prone situations are present throughout life, and constant anxiety is the number one element which humans try to avoid.

Faulty interpersonal relations are a source of great anxiety because they interfere with or interrupt one's communal existence. Sullivan's theory of stages of personal identity development is connected to anxiety and communal existence. About communal existence Sullivan notes:

> The principle of communal existence refers to the fact that the living cannot live when separated from what may be described as their necessary environment . . . the fact is that the living maintain constant exchange through their bordering membranes with certain elements in the physicochemical universe around them; and the interruption of this exchange is tantamount to death of the organism. Thus by the principle of communal existence I mean that all organisms live in continuous, communal existence with their necessary environment.[30]

Communal existence, as understood by Sullivan, does not relate to humans alone but to all that surrounds them. This author's understanding of the above statement by Sullivan is that all living things, including humans, depend upon each other for survival. Lack of exchange with other organisms (air, water, trees, soil etc.), Sullivan says, may cause death in human beings. We are interdependent upon our "universe" and "necessary environment." For human beings, the necessary environment is the human culture and that which surrounds them.

He also perceives communal existence as meaning those interpersonal relationships, which exist between humans. Without communal existence or other humans, Sullivan says, the human personality would deteriorate:

> . . . it is possible to think of man as distinguished from plants and animals by the fact that human life—in a very real and not only a purely literary or imaginary sense—requires interchange with an environment which includes culture, . . . man is distinguished very conspicuously from other members of the biological universe by requiring interchange with a universe of culture, this means, in actual fact, since culture is an abstraction pertaining to people that man requires interpersonal relationships or interchange with others . . . It is a rare person who can cut himself off from mediate and immediate relation with others for long spaces of time without undergoing a deterioration in personality.[31]

30. Sullivan, *The Interpersonal Theory*, p. 31.
31. Ibid., p. 33.

In other words, Sullivan is suggesting that "no person is an island." To survive and to have an identity, humans need a culture and need to engage in interpersonal relationships. He further argues that:

> If one scrutinizes the performances of any child it will be evident that the child as a creature is existing in communal existence in or with an environment now importantly cultural in its composition. The cultural entities, so to speak, are part of the necessary environment. The human being requires the world of culture, cannot live *and be human* except in communal existence with it . . . Other people are, therefore, an indispensable part of the environment of the human organism.[32]

Sullivan notes that even in adulthood the idea of the "individual" (to use his term) is an illusion. He notes,

> . . . the study of individual personality did not seem to be within the field of science, the only thing that seems amenable to scientific approach being the actions in interpersonal situations; that which someone does with me, that can be observed, both by me and by some objective third person—what goes on in that person, the unique peculiarity of his personality, seems to escape any method of science . . . [33]

Sullivan maintains his argument that the development of personality and identity must be closely connected to communal existence. He is saying that we cannot have an individual or the study of the meaning of an individual outside of his or her community of existence or interpersonal relations. For Sullivan it would be therefore a misconception to speak of an individual outside the community. Individuality can only be understood within the context of interpersonal relationships. How then are Sullivan's concepts of anxiety, interpersonal relations, and communal existence related to Sullivan's stages of personal identity development?

INTERPERSONAL RELATIONSHIPS IN SULLIVAN'S STAGES OF PERSONALITY DEVELOPMENT

The purpose of this section is to present the connection between interpersonal relationships, anxiety, and communal existence in some of Sullivan's

32. Sullivan, *Conceptions*, p. 18.
33. Ibid., p. 23.

stages of personal identity development. Beginning with conception and continuing through adulthood, it is how the mother, siblings, peers, and other adults interrelate and interact with an individual that helps the individual to develop a personal identity. In short, Sullivan is saying that communal existence, that is, the individual interaction and relations within his or her "community of embeddedness," formulates personal identity.

Sullivan outlines seven stages of personality development before one reaches maturity. In these stages of development, Sullivan argues, interpersonal relationships play a central part. At each developmental stage the child, or adolescent, has to acquire healthy interpersonal relations in order to have a positive personal identity. Sullivan's developmental stages include infancy, childhood, the juvenile era, pre-adolescence, early adolescence, late adolescence, and adulthood or maturity. He does not elaborate on adulthood or the stage of maturity. Sullivan talks about the roles adults are expected to play in the other stages of human development (infancy through late adolescence).

Sullivan addresses how a child develops a sense of self based upon one's relationship with the mother in the developmental stage of infancy.[34] He talks about three aspects of a sense of a "*me*," "the good me," "the bad me," and "the not me," present from the time of infancy. He suggests:

> . . . these aspects of interpersonal cooperation require acculturation or socialization of the infant. Infants are customarily exposed to all of these [forms of anxiety-prone interpersonal situations] before the era of infancy is finished. From experience of these three sorts—with rewards, with the anxiety gradient, and with practically obliterative sudden severe anxiety—there comes initial personification of three phases of what presently will be me . . . Now, at this time, the beginning personifications of me are good-me, bad me and not me.[35]

According to Sullivan, the development of the *me* depends on the baby's sensing the anxiety in the mothering one. He says that even though it is complex or impossible to trace scientifically the anxiety from the baby to the mother, it is present. The "good mother," who has a good relationship

---

34. Sullivan is writing in the 1950's when gender roles are clearly defined in terms of the mother taking care of the baby, unlike today where fathers can assume the role of the caretaker. What is important here is not the question of who is caring for the baby, but the key is the context of the community or the nurturing one who provides healthy interpersonal relations.

35. Sullivan, *The Interpersonal Theory*, p. 161.

with the infant, helps the infant *incorporate* in him/herself an image of the "good me." He also believes that children who grow up in nurturing environments with good interpersonal relations develop high self-esteem and a good "self-system, which is the same as a good-me."[36] The low level of anxiety in the interpersonal relationship between the mother and the baby helps the infant develop a sense of a "good me."

He says that an interpersonal relationship between the two is important or the infant will be anxious and develop a negative personal identity or the "bad-me." Constant anxiety caused by the tension in relationship between the mother and the infant, or the absence of a relationship, has a negative impact on the personality of the infant. What Sullivan calls the "nasty mother" is the mother who constantly exposes the baby to tension relationships or situations. The baby reflects to the self the image of "bad me" from a "bad mother." Sullivan notes: "*Bad-me*, on the other hand, is the beginning personification which organizes experience in which increasing degrees of anxiety are associated with behavior involving the mothering one in its more-or-less clearly prehended interpersonal setting."[37] From poor interactions, one develops poor personal identity with a very low self-esteem.

In an environment where the mothering one is absent or is persistently and extremely anxious, the mother is perceived as the "evil mother." The relationship is so extremely anxious that the baby develops a sense of "not me." Sullivan notes:

> The rudimentary personification of not-me evolves very gradually, since it comes from the experience of intense anxiety—a very poor method of education . . . . these experiences are largely truncated, so that what they are really about is not clearly known. Thus organizations of these experiences are marked by uncanny emotion—which means experiences which, when observed, have led to intense forbidding gestures on the part of the mother, and induced intense anxiety in the infant . . . [38]

Sullivan goes on to suggest that people exposed to this intense anxiety develop a "not me" and this type of *me* easily develops dissociative behavior. Pathology may develop as a result of the relationship between the mother and the infant combined with the level of anxiety to which the infant is constantly exposed.

36. Ibid, p. 164.
37. Ibid., p. 162.
38. Ibid., p. 163.

The child makes the transition into childhood at two to five years of age, when one of the key factors becomes the development of language. Sullivan believes the little boy identifies with the male gender and the girls with the female, as prescribed by the society, at the same time. The child is now developing interpersonal relationships with others, other than the mother and the siblings. Sullivan says:

> During infancy, he [child] learns the grossest culture patterns about zonal and general needs. But throughout the era of child-hood there is an increasing demand for his cooperation. The child is expected to do things which are brought to his attention or impressed on him as requirements for action by the authority -carrying environment—the mother, increasingly the father, and perhaps miscellaneous siblings, servants and what not.[39]

Childhood is a period in which the child is starting to be held accountable and responsible by those in authority. The authority figures are more than the mother and the father, and include the community at large. To use Sullivan's words, these are the "siblings, servants and what not." By the phrase "what not" I assume that Sullivan is referring to other persons in the community who may impress communal values, rules, and norms upon the child.

The juvenile stage, five to eight years, is school age. This is the stage in which the child learns about social relations and the respect of social norms, values, and rules, what ostracism means, co-operation, competition, and group feelings.[40] The child internalizes these values and rules in the further development of a sense of self. In addition, the child understands ostracism as brought upon him or herself if s/he chooses to be indifferent to the societal and community norms and values.

The next stage, pre-adolescence, from eight to eleven years, is marked by the need for intimate interpersonal relationships. One of the persons important at this stage is the "chum."[41] This is a person who is of the child's same sex but older, and who acts as a role model with whom the child can confide and identify. Peer relationships are also important for the child. Ac-

39. Ibid., p. 203. By zonal needs Sullivan is referring to physiological needs mostly realized through the senses, such as the need to be touched, eating (sucking on the mother's breast) etc., and to put it in Sullivan's words this is "organization of special sense apparatus, such as sight, special tactile sensitivities, gustatory or taste sensitivities, olfactory or smell sensitivities."

40. Ibid., p. 227ff.

41. Ibid., p. 245ff.

cording to Sullivan, pre-adolescence and early adolescence tend to overlap since people develop at different rates; some may reach these stages earlier than others.

Early adolescence, from twelve to fourteen years, is important for the development of sexual orientation. According to Sullivan, erotic needs are supposed to be met through the relationship with the opposite gender. The chum, as stated earlier, is a role model of the same sex as the adolescent and with whom the adolescent confides and develops attachment. If one does not make the transition or remains stuck with the chum, one may display homosexual tendencies.[42] The conflicts that the child experiences at this stage are those of sexual gratification, security, and intimacy. Sullivan notes:

> . . . making very much sense of the complexities and difficulties which are experienced in adolescence and subsequent phases of life, depends, in considerable measure, on the clarity with which one distinguishes three needs, which are often very intricately combined and at the same time contradictory. These are the need for personal security—that is, for freedom from anxiety; the need for intimacy—that is, for collaboration with at least one other person; the need for lustful satisfaction, which is connected with genital activity in pursuit of the orgasm.[43]

Late adolescence, from fourteen to eighteen years of age, he says, ". . . extends from the patterning of preferred genital activity through unnumbered educative steps to the establishment of a fully human and mature repertory of interpersonal relations, as permitted by available opportunity, personal and cultural."[44] The late adolescent is discovering his/her "genital behavior and how it fits into the rest of life." He or she continues to learn about how inappropriate and inadequate interpersonal relationships produce anxiety. In other words, he/she is learning about how to minimize anxiety as well as about self-respect and human maturity. There is a realization in the late adolescent that communal existence is important in one's personal identity.[45]

---

42. Ibid., p. 277. Sullivan says that there is not enough evidence or "actual facts" to support his theory of sexuality development leading to homosexuality in the adolescent boy. I have not, however, seen any studies countering specifically Sullivan's theory about the development of sexuality.

43. Ibid., p. 263-264.

44. Ibid., p. 297.

45. Ibid., p. 297ff.

After late adolescence, a person moves on to the final stage, adulthood. The stage of adulthood is one in which a person is expected to have reached maturity. Social expectations allow for a person to marry and have a family. Interpersonal relationships continue to be central in adult life.

One of the key thoughts of Sullivan's developmental theory is that, due to different experiences and interpersonal relationships, a person is transformed. He did not believe that one's personality is set at an early age. In fact, new experiences and new interpersonal relationships can cause changes in one's personality. In other words, one's interpersonal relationships and the amount of anxiety experienced within those relationships affects one's personal identity throughout life. Sullivan says personality is "the relatively enduring pattern of recurrent interpersonal situations which characterize a human life."[46] Interpersonal relationships, which are part of everyday human experiences occurring throughout life, are the basis of the formation of one's personality. The disruption of interpersonal relationships or the lack of a community of embeddedness to foster healthy personal identity development, according to Sullivan, will result in anxiety. In this book, this author is arguing that due to the changes taking place in the urban Shona context, the lack of healthy interpersonal community relations is causing anxiety in individuals' sense of personal identity.

As demonstrated throughout the stages of development, the key aspects of Sullivan's theory are interpersonal relations, anxiety, and communal existence. Sullivan's theory speaks to the lack of communal existence, interpersonal relationships, and anxiety as a factor that would drive people to seek help or counseling. In light of Sullivan's understanding of human beings and personality development, we will now turn to the African Shona context's understanding of these concepts. A counselor or pastoral caregiver, who has an understanding of a Western theory such as Sullivan's and Shona African approaches, would be better equipped for integrative work in the African contexts.

A SHONA AFRICAN PERSONAL IDENTITY DEVELOPMENT THEORY

The general African philosophical understanding of a person includes, according to Mbiti, an African theologian from Kenya, "the unborn members who are still in the loins of the living; and the living-dead . . . who are

46. Sullivan, *Conceptions*, p. vi.

thought to be still interested in the affairs of the family to which they once belonged in their physical life . . . People give offerings of food and libation to the living-dead because they are still part of the family."[47] In other words, the African understanding of a person is not limited to those that are still physically alive but include the dead who are considered as the "living dead."

The key to understanding the person in the African context is community. Without a community of embeddedness, the person is not considered whole. However, without individuals there is no community. Both the individual and the community are integral parts of understanding persons in the African context. Mbiti says the following about the African understanding of person (which includes the Shonas):

> In traditional life, the individual does not and cannot exist alone except corporately. He owes his existence to the other people, including those of past generations and his contemporaries. He is simply part of the whole.
>
> The community must therefore make, create, or produce the individuals, for the individual depends on the corporate group. Physical birth is not enough: the child must go through rites of the incorporation so that it becomes fully integrated into the entire society. These rites continue throughout the physical life of the person, during which the individual passes from one stage of corporate existence to another.[48]

Africans traditionally develop an identity or personality through the involvement of the community. The biological influences and personal endowments in the African society are not overlooked. Instead, they are assumed to be present, but alone do not make a person. In the above statement Mbiti underscores that, "physical birth alone is not enough." He goes on further to say, "Nature brings the child into the world, but society creates the child into the social being, a corporate person. For it is the community which must protect the child, feed it, bring it up, educate it and in many other ways incorporate it into the wider community. Children are buds of society, and every birth is the arrival of 'spring' when life shoots out and the community thrives."[49]

---

47. Mbiti, *African Religions*, p. 139.

48. Ibid., p. 141.

49. Ibid., p. 143.

The person, or one's personal identity, is believed to be highly influenced by the community or social systems within which one develops. Taking into consideration the biological influences on the concept of a person, the Africans believe that it is the society, which gives one an identity or molds one's personality. One is not just a biological entity, but is also a proactive person who reacts to and internalizes the community values and norms in the formation of one's personality.

Mbiti illustrates the importance of the community in individual development when he says, "The individual can only say, 'I am, because we are, since we are, therefore I am.' This is a cardinal point in the understanding of the African view of man."[50] This African philosophical understanding of "person" is quite contrary to Western thought. This is basically because the Western philosophy's understanding of the person emanates from the individual to the society, while the African view is vice versa. Mbiti's statement is equally true in the Shona context; a person is defined within their social context, and in the community. The key to being human therefore lies in interacting within communal interpersonal relationships. Oduyoye, an African woman theologian, suggests this when she notes:

> Africans recognize life as life-in-community. We can truly know ourselves if we remain true to our community, past and present. The concept of individual success or failure is secondary. The ethnic group, the village, the locality, are crucial in one's estimation of oneself. Our nature as beings-in-relation is a two way relation: with God and with our fellow human beings.[51]

Likewise Muzorewa, a Shona theologian, notes the difference between how the West and Africans perceive a person when he says: "Strains of Western thought which have been influenced by Descartes's, 'I think therefore I am,' (cogito ergo sum) and Albert Camus's 'I rebel therefore we exist,' contrast with African concepts of humanity."[52] Muzorewa suggests the Shonas have the community as their starting point in the definition of a person (human) in contrast to the West's individual as a starting point. All the authors, Oduyoye, Muzorewa, and Mbiti, address the importance of community in the development of an individual as a person. It is important to examine how the traditional Shona context did understand communal interpersonal relationships

---

50. Ibid., p. 145.

51. Oduyoye, "The Value of African Religious Beliefs," p. 100-101.

52. Muzorewa, *The Origins*, p. 30-34.

of personal identity. Only then can we examine the anxiety created in the Shona context as a result of the influence of Westernization.

TRADITIONAL SHONA AFRICAN PERSONAL IDENTITY DEVELOPMENT

Little has been written from the Shona context tracing the stages of personal identity development. Due to lack of written material from the Shona context tracing stages of personal identity development, this author will depend mainly on two different books, one written by Gelfand and another edited by Mutswairo.[53] Gelfand was a medical doctor and writer who taught at the then University of Rhodesia starting from about the 1960s. The editor Mutswairo, currently Professor at the University of Zimbabwe in the Department of African Languages and Literature, specializes in Traditional Oral Literature in Africa. Based on the lack of sufficient material, the author will also use relevant written material from other African contexts and some personal experiences, which illustrate the Shona traditional situations.

The belief of the traditional Shona notes that the individual exists because of the community; however, the community cannot be without individuals. In this book, I am not focusing on the debate of individual versus community rights; rather, the concern is about the involvement of the community in the molding of the individual and the development of a personal identity. A person attains personhood through socialization, passing on of communal beliefs, values, norms, and mores. One cannot claim to "be" without the community. The Shona saying, *Munhu vanhu*, which means a person is because of other people, illustrates that individual identity depends on the corporate community. The values, beliefs, and norms an individual internalizes from the community are those, which help one formulate individual identity. The community supplies or equips individuals with the things necessary for identity development. Lack of these interpersonal relationships, as posited by Sullivan, causes anxiety, and can be detected in the urban Shona context today.

53. Gelfand, *Growing up*. In this book Gelfand presented how children grow up in the Shona context. To test the impact of the change taking place in urban areas, he did research in different schools in Harare. He also researched how the children who were being raised in the cities were learning about the traditional culture and life in the rural areas. Some of Gelfand's findings were issues of "bi-culturalism" or of children raised in the cities, not being able to "fit in" in rural area settings. See also Mutswairo ed., *Introduction*, p. 44-62. Traces development and training from conception to adulthood.

Having stated the influences of communal interpersonal relationships in personal identity, I will present the traditional Shona stages of personal identity development, mainly drawing on Gelfand and Masasire. The late Masasire, who was teaching at the University of Zimbabwe in the Department of African Languages and Literature, contributed a chapter focused on issues of growing up in the traditional Shona context in the book edited by Mutswairo.[54] Relevant material from Mbiti's writing will also be utilized.

In traditional Shona culture, from the moment a woman realizes she is pregnant she goes to the elderly women of the community who know about the herbs and the charms the pregnant mother is supposed have. The mother takes herbs and wears protective charms to prevent harm to the fetus. In some Shona communities, sex between husband and wife will cease when the mother is in her final month of pregnancy. A pregnant woman is held with respect and not allowed to overwork in case harm may occur to the life of both the mother and fetus. As Masasire illustrates:

> During pregnancy the wife continues with her normal activities, although she may discontinue heavier work in the later months. Many taboos and avoidances must be observed by pregnant women, usually to protect the child, but sometimes, also to ease the pregnancy and labor ... Women are often given medicines during pregnancy to relieve the pains and sickness, to facilitate the birth or to protect the foetus against harm *(mishonga yamasuo)*.[55]

Naturally, following pregnancy comes the birth of the baby. The next section covers the period up to five years of age. The cutting of the umbilical cord is of significance to the Shona in that it is a sign of separation of the baby from the mother. In most cases, the umbilical cord is disposed of by burying it. The child is separate from the mother but is also in close proximity to the mother. According to Masasire:

> The cord is cut at birth, and then after birth is buried secretly to prevent strangers or witches from tampering with and causing harm to the child. The infant is washed and often given a little porridge, or medical infusion soon after being born. For some time after birth, the baby is believed to be very weak and rituals may be performed to strengthen and protect it. The rituals link the new member to the whole family. The mother and the infant

---

54. Masasire, "Kinship and Marriage," p. 46.
55. Ibid., p. 46.

remain secluded in the hut for a period varying between six days and ten days.[56]

During the time of seclusion, the involvement of the midwife, and in many cases the grandmother, is now a sign that the baby no longer belongs to the mother only but to the whole community. At the end of the six to ten days of seclusion of the mother, baby, grandmother, and midwife, the cord is expected to separate from the navel *(kudonha chikuvhu)*.

A ceremony is performed which in some cases combines with the naming ceremony called *kubudisa mwana* (meaning "bringing the child out to the community"). The child is named and given or presented to the community to raise. In other communities, the child is named and then a ceremony of presenting the child to the community is done. The name one is given at birth or in infancy, in most Shona communities, has a meaning. In most cases the name is connected to, or describes the personality or character of, the child. Sometimes the name may be descriptive of the family's relationship with relatives or others in the community or related to a crucial event surrounding the pregnancy or birth of the child. The name of the child might also be symbolic of what is perceived as the quality of the child's character or personality. Mbiti says about the incorporation of a child into the community:

> The child has, however, begun its journey of being incorporated into the community, so that the separation between the individual mother and child continues to widen as the child's integration into the wider community also increases . . . Paradoxically, then, the child is near the mother and yet begins to get away from the individual mother, growing into the status of being 'I am because we are and since we are therefore I am' . . . the child is now public property, it belongs to the entire community and is no longer the property of one person. It has died to the stage of being alone in the mother's womb: but now it has risen in the new life of being part of the human society.[57]

It is no longer the sole responsibility of the immediate family to raise the child but the responsibility of the community. The belief that "It takes a village to raise a child" is also prevalent among the traditional Shonas.

In most communities the child is allowed to breast feed until about the age of two. The following, of what Mbiti says, is true of the Shona context:

56. Ibid., p. 45.
57. Mbiti, *African Religions*, p. 147-148.

"During the nursing period, the child is carried on the back or bosom of the mother or of another female member of the village. The direct contact between the mother and child gives the child a deep psychological sense of security."[58] The older sisters, cousins, grandmothers, and aunts also share the task of carrying the baby. As the baby grows older, it starts to realize that it does not belong to the mother alone but develops attachment with others (community).

Until the age of two to two-and-a-half years the child still sleeps with the parents. The child is expected to acquire a language, walk, and be toilet trained by the end of five years. Among the Shonas, the end of this phase and the beginning of the next may overlap since these phases are arbitrary and may be attained at different rates by each child. Toward the end of this stage the child is starting to sleep with children of the same sex as him/herself or of the same age, separate from the parents.

During the ages of about six to twelve, the community starts training the child about community expectations and responsibilities. Gelfand, basing his information from the traditional Shona context, notes:

> At this stage the children no longer sleep in the same room as their parents, they are taught the difference between good behavior and bad behavior and they also learn to avoid a number of taboos . . . If they sit on the road they will develop boils on their buttocks. They may meet a lion if they walk backwards. Peeping toms will develop sties, . . . Dust must not be swept out of the hut at night . . . Children are forbidden to whistle or call at night lest they attract witches.[59]

With the aid of and training by older siblings, the child starts to look after the family animals and sometimes those of the extended family. The child is starting to learn responsibility, even though he or she is not considered a mature person. The taking of duties similar to those of adults gives the children the sense that they are passing through the stage of being a baby to another stage of childhood where the child is responsible to the community.

The boys at this stage are expected to learn to take care of the animals, make and use weapons, help weed the fields, water the gardens, and feed the chickens and their dogs. Toward the end of this phase, the boys sit outside in the open air, a place around the fire, *kudare*, where the elderly men teach the young people about life and being a responsible communal human being. The women stay inside the house with the girls and do the

58. Ibid., p. 156.
59. Gelfand, *Growing up*, p. 12-13.

same. Girls at this age start to learn about cooking, cleaning the house, and taking care of younger siblings. Stories using animal characters (such as the baboon, hare, lion, hyena, etc.) are told at this phase to emphasize good character, language, and manners.

The children are taught a lot of proverbs, riddles, and stories to help them learn to be responsible people in the community and to build character. This is a time when children are corrected in the presence of others so that others may learn from the mistakes of some. They are taught about taboos. A taboo is a prohibited, restricted, or forbidden behavior. If someone is to commit such an act (taboo), he or she receives automatic consequences through natural laws, the spirits, or God. The children are taught the importance of maintaining good interpersonal relations, with animal stories as illustrations. Good interpersonal relationships must be maintained with others in order for harmony to exist.

What the children are taught by their grandparents, aunts, uncles, or elders of the family is constantly reinforced in the community. Any elderly person can discipline any child in the community if a child is found misbehaving. The reinforcement of values, norms, and character building also happens in the in-groups of the girls or boys. They remind each other of the taboos since most of the taboos will affect not only the one who breaks them but the whole family or community as well. One is said to be developing a good *unhu* (character or personhood); for example, having respect for the elders (*ano kudza vakuru wake*), or *kutumika*, which means being sent and doing it ungrudgingly. In addition, children must not use bad words or language, learn to ask questions about things of which they are unsure, admit when they are wrong, and be helpful to strangers. Having a good relationship or being helpful to a stranger is a way of creating harmony with that stranger's community. The stranger will spread news to his/her community of the hospitality given him or her at a time he/she needed it, rather than vice-versa.

This is the point at which the children are taught proverbs such as, *Varume ndevamwe, kutsva kwendebvu vanodzimurana*. Hamutyinei, a Shona literature writer, translates the proverb "(Men should show a spirit of cooperation and sympathy. They should help one another in times of difficulty and danger). At times, this proverb is quoted as an encouragement to work together. It also serves as a reproach for people who are reluctant to give a hand to those who need it."[60]

60. Hamutyinei, *Tsumo Namadimikira*, p. 39.

Another proverb which would apply to respecting people regardless of, for example, one's disabilities is, *Munhu, Munhu asina kubarwa ndiyani?*, which translates as, "A person is a person, is there one who was not given birth to?" *Munhu vanhu* (a person is because of others) also teaches the child that s/he is because of others or the community, without which s/he ceases to *be*.

As Gelfand says, the next arbitrary phase extends from about twelve to eighteen years of age. Among the Shonas, this phase includes the physical and/or mental developmental changes in the child. Girls develop breasts and they have their menstruation. Boys develop deeper voices, pubic hair, and sometimes they experience their first ejaculation. This is a period in which the aunts, uncles, or grandparents do a lot of work to educate the adolescents about adulthood. The education is mostly done during the evenings. Usually the boys and girls in this age group are separated, but sometimes they are taken together and given a series of lessons about manhood and womanhood. Boys in the early part of adolescence are known as *kajaya* and girls are known as *kamhandara*. At the late part of this phase (18 years old), a boy is *jaya* and girl *mhandara*, which is adolescent. Both boys and girls are taught about sexual relationships. Sexual intercourse before marriage is highly discouraged. This is a period where *kuzvibata* (self-control, self-respect) is emphasized and tested. One might hear statements being used, such as *mwana asina hunhu*, meaning "a child without character or having bad behavior." The implication of this is that the child is developing a bad personality, and the saying can be used when a child is being disrespectful of his or her elders.

Gelfand gives the following list of things girls are to learn at this age: "The girls are taught how to take care of children, use of clean language, cleanliness, temper control, how to react to courting proposals, and how to relate to one's in-laws."[61] For girls, one would hear proverbs such as *musha mukadzi*, which translates as "a stable home is because of the wife." The training regarding marriage, procreation, sexual life, family responsibilities, allowance of full privileges, and duties to the community occur in the context of the home. The aunts, uncles, and grandparents act as mentors to this age group until its members are ready for marriage.

There are times when elders in the community, who are not necessarily related to the boys or girls by blood, would provide the same educational duties in their homes. In some traditional Shona communities this is the

61. Gelfand, *Growing up*, p. 27.

time when the initiation ceremony, which includes circumcision, takes place. Again, any of the adults or elders of the community, especially those of the same sex as the adolescent, constantly reinforce the things, which adolescents are to be taught. Similar to Sullivan's theory, these elders act as chums.

The next stage is that of marriage and procreation. One goes through the period of courtship. When ready to be married, a man must have accumulated some money or gifts to give to the family of the bride (bride wealth/ dowry). If the man has brothers, they would also contribute towards the dowry. A woman is married into a family; a man likewise marries into a family. Marriage is not just the union of two individuals, but the uniting of two families. It is a rare case in the Shona traditional culture in which marriage is an agreement only between two people, without the involvement of the families or community. Marriage makes one creative and reproductive. The children born to the marriage become the link between the parents in the marital relationship, the extended families, and with the departed (the past) and the generations to come (the future). This is also a period in which one engages in the responsibility of family and becomes a senior to all those who are unmarried (younger adults) of the community. One assumes leadership positions in the community (mentoring/ apprenticing younger members of the community), advocates for good communal interpersonal relationships, and makes decisions on behalf of one's family. Chapter five will go into detail about marriage among the Shona.

As one grows older in wisdom, character, wise counsel, and experience, one is elevated to eldership in the community. In many communities there are no rituals connected to this stage. With experience and age, one is believed to attain the position of elder. One of the key roles of the elder is to make sure healthy interpersonal relationships are maintained within the family or the community.

Again, the lack of communal interpersonal relations deemed central in both Sullivan's theory and the traditional Shona culture (village setting) has become a source of anxiety for the contemporary urban Shona people, requiring pastoral caregivers with an integrative consciousness to serve in this context.

PERSONAL IDENTITY IN THE CONTEMPORARY URBAN SHONA AFRICAN CONTEXT

The advent of urbanization and Westernization upset the traditional village structure. Bourdillon (who has written much about the Shona), Gelfand, and Mbiti note that urbanization changed the traditional cultural and religious ways of life. The urban setting does not encourage communal living. Most of the upper middle class families in the city have both parents working outside the home. The mothers leave their babies early to return to work, and the nanny then raises the infants and children. Remember that, according to Sullivan's findings, the mother's consistent absence can produce anxiety or a "not me" personality in the infant. The situation has changed from the traditional context in which the mother was present, nursing, and carrying the baby for up to the age of about two years.

These nannies are mostly teenagers themselves, who are not well vested in the Shona traditional culture or moral values. Some of the nannies are still probing their own identity or sexuality about which no one might have educated them; they therefore lack the wisdom with which to teach the children of the household about adulthood. Because of the fast-pace of life in the cities, some parents do not have the time to teach their children about life and sexuality; instead the television movies inform children before the parents do. There is lack of adult supervision since both parents are working. Masasire notes about the impact of change in the urban setting "Much of the success of traditional methods of socialization rested on the homogeneity and relatively static nature of society. With the accelerating rate of change in these societies [urban Shona] today, child-rearing techniques have gone through many changes."[62]

The setting in the cities is different from the traditional villages in which any adult could discipline the youth. In the cities, the children are under no obligation to listen to a stranger. Life in the cities is based on competition, not cooperation. The children are without the luxury of having elders to train them about adulthood in the traditional sense; therefore some children grow up without personal role models who could act as "chums" for them. The substitute role model they have might be, singers, etc., on the television, for example, Michael Jordan, LeBron James, Steven Curry or Nicki Minaj, Justin Bibber, thousands of miles away from their context.

---

62. Masasire, "Kinship and Marriage," p. 45.

Kapenzi, a Shona, writing on the clash of cultures in the Shona context says, "Conflicts between the old and the new social principles are producing new rivalries unknown in the traditional tribal order. Industrialization and urbanization have released new forces and created new groups. Members of a family are isolated more and more from each other. Men and women are taken far away out of their families and kinship groups, where they become involved with strangers within a whole system of impersonal institutions."[63]

Kapenzi's argument on the cultural clash is quite apparent in the urban context today and this is what sets the Shonas in a personal identity conflict. In the cities, kinship such as that in the village setting is no longer primary. Having small families is being encouraged in the name of economic feasibility.

In their research on the Zimbabwean cities (mostly Harare), both Gelfand (cited in Chapter One) and Bourdillon found that most urban parents try to have their children educated about the traditional Shona culture by sending the children to the rural areas.[64] However, this has proven ineffective since the children have the tendency to perceive rural life as backward. In turn, the rural folks, especially the elders, look at these city children as modernized and lacking an understanding of or respect for the Shona traditional life, morals, values, and culture. Bourdillon notes:

> One result of the weakening links between parents and children, and between children and traditional society, is that people born and brought up in town often do not know how to behave correctly when they visit their relatives in the country. They have not learnt the details of traditional social patterns . . . Besides, they are likely to have a higher standard of living than the rural kin and children in the towns are more aware of wealth differentials than absent patterns of kinship: parents of such children may find it difficult to persuade them to pay due respect to rural elders which may involve sitting on the ground soiling their smart town clothes.[65]

Most children growing up in the cities are of the opinion that the traditional beliefs are oppressive and backward. Mbiti also argues that the cultural change, taking place in the African context in general, is producing "half-cultured people." He notes, "Modern change tries to plant a form of culture which is shallow at least on the African soil. It is a culture of the alphabet and

---

63. Kapenzi, *The Clash of Cultures*, p. 47.

64. Bourdillon, *The Shona Peoples*, chap. 2 and 4 passim.

65. Ibid., p. 318.

comics, of pop music and transistor television and magazines with pictures of semi-naked women, of individualism and economic competition, of mass production and ever accelerating speed of life. Men and women are forced to live in two half cultures which do not unite to form one culture."[66]

The point Mbiti is making is similar to the one argued earlier about the contemporary urban Shonas lacking a culture which can provide the children and youth with a strong foundation. The church has not prepared pastoral caregivers serving the urban generations for helping them to handle the changes taking place in these people's lives, and the Western culture is not a legitimate substitute for the traditional culture. The urban culture places more emphasis on the individual, and the training of boys and girls, a task which used to be given in the traditional Shona culture, is no longer available or is perceived as not suitable for the urban context.

Some parents in the urban areas are uncomfortable talking to or teaching their own children about sexual matters since this was the aunts', uncles', and grandparents' role. These people (aunts, uncles, etc.) are not readily available in the cities. At the same time, there is no one else to teach their children about sexual issues except for the television and popular sexually explicit lyrics heard over the radio. In such a setting, the children end in confusion about developing a personal identity; there is no one to provide structure and accountability as there was in the traditional context. The education, which is provided by foreign Western culture through the media (emphasizing I, me, my, and mine), is not fully understood either.

In the cities, children do not have to live by the traditional rules such as respect of one's elders, respect of the community values and morals, believing the common African world-view such as, "I am therefore we are, since we are therefore I am," or "One tree does not make a forest." Anxiety strikes when the adult or the child growing up in the city realizes that s/he does not have a community support system founded in interpersonal relations. The children growing up in the city realize the lack of communal support and do not have that sense of community internalized or ingrained in them because the ways in which they were brought up are individualistic. Anxiety also arises primarily when the child realizes a lack of community support and has to deal with relatives who live in the village setting where there is that sense of communal support. The traditional Shona society's stages of development have no place or are not regarded in the urban context. The Western individualistic

66. Mbiti, *African Religions*, p. 288-289.

educational system plus the media have replaced the traditional educational systems without providing all the benefits of the traditional society.

THE MISSING LINK IN THE URBAN SHONA SETTING

The missing link for the urban population, in line with Sullivan's theory of interpersonal relationships and communal existence, is the lack of a sense of connectedness or communal interrelatedness. People are connected to their wealth more than their interpersonal relationships. The children growing up in such a context tend to internalize economic values of competition more than kinship values. One lives a life of competition more than of harmony. The idea of "I" is valued more than that of "we." Having grown up with an individualistic mode of life, the children find that non-communal frame of reference detrimental when they ask the questions regarding one's identity, the relational connectedness of one's roots, and one's history and origins.

I agree with the conclusion reached by Mwikamba, a Catholic priest as well as a lecturer in the Department of Religious Studies at Nairobi University. He notes:

> . . . it is clear that the Western identity and the African identity differ, and that they have different emphases. Friendship, solidarity, respect for nature, respect for human dignity, the right relationship within community and extended family, which includes both the living and dead, are values regarded with high esteem in African traditional society. However, these values seem to be fading away from 'modern' African society.
>
> Many of the so called 'modern' Africans are strangers to themselves, to other people and to nature. The harmonious and symbiotic relationship between a person and the object, between a person and the world, seem to be breaking down. In the past, the symbiotic relationships made an African world of experience to be personal, for the world could not be separated from the self. The self could not be separated from other people or from the world; and all of them could not be separated from God.[67]

The upper middle class urban Shonas are ashamed to go back to the "backward" way of life to get their sense of personal identity, and at the same time they find that having chosen a life of individualism has led them

---

67. Mwikamba, "A Search for," p. 99-100.

to living a lonely life. Their personal identity is based on their economic possessions and not on interpersonal relationships.

In their book, Sue and Sue talk about five different types of cultural orientations that native people in the North American context experience and this author would add that people from indigenous contexts such as Zimbabwe experience similar.

> *Traditional:* The individual may speak little English and practice traditional customs and methods of worship. 2. *Marginal:* The individual may be bilingual but has lost touch with his or her cultural heritage yet is not fully accepted in the mainstream society. 3. *Bicultural:* This person is conversant with both sets of values and can communicate in a variety of contexts. 4. *Assimilated:* The individual embraces only the cultural *mainstream* values *(need to note that in other indigenous contexts outside of Western world, the assimilation is not of traditional values but of the Western cultural values).* 5. *Paratraditional:* The individual has been exposed to and adopted *Western* values but is making a conscious effort to return to the old ways.[68]

The traditional person may struggle with the urbanized life but would fit well in the rural environment where they can easily practice their traditional beliefs and live communally. Those who are marginal and assimilated would find it hard to live in the rural areas and may have conflict in the self-identity. Sue and Sue say the following about the marginalized and the assimilated:

> . . . they may face issues such as (a) lack of pride in or denial of "native" heritage, (b) pressure to adopt "Western" cultural values (c) guilt over not knowing or participating in the "native or indigenous culture, (d) negative views regarding "natives or indigenous people" and (e) a lack of an extended "family" support or belief system.[69]

Many of the contemporary Shona living in the urban areas find themselves in the marginal and assimilated groups. As argued above, they feel the full pull of the traditional and Western way of life and don't fit either one.

When anxiety sets in, those who belong to Christian families may choose to go to a counselor or to their pastors for help. This author agrees with Sullivan that anxiety is one of the main reasons why people seek help,

---

68. Sue and Sue, *Counseling the Culturally Diverse*, p. 387.
69. Ibid, p. 387.

including in the Shona context, that is, when interpersonal relations are ignored:

> . . . it is necessary to appreciate that it is anxiety which is respon-
> sible for a great part of the inadequate, inefficient, unduly rigid,
> or otherwise unfortunate performances of people; that anxiety is
> responsible in a basic sense for a great deal of what comes to a
> psychiatrist for attention.[70]

There are many reasons why people need help, as stated above by Sullivan; however, Sullivan also believes that faulty interpersonal relations, or threats to one's security or personal identity, are other ways in which people become anxious. A pastor with an integrative consciousness who is cognizant of the Shona traditional culture, the Western culture, and/or the integration thereof, is equipped to help youth or individuals going through such a personal identity crisis. Sullivan's theory provides a pastoral caregiver reasons to explore issues of interpersonal relationships and communal existence, which might be causing anxiety to those living in the urban Shona context and a theoretical framework within which to do so.

For the Shona there is also the spiritual or religious aspect of being involved in interpersonal relationships to assure personal wholeness.

The following case illustrates the importance of interpersonal relations and how identity confusion can create anxiety in individuals in a Shona African context.

A CASE OF RELIGIO-CULTURAL REFUGEES

Nhamo and Netsai are a young couple in their thirties. They live in one of the suburbs of Harare. Nhamo is a very independent man who has assimilated many Western cultural and economic values and who owns a very successful business. He is highly educated with a master's degree and also went to a highly rated boarding school for his secondary education. The couple decided to consult their "spiritual father," after continual illness of their son, difficulties in their marriage, and the husband's depression.

Their problems started when Nhamo went to introduce Netsai to his parents. Nhamo's father openly rejected Nhamo's intentions to marry Netsai. Nhamo's father said he had heard that Netsai's family was accused of being

---

70. Sullivan, *Interpersonal Theory*, p. 160.

witches and that the family was being hounded by a ngozi (avenging) spirit. Nhamo asked his father to reconsider but the father put his foot down.

At a family meeting, Nhamo's father restated his reasons for refusing to approve of Nhamo's proposed marriage. Nhamo became angry and started to speak in English. The uncles and grandfather registered their complaint that they felt disrespected by Nhamo, and could not help him since he was speaking in English. He told them they (including his father) were not Christian and were uncivilized. Nhamo told everyone at the meeting he was now attending a church and had acquired a new name through his church. He was now the "son of prophet Mugandiwa." He said he believed in Jesus' response when the mother and brother were looking for him:

> "While Jesus was still speaking to the crowds, His mother and brothers stood outside, wanting to speak to Him. Someone told Him, 'Look, Your mother and brothers are standing outside, wanting to speak to You.' But Jesus replied, 'Who is My mother, and who are My brothers?' Pointing to His disciples, He said, 'Here are My mother and My brothers. For whoever does the will of My Father in heaven is My brother and sister and mother.'"[71]

Nhamo said his new Christian family was now the church and his "spiritual father" the prophet could suffice for he and Netsai. The father told (he) Nhamo that since he had chosen to sever his family relationships and had chosen "the prophet or spiritual father," as his new father, he was now on his own. Some of the elders at the meeting tried to convince Nhamo to take back his words and re-consider to which he burst out more in anger and told everyone he did not need them and they were just a bunch of uneducated heathens. The meeting ended and Nhamo left for the city where he was working.

Nhamo proceeded without the support of his family of origin to marry Netsai. They were well known in their church as "the son and daughter of prophet Mugandiwa." The prophet also always elevated them since they were a very well to do couple. When the couple moved into their suburban home they found a horn filled with blood, hanging in a tree next to their bedroom window. They invited some church members to help them burn the horn. The horn, however, would not burn.

The couple's first pregnancy ended in a miscarriage, despite Netsai's having received prenatal care. Zvitendo (now three years old) was born from the second pregnancy, but is a sickly child. At one point, when Zvitendo was seriously ill, the couple went to several European doctors and were told by one of the English

---

71. Matthew 12:46-48, NRSV.

medical doctors that the root cause of the illness was traditional "zvechivanhu."
In other words, the doctor said the health problems seem to be "culture bound
syndrome" or a cultural explanation or perceived cause."[72] The doctor said the
solution could be found in the Shona traditional religious culture. He advised
them to go back to their families of origin to get help or to look for a tradi-
tional medicine person. Nhamo responded that they would not seek the help
from "a bunch of uncivilized heathens or of a medicine person since they were
Christians. He declared that "Christ and their spiritual father" would see them
through all their problems. However, after the visit, the wife secretly took the son
to a traditional medicine person. The medicine person in his "kushopera"—the
traditional casting of the divining bones—told the wife that he saw that there
was a "wandering spirit" and that something was wrong within the family rela-
tions of both of the couple's families of origin. He said he could only give details
of the problems if Netsai's husband was present. The medicine person prescribed
"muti," medicinal roots for Netsai to give to the child. The child appeared to
respond positively after two days of being on the prescribed medicine from the
medicine person. Prior to the medicine he used to sleep only three to four hours
and would then wake up the rest of the night due to nightmares. Unlike in the
past, he slept throughout the night after Netsai gave him the "muti."

A week after Netsai's visit to the medicine person, Nhamo found the
"muti" (medicinal roots) prescribed for the son and he threw them away. That
same day Zvitendo could not sleep. Nhamo told his wife that he did not want
his wife going to visit with her family anymore because he was convinced
that they were the ones who had influenced her to see the medicine person. In
addition, he also accused Netsai's family of not being Christian, of being poor
and lazy, and of milking him of his wealth. Netsai's relatives needed to know
Nhamo had big medical bills to pay to get his son well. He was tired of taking
care of "a whole village," he said. Netsai shared this with her aunt who, in
turn, shared the story with Netsai's family of origin. Netsai's family responded,
"Achazviona, anodada netuhupfumi twake itwotwo. Ukama hunopfuura
hupfumi. Akaona tichitsika kumba kwake atibvunze." This translates to
mean, "He will have to face it, he is proud of his small riches. Relationships
are more important than wealth. Let him ask us if he will ever find anyone of
us paying him a visit again."

---

72. APA, DSMV, p. 14. (A label, attribution, or feature of an explanatory model that
provides a culturally conceived etiology or cause for symptoms, illness, or distress . . . Ca-
sual explanations may be salient features of folk classifications of disease used by healers.

Nhamo also told his wife that her act of visiting the medicine person could be grounds for divorce and that she was a backsliding Christian. Netsai told Nhamo what the medicine person had said and that the medicine person wanted to meet with Nhamo as well. Nhamo responded by saying, "Not even over my dead body would I consult a medicine person."

During this time, word also reached them that Nhamo's father was seriously ill. Nhamo started having re-occurring dreams and nightmares of his father dying without having set things right with him. The couple noticed that the days when Nhamo's depression was better the son was ill the most and vice versa. Zvitendo started having terrible nightmares. The son talked about seeing a horn, a frightening ugly human-like figure and hearing a voice asking why the father burned the horn. The voice said that Zvitendo would suffer the rest of his life to pay for his father's deeds. This caused Nhamo to be even more depressed, and he also continued to have re-occurring dreams of the father dying without reconciliation. In the dream Nhamo's father's spoke the words "ndikafa zwinhu zwakadai uchazviona," which translates as "if I die with things the way they are (conflicted relationship) Nhamo would have to face the consequences."

Nhamo became depressed and would not go to work or to church. At this point they decided to call their "spiritual father." The young "spiritual father, Mugandiwa" was someone who had been born and raised in the city, and who had not received any pastoral training. He did not believe in the Shona traditional world-view. The first time the "spiritual father" heard about the couple's situation through "the grapevine," he used the couple's situation as an illustration during a worship service saying he had heard that there were some members of the church who had visited a medicine person. In his preaching he condemned "such members and that he could easily disown them as their spiritual father." He characterized them in front of the congregation as being weak in faith and headed for hell and condemnation.

SOCIO-CULTURAL ISSUES

The socio-cultural analysis of Nhamo and Netsai helps a counselor or pastoral caregiver in assessing the main cultural influences affecting both of them, and determining how these influences have affected their interpersonal relationships. Nhamo is someone who has assimilated Western cultural values, is a successful businessman, and focuses on economic success rather than on his communal interpersonal relationships. Nhamo grew up in the mission schools where he was prevented from assimilating the Shona traditional religio-culture. He acts more Western than Shona. Nhamo functions at the level of naive consciousness. He has assimilated Western values to the extent that he does not analyze when to apply those Western values. He speaks to his grandfather and uncles in English, despite the fact that they have told him they felt disrespected when he did so.

Due to the crisis in his family, Nhamo now realizes that the Western socio-culture of economic success cannot provide him with the support he now needs. He has money, but the money is not providing him with the sustenance of an extended family support system. Nhamo is also now experiencing cultural dissonance.

The couple loves their son, but have no other relationships other than their nuclear family. Nhamo has spent a lot of money on the treatment of his son. The son's illness is a factor in the severance of relationships with both of the extended families. In addition, their "spiritual father" has condemned the couple as of weak faith. This has also left them with no to poor support system in terms of their church family.

ANXIETY, ITS SOURCE, AND PSYCHOLOGICAL ISSUES

A counselor or pastoral caregiver can explore at least three different sources of Nhamo's and Netsai's anxiety. First, Zvitendo's illness appears to be one of the main sources of anxiety for the couple. The nightmares Zvitendo is experiencing appear to be pointing to Nhamo's relationship with the father and family of origin, which involves the African traditional religio-culture practices of reconciliation, which Nhamo vehemently despises as pagan and heathen. The wife went to a *nganga* (medicine person) with their son, Zvitendo. The medicine she was given for Zvitendo appeared to work, and the wife was told to bring her husband to the *nganga* for further information. Consulting a medicine person is one of the things Nhamo is opposed to, but now he appears to be in a dilemma, after hearing what the son is telling them about the nightmares. During the nightmares, the spirit asks why Nhamo burned his "stuff." The solution points to Nhamo having to shift his beliefs and accommodate some of the African traditional beliefs and solutions. The church already condemned them as an unworthy Christian family. As much as Nhamo condemns African traditional beliefs, he does not know what to do with the situation surrounding his son's, and his own, illness. The doctors have diagnosed the cause of Zvitendo's illness as "a culture specific syndrome." The illness has shaken the grounds of Nhamo's Christian faith, and the church has not provided him with the type of support system he expected during this time of need. The doctors and his Christian faith have not been able to provide him with solutions to the problems, and Nhamo is anxious about the idea of having to look for resolution in that which he condemns as pagan and heathen. In short, Nhamo is experiencing religious-cultural dissonance. He has become a *refugee* both religio-culturally.

Second, a counselor or pastoral caregiver must explore with Nhamo the issue of his father's illness, and how their faulty dysfunctional relationship is affecting Nhamo. Nhamo has constant dreams of his father dying without being reconciled with him, which is another source of great anxiety. Nhamo realizes there will be added consequences if his father dies without reconciliation being achieved. He does not know how to go back and address the situation of his broken relationship with his father.

The third source of Nhamo's anxiety which a counselor or pastoral caregiver can help address is his broken interpersonal relationships with the extended family. The extended family members from Netsai's family side have vowed never to step in Nhamo's home again. They have told Nhamo that his foolishness lies in failing to realize that relationships are more important than riches. It is Nhamo's behavior and words, which severed his relationship with his own family of origin, including his extended family members. He condemned their Christian beliefs as "heathen" and said he did not need anyone except Christ and his "spiritual father."

Netsai's anxiety is based on lack of control. She has been condemned by her husband and the church for going to the medicine person. In addition, she is not allowed to have any relationships with her extended family. She has not been able to free herself from oppression in this marriage. Netsai's beliefs (consulting the medicine person) have been condemned by both the church and her husband, even though she is convinced that the medicine prescribed by the medicine person for their son was working. I agree with ma Mpolo that a counselor or caregiver must explore the problem from the careseeker's point of view. He notes:

> As a starting point, the therapist should accept as valid the experience of the patient. This therapeutic encounter lowers the distance separating the patient and the therapist. By accepting the diagnosis

of the patient, his/her world view is at the disposal of the therapist who, with analytical mind, can explore it in depth.[73]

Netsai has never been given an opportunity to tell her story and what she believes about Zvitendo's illness. Netsai needs to be allowed to present her point of view. A counselor or pastoral caregiver must be attuned to psychological issues with which this couple are struggling and examine how they pertain to the issues of bi-culturalism and bi-religiousness. Netsai does not appear to have any problems mixing the two religions, Shona traditional religion and Christianity. Nhamo, on the other hand, is totally opposed to Shona traditional religion. That to which Nhamo is opposed appears to be what works, insofar as was proven by the useful medicine Netsai got from the medicine person for Zvitendo.

Nhamo and Netsai seem to be caught between issues of success within their relationships. This has caused them much misery inasmuch as they have become an "island unto themselves." They cannot seem to fit well with the Western nor the Shona traditional culture. As stated earlier, this has created anxiety in terms of a lack of an available relational support system. Psychologically, they are struggling with a lack of both cultural and spiritual grounding. They have no "home" psychologically or culturally. The two now feel isolated and live as *refugees* culturally and religiously. The Christian foundation they have always depended upon appears to have been shaken. In addition, Nhamo is depressed and confused, and appears to be questioning his religious beliefs.

RELIGIOUS OR THEOLOGICAL ISSUES

A counselor or pastoral caregiver utilizing an integrative consciousness must be attuned to the different diagnoses being given by Nhamo and Netsai. One of the main religious issues with which this family is faced relates to the cause of Zvitendo's illness, which the doctors named "culture-bound syndrome." Coupled with the physical illness and Zvitendo's nightmares (which in the Shona religious understanding are an indication of an unsettled spirit of a dead person who needs recognition or reconciliation), Nhamo's problem is that he does not entertain or allow any Shona traditional religio-cultural values to be mingled with his Christian beliefs. Nhamo appears to be in a significant struggle insofar as acknowledging the

73. ma Mpolo and Kalu, eds., *The Risk of Growth*, p. 5.

power of the spirit, since he considers such a belief an influence of the pagan world. A counselor or pastoral caregiver must explore whether Nhamo might feel that a diagnosis of Zvitendo's illness, as related to an influence of a spirit hounding him, would be condemned as an indication of shallowness in Nhamo's own Christian faith. He also may fear being viewed as a weak or unfaithful Christian, due to the perception that his family is being attacked by the pagan powers.

Nhamo's nuclear family's relationship with the spirit connected to the horn is an issue, which needs to be addressed, since it appears to be directly related to Zvitendo's illness. It is easy to conclude from the Shona traditional world-view that Nhamo cut down a tree which might have ritually been given as a home to a spirit. Nhamo burning the "stuff"- the container with a horn filled with blood—was a mistake. There is a high possibility that the "stuff" belonged to the previous owners of the house, and Nhamo could have consulted with them and let them take their "stuff," if it belonged to them. If the previous owners of the house were not associated with the container, Nhamo could have asked the help of other Christians to ritually remove the "stuff" and request that the spirit move elsewhere, since they did not know the spirit or have any relationship with it. They did not need to burn the container. By attempting to burn the container, Nhamo committed a violation against the spirit. Some form of acknowledgment or reconciliation needs to happen between Nhamo's nuclear family and the spirit.

Nhamo needs to be questioned about what he believes about the "spirits." The best place to start may be to refer him to the Biblical stories referring to when Christ was casting out evil spirits from people. It is not unchristian to believe that evil spirits exist. The questions about Nhamo's biblical images or stories with which his family identifies need to be explored. How are these biblical stories being used or misused in Nhamo's and his family's experience?

There are also issues of communal interpersonal relationships between Nhamo's family, the church, and God. In addition, Nhamo must address issues of his interpersonal relationships with his wife, father, and the general extended family on both sides. Both are seeking healthy interpersonal relationships.

At this moment of crisis, Nhamo and Netsai need to explore their interpersonal relationship with God. Where do they see God at work or not at work in their lives? What needs to change pertaining to how they perceive God? Is God wrathful and unforgiving? Is God punishing them by making

Zvitendo sick? Does Nhamo perceive belief in the power of an evil spirit as something God will judge him for as an unforgivable sin? Could God use the Shona traditional methods (not contrary to Christianity) to help heal Zvitendo? Nhamo and Netsai need to re-examine the ways in which they relate to God, and explore ways God could bring healing to their family.

Netsai's and Nhamo's marital relationship needs attention. Netsai needs the freedom to tell her story and articulate her religious beliefs. How does it feel for her to be married to Nhamo? How does it feel for her to have been condemned by both the church and her husband? How is she handling the fact that she is not allowed to have any contact with her extended family? What does she wish could change? Netsai is to be given the freedom to narrate how she feels about Zvitendo's illness, and to express her opinions regarding viable solutions to the illness.

The issue of the relationship with the church or congregation is one which is hard to address. A counselor or pastor with an integrative consciousness is to be involved in such a case. The "spiritual father" must have fully understood that his condemnation of his parishioners in a sermon, without having provided pastoral care to them, was a poor approach. The first thing the "spiritual father" was supposed to do was to meet with the couple and hear their story. A counselor or pastor with an integrative consciousness can work on theological, religious, and pastoral care issues present in the case.

A counselor or pastoral caregiver's next task for Nhamo and Netsai involves working on their relationship with the extended families. The starting point lies with Nhamo's father, since he is in very poor health. Nhamo must swallow his pride and ask for forgiveness for the things Nhamo said to his father and extended family. Nhamo has to realize that his father's belief in some things from the traditional religion does not mean he is "not Christian or an uncivilized heathen." Nhamo used his own Christian ways as the yardstick with which to judge his parents and relatives. In addition, there was no reason for Nhamo to disrespect his father by telling him he was an uneducated heathen. The source of Nhamo's dreams could well be a manifestation of his guilty conscience about his relationship with his father.

Nhamo needs to realize that his assimilation of Western values and Christianity appears to have gravely interfered with his relationship with his father and his extended family. As someone who is educated, Nhamo appears to exhibit a naive consciousness in that he does not analyze the situation and context and subsequently apply the best approach. The same inadequate naive approach was applied by Nhamo in the way in which he responded to his uncles and grandfather, telling them they were "a bunch of uncivilized heathens."

Nhamo needs to comprehend that his "holier than thou" attitude toward extended family members is the main problem impeding the progress and success of his communal interpersonal relationships. It is Nhamo who needs to take the first step of asking for forgiveness. He needs to learn what Christianity says about forgiveness and relationships with both Christians and non-Christians. If Nhamo's relationship with his family and other Christians is not right, can it be right with God? From the Christian understanding, Nhamo can be encouraged to engage in a process of rebuilding his relationship with his extended family. Jesus set a process of forgiveness in which one goes to the person who has committed sin, before offering a gift at the altar if he/she remembers the fault; then, to leave the gift at the altar, go and resolve the issue and so forth (Matthew 5:21-25).[74]

Nhamo and Netsai need help to explore issues around Zvitendo's illness, their communal interpersonal relationships with God, the spirit world, extended family relations, and with their church family. The process will also help Nhamo and Netsai re-evaluate their Christian values, as well as their marriage relationship. In the final analysis, the question of interpersonal relationships or estrangement from God, spirit world and others, brokenness, forgiveness, accountability, justice, and restitution need to be resolved before Nhamo's and Netsai's family can feel whole again. What van Beek, a pastoral counselor and theologian, concludes about the clash of worldviews in one of his case analyses holds true to Nhamo's and Netsai's situation. He says:

> The clash of meaning providing processes has reached a crisis point. They are riddled with guilt, plagued by fear, and jolted by anger . . . Worldviews rub against each other like crusts of land riding on restless continental plates. Everything is affected, the way they see the other, themselves, the people who raised them, the God they believe brought them together so irresistibly.[75]

74. Matthew 5:21-25, *NRSV*.
75. Van Beek, *Cross-Cultural Counseling*, p. 45.

SUGGESTED PASTORAL RESPONSE

In this case, one of the main tasks of a counselor or pastoral caregiver is to help Nhamo and Netsai realize the need for reconciliation between them and the spirit which is appearing to Zvitendo in the form of a nightmare. The action Nhamo and his friends from church performed in attempting to burn the container is the rightful ritual acknowledged by the Shona Christian church today. Since this action brought not peace, but rather more psychological and spiritual chaos to Nhamo's family, I am proposing an alternate solution which incorporates aspects from the traditional Shona world-view. The basis or criterion of the alternative solution is based on Shona traditional relational theology, which recognizes that, by burning the container, a violation was done to the spirit by Nhamo and his church friends. The spirit's home (the tree) was cut without announcement. Since the spirit is talking through Zvitendo's nightmares, the spirit can be asked who ritually placed it in the tree, and who its owner is so they can be send back and be reunited with its owner. After such a ritual, the spirit can then be exorcized and sent forth to its rightful place.

A counselor or pastoral caregiver must also take the lead in helping Nhamo and Netsai address their interpersonal relationships with their extended families. The family gathering(s) will allow opportunities for those with grievances against Nhamo to air them. Since there were no previous strong relationships between the two families, this might also provide an opportunity for the families to begin a better relationship. To a certain extent, Nhamo will be used as a scapegoat in the process; however, this will also bring to the fore, unresolved issues which the families can identify and pursue in the hope of eventual reconciliation.

CHAPTER FOUR

Shona African Traditional Relational Theology

HUKAMA, WHICH TRANSLATES AS kinship "relations by blood or marriage," and also sometimes translates as one's "interpersonal relationships," is one of the key elements tying the Shona communities together. This concept influences the world-view of these communities, particularly how they perceive life and being human. *Hukama* signifies many facets of one's relational interconnectedness, affiliations, interdependence, communal existence, ties to one's family and community, and integration of these factors into one's being. In addition, the concept of *hukama* is central to how the Shona relate to God and the Spirit World. Illustrative of this centrality is the Shona saying *Hukama hwakanaka hunopfuura hupfumi*, which literally means "having strong relationships is better than being wealthy." This saying is common among the Shona. For the Shona, a person who has good interpersonal relationships can rely on the support of his or her relatives, instead of having to rely on one's wealth in times of need. Thus, in the Shona world-view, one's interpersonal relationships are of great value to one's sense of being. One of the goals of this chapter is an attempt to demonstrate that communal interpersonal relations between God, humans, and nature, in the traditional Shona society, are predicated on religion. For instance, the way to relate with creation, such as land and trees, is based on traditional Shona religious understanding. Another goal is to illustrate the conflict that was created by the coming of colonization, Westernization and Christianity. The contemporary context has people caught in between traditional cultural practices, Christianity and capitalism at the expense of relationships.

INSTINCT TO RELATE IN TRADITIONAL SHONA RELIGION

The traditional African religio-culture, and more specifically for the traditional Shona people, believe that "humans are born with an instinct to relate."[1] In addition, in the traditional Shona worldview, the 'human instinct to relate' extends to an outside power, God. This way of understanding how humans relate to God is readily recognized as such in the general traditional African societies. One of the key aspects to indicate the difference between the West and the traditional African context is the presence of formal instructional structures (Sunday School) to teaches children about religion in the West, and the lack of such structures in the traditional African or Shona societies. Thus religion becomes "folk knowledge," practiced through relationships, participation and observation.

There is in the traditional Shona understanding a "spiritual instinct to relate" to a power outside of oneself, such as relating to *Musiki* (the Creator) or *Mwari* – (God), and the Spirit World. Moyo, a former professor at the University of Zimbabwe, without using the word "instinct" in describing traditional African religion, implicates:

> In African traditional thought, religion is not just another aspect of the culture but something inseparable from it (spiritual instinct to relate): a way of life, which embraces all aspects of human relations. Zimbabwean traditional thought cannot conceive of a human being without religion and without participation in the life, beliefs and practices of the community. Religion and culture are as it is were interchangeable. No African language of which I am aware, particularly in southern Africa, has a word equivalent to the English term "religion." The idea of such a thing, isolated from the rest of life and practiced on its own, does not exist. In the holistic worldview characteristic of all Africa, there can be no separation between the sacred and the profane, the spiritual and the material. Religion interweaves everything; hence, asking an African "What is your religion?" is like asking "What is your way of life?"[2]

---

1. The author realizes that the word instinct has been used in many negative ways against the African people. There are dangers in using the word in that one could read the author's use of the concept instinct as reducing the traditional Shona religion to an instinct. Religion as an instinct is not defining the religion in and of itself, but the tendencies or inclinations people have in becoming religious. The words "to relate" qualifying the word instinct are central to the use of this concept.

2. Moyo, *Zimbabwe*, p. 1-2.

Setiloane, even though writing from the South African context about African theology, wrote a subsection entitled "Religion as an Instinct" in addressing his understanding of African religion for the African people:

> The three seem to fall upon him/her all at the same time: Consciousness of self, consciousness of the community of humans and animals, and consciousness of Divinity as the Cause of being. So like the sense of being human or the sense of community, religion, a sense of a Power other than self, at work and determining existence, its origins and vicissitudes, is not something acquired. It is as old as being human itself; it is of the human's very nature. Hence the difference between Africa and the West in their attitude towards religion. There is actually no African word to translate 'religion.' At best it is translated as 'a people's ways' or 'customs' (mekgwa/amasiko) something lived and practiced, not discussed and discoursed about.[3]

Setiloane is arguing that the sense of relating to an outside power, outside of the self, is one which is part of human nature. The main idea I borrow from Setiloane is the fact that religion for the Africans is something, which is practiced and lived; it is a way of life. As instinct, it is part of the human inclinations and tendencies to relate to a power outside of themselves, present from the time of infancy. I add that as one grows older, the tendencies or inclinations to relate to God increase through living and practicing.

DEFINING SHONA TRADITIONAL RELATIONAL THEOLOGY

The advent of Christianity, and the condemnation of traditional Shona religion by Christianity, resulted in limiting some of the relational theological grounding on which the urban contemporary Shona pastoral caregiver can draw. What is relational theology from the traditional Shona context? How does it differ from other relational theologies? The Shona relational theology is informed by the traditional communal religio-cultural values of the Shona traditional society. As aforementioned, these values are grounded upon one's relationships with God, humans, and nature through the community. The redemptive plan of Shona relational theology is holistic rather than individualistic. In traditional Shona society, it is through relating to God, others and nature that one gets a sense of the spiritual self.

3. Setiloane, *African Theology*, p. 41.

There are different types of Western relational theologies. One of the fundamental values of Christianity is the belief of maintaining a relationship with the One Supreme Being, God. However, the one God is holistic in three persons: Father, Son, and the Holy Spirit. Christians, however, do not relate to the three as different entities but as One being (Trinitarian theology). Then, there is also eco-theology, which focuses on human relationship with creation or nature.[4] Another type of theology is anthropological theology, which emphasizes human nature, destiny, and human relations to the divine. In these other relational theologies, the relationships are not equally balanced, while in the traditional Shona relational theology, all the elements (nature, humans, Spirit World), are equally interdependent. What affects nature affects humanity, what affects humanity affects the Spirit World, and vice versa. The traditional Shona relational theology is one that seeks equilibrium in all of the relationships. Failure in any of the relationships produces a "domino effect" on the other relationships, resulting in disequilibrium in the community.

"Life in community is seen in terms of a triangle of relationships. These relationships help one understand who one is, and gives one a sense of their existence. The following fig is an illustration of how people in these communities try to live out their theology and how they understand their theology of relationships." [5]

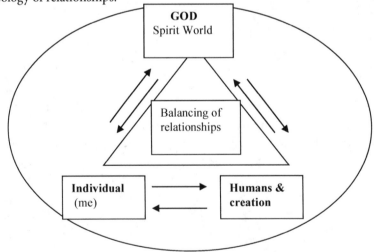

Fig 1 Communal Relationships: Theology of Life

4. Rasmussen, *Earth Community*.

5. Mucherera, *Meet me at the Palaver*, p. 89.

RELATIONSHIPS AND RITUALS IN TRADITIONAL SHONA SOCIETY

Rituals and relationships are central in religious beliefs and customs of the Shonas. Rituals are believed to be a means to right the wrong caused by faulty relationships. In the traditional Shona context, interpersonal relations take the form of interaction, relatedness, interdependence, or interconnectedness between "one" and the "other." The "one" or the "other" may refer to humans, nature, God, or Spiritual beings. The words "interpersonal relations" and "relationships" are used interchangeably since they draw the same meanings for this book. A key assertion in this chapter is what Maimela, a South African theologian, suggests about relationships and rituals in the African context:

> Africans are taught and expected to engage themselves in those activities that will enhance the total welfare of the community of which they are a part by: (a) avoiding bad relationships with those among whom the individual lives so as to make self-fulfilment in life by all those concerned possible; (b) engaging in various religious rites which maintain the well-being of the community, because failure to comply with them will release evil forces that will bring illness or misfortune of one kind or another.[6]

Maimela's claim is central to many traditional Africans including the Shona people. Rituals become a main avenue by which relationships between humans, creation, and the Spirit World are maintained. Malidoma Some, from Burkina Faso, in writing about form and function of ritual among the African communities, summarizes it well:

> Ritual is by its nature a communal activity and an act of creation. The people involved must develop these details themselves to fit the particular need that is being addressed. The ritual must create a certain kind of energy that can embrace individuals involved, allowing them to expand their awareness and undergo the transformation necessary to become healed . . . Ritual, community, and healing—these three are so intertwined in the indigenous world that to speak of one of them is to speak of them all. *Ritual*, communally designed, helps the individual remember his or her purpose, such remembering brings healing both to the individual and the community. The *community* exists, in part, to safeguard the purpose of each person within it . . . *Healing* comes when the

---

6. Maimela, "Salvation in African," p. 67.

individual remembers his or her identity—the purpose chosen in the world of ancestral wisdom—and reconnects with that world of Spirit. Human beings long for connection, and our sense of usefulness derives from the feeling of connectedness. When we are connected—to our own purpose, to the community around us, and to our spiritual wisdom—we are able to live and act with authentic effectiveness.[7]

The meaning and function of ritual described above by Some is the same as found in the traditional Shona context. The purpose of ritual is to transform and bring healing to dysfunctional interpersonal relations.

It is not unusual to hear Shonas say: *Ida hama dzako, mombe hai-kuchengeti,* which translates as, "Love or be in good relationship with your relatives for a cow (a symbol of one's possessions or wealth) won't take care of you." Even if one had the money to go to the most expensive doctors, the idea is that one still needs relational support. For example, only one's relatives can accord a person proper burial if one dies. If one is not accorded a proper burial, one's spirit wanders around. One has to be accorded the full burial ritual to become an ancestor or join the community of the Spirit World. The worst thing that can happen to a deceased person's spirit, or to a living human being, in the Shona context is to be cut off from the Spirit World or one's community respectively, since one's personal identity is based in one's community of embeddedness.

While relationships are valued more than wealth, being wealthy is not evil. However, people are expected to share their riches with those in need within the family or community. Sharing is not only the right thing to do, it is also believed that the sharing of one's wealth with the poor or others strengthens relationships and is a sign of a good communal spirit. Another saying among the Shona, *Hukama igaswa, hunozadziswa nekudya,* translates as, "a relationship is only partial until one shares a meal with the other." Illustrative of this belief is that in any reconciling ritual or ceremony, the two reconciling parties/families must prepare a meal together and share the meal in order to seal the conciliation or the new relationship. In these ceremonies, the ancestors and God are also involved as libation is poured out and some of the food is offered to them. Through the ancestors, the name of God is invoked as part of the ceremony and peace meal. The process of reconciliation is important in relationships because it functions as a seal of reparation for past broken relationships. Rituals repair

7. Some, *The Healing Wisdom of Africa,* p. 35-36.

shattered relationships, bridging them to renewed healthy relational beginnings. When relationships become broken, rituals are performed to bring the community to equilibrium. Maimela also says of the African society in general, in terms of rituals:

> In order to help save people from anxieties that are experienced due to life's contingencies, from the vagaries of nature, from potential impotency, from bad luck and from the malevolent spirits, witches and sorcerers, the African Traditional Religions have designed a variety of protective rites   and rituals . . . Furthermore, there are purificatory rites to cleanse those who are defiled so as to avoid impending destruction of the individual concerned as well as the threatening of the well-being of one's corporate existence. In addition, a variety of sacrificial offerings have been developed over the years to atone for whatever wrong or sin an individual or the community might have committed. [8]

Maimela echoes the fact that rituals, rites, and sacrifices are key to how Africans maintain their relationship with God. God is experienced in terms of interpersonal relationships, which is the Shona community's core of existence. Re-evaluating rituals and rites in the church offers the opportunity to integrate and reclaim some of the traditional religious practices inasmuch as rituals play such a central role in interpersonal relationships and in the Shona world-view. There is the need for rituals to be essentially cooperative and communal rather than individualistic in their function.

Sacrifices and rituals are thus means by which order is restored. There is a ritual for almost every little thing, performed so as not to disrupt life in relationship with God and the "other." Thus, most of the missionaries, when observing life in African communities, said the people were "notoriously religious."[9] Partly, the religiousness of the African communities is due to the need for maintaining their relationship with God, which is also a sign of humanity's dependence on God.

SHONA TRADITIONAL ATTRIBUTES AND CONCEPTS OF GOD AND ANCESTORS

It is a general understanding of those who have studied the Shona religion that the Shonas believe in One Supreme Being, God (*Mwari*). The word

8. Maimela, "Salvation in African ," p. 69-70.
9. Mbiti, *African Religions*, p. 1.

Mwari, when broken down, is *Mu—Ari*, and literally translates as "One Who Is." Daneel, who has studied and written about Independent churches, says,

> "The Shona concept of the Supreme Being has never been poly-theistic. The great number of names designating the Supreme Be-ing reveal a variety of functions and the association of the Divine with different phenomena of the nature rather than suggesting the existence of a number of deities. For centuries the Shona have believed in Mwari as the final authority above and behind their ancestors . . ."[10]

As Daneel intimates, God is known by different names and attributes. The different names for God imply the type of relationship the Shonas have with God and/or how they see God relating to them. Some call God *Samasimba*, which means the One who has all the power or is the source of power, or All powerful. Others refer to God as *Nyadenga* (One who possesses or who resides in the skies/heavens), *Wokumusorosoro* (the One who is above), *Mutangakugara* (the One who was first in the beginning), or *Muwanikwapo* (the One who was found already in existence). *Musiki* refers to Creator or the One who created everything. As creator, God is also known as *Musikavanhu*, specifically meaning that God is the creator of humanity. Another name, *Chidzachopo*, refers to God as the One who has always been there and/or the One who is Ageless. "*Dandemutande ngawi rakatandira nyika*" translates to "the web that surrounds the whole world." *Dzivaguru* means the Great Pool, with the connotation being that God supplies people with water or rains. God is also known as *Tateguru*, which means the Great Great Great Grandmother, suggesting that God is the source of life, the One who gave birth to all of humanity. Sometimes God is also known as *Jenandebvu* (the One with the white beard), depicting a God who resembles an old grandfather. In this theology, the Shona believe that there is no point where in one's life where God is not in relationship with humans. Our Spirit start with God, then they take the human form when we are born into this world. After we are dead physically, one's spirit re-joins the Spirit world.

In the Shona traditional religion, ancestors are of great importance; ancestors act as the mediators between God and humanity. As Mbiti says about the ancestors in all African contexts "They have both feet in both worlds, this world and in the spiritual world."[11] In addition, when the Shona Christians read in Exodus 3:6 "I am the God of your father, the God

---

10. Daneel, *Old and New*, p.80-1.

11. Mbiti, *African Religions*, p. 25.

of Abraham, God of Isaac, and God of Jacob," they believe this is the same God to their ancestors as well. He is the God of their fathers, of/in the lineage of father Abraham, since we are all descendants of Abraham. Thus, when praying to God, the Shona people always prayed through the ancestors to the one and only God—*Mwari*.

There might be many reasons for this way to approach God, but I will posit two reasons, which might be the major influence for the Shona who use these methods of praying through the ancestors. The first reason involves the sense of respect people carry for God's name and to note God's place. There is always a hierarchy in how elders and those with greater honor and age are addressed. At the conclusion of a prayer, God's name is used, both out of respect and to acknowledge God's position at the top of the hierarchy of respect and reverence. Illustrative of this is the following prayer: "*Nemi watisikachizivi motisvikisirawo munamato wedu kuna SaMatenga, Mwari, Musiki wedu.*" This prayer translated to English says, "And you (the ancestors) we no longer remember by name, please pass our prayer of thanks or requests to the One who possesses the heavens, God our Creator, and to the One Who who Is."

A second reason for praying through the ancestors is closely connected to the idea of respect and honor, and the traditional Shona understanding of death. It is believed by the traditional Shonas that a father or mother who cares for and loves his/her children must be well informed of the children's struggles and joys. In addition, parents are expected to intervene (if need be) or rejoice with the children, if there is cause for joy. The caring for and loving of one's children is not ended by death since the dead are considered to be "the living dead" or "living timeless." As they used to be informed of the struggles and joys of their children when alive, parents must continue to be informed of such pain and celebration after death. They are still living, in another form, the spiritual form, and now they can mediate for their children since they are closer to God. One would pray tracing the hierarchy (paternal side), beginning with one's father (if deceased), then the grandfather, and so forth, to the point of the name of the last person remembered in the hierarchy. At the end of the prayer, one calls upon all the other ancestors, no longer remembered by name, to take one's request to God. Bishop Hatendi notes the following:

> A person is inextricably and indissolubly one with the past, present and the future. The time concept is the observance of the collective personality. The family-group includes the dead who are

revered because they are believed to be nearer the source of life; but they are never deified. They play the role of the 'go-between' as in Shona marriage and royal protocol. It is this sense that the Shona pray 'through the dead.'[12]

The traditional Shona believe that the ancestors are present to them, but they have no power to change situations. The ancestors are dependent on God's will, taking the role of mediators. It is believed that the ancestors can speak to God on behalf of their loved ones, but they cannot change the will of God.

Since the Shona society is patriarchal, the prayers are presented through the father's lineage. However, women who are dead are also ancestors and are part of the Spirit World. The spirits of both the father and the mother are expected to play the role of protecting the children and grandchildren from harmful things. These spirits can also cause illness (as a way of getting attention) if they are not remembered.

It was and is easy for the Shonas who converted to Christianity to see no contradiction in Scriptures about praying through Christ instead of the ancestors. The supremacy of Christ is now seen as above the ancestors. Christ is now the ultimate revelation and the one who the converted Shonas should now worship through as opposed to the ancestors as stated in Hebrews Chapter One.

> "Long ago, at many times and in many ways, God spoke to our forefathers (ancestors) by the prophets, but in these last days he has spoken to us by his Son, whom he appointed the heir of all things, through whom also he created the world. He is the radiance of the glory of God and the exact imprint of his nature, and he upholds the universe by the word of his power. After making purification for sins, he sat down at the right hand of the Majesty on high, having become as much superior to angels as the name he has inherited is more excellent than theirs." [13]

The missionaries who did well were the ones who started with the religion that the Shona people knew and believed like the Apostle Paul it pointed them to the "unknown God." Those who advocated for the throwing away of everything African sent those who had converted into a turmoil. These were the ones who became Christians by day and Africans by night.

12. Hatendi, "Shona Marriage," p. 146.
13. Hebrews 1:1-4, NRSV.

INTERPERSONAL RELATIONSHIPS: NATURE, EVIL SPIRITS AND HUMAN BEINGS

There are sacred places or things, such as caves, dams, mountains, and trees, but they are not worshiped. Most missionaries confused this belief with animism, thinking that Africans believed that trees have souls similar to those of human beings. While an evil spirit may reside in a tree, it is not believed to be part of the makeup of a tree. Similarly, a tree may be sacred because of events that may be performed under it, but does not have a soul as part of its essential makeup. It is believed that what affects nature affects humans, and vise-versa; therefore, a lot of emphasis is put on harmony with nature. Harmony is very important to the way of life of the Shonas and includes co-existence with nature, humanity, God, and the Spirit World.

Evil spirits exist as part of creation and can live in caves, trees, river-banks, and elsewhere. The Shona believes that it is therefore advisable that one not cut down trees at random in certain areas since these might be dwelling places for evil or for wandering spirits. For example, a wandering spirit, *shavi*, can be the spirit of a dead person who was not accorded proper burial. The only way this person's spirit can find rest is if the family accords the person proper burial, with a ceremony to send this spirit off to the Spirit World.

The traditional Shona religion holds that humans are basically born good, but they have the potential to be bad. Everything good and bad were created by God. The dualism of believing in a devil, who is the source and cause of evil, and a God who is good is not held to. There are no Shona words for 'Devil' or 'Satan.' Illustrative of the influence of the Christians' world-view are the direct translations from English *(Satani or Diabori)*. In the Shona language, an attribute, *Chirazamavi namauya*, is used in reference to God as the one who is the source of both good and bad. Murphree, in discussing the Shona beliefs in Mwari, talks about *Chirazamauya*, "The One who provides for good and bad."[14] The attribute *Chirazamauya* (cited by Murphree) describes a God who is the giver of good, *mauya*. To make a correction on how Murphree presents the attribute, I argue that Murphree left out the word *mavi*, which means bad. The full attribute would therefore be "*Chirazamavi namauya*," which means provider of good and bad.

In addition, humans, such as witches, can manipulate the forces of evil to use it against other humans. In other cases, one can become evil because the family so chooses to place an evil spirit on one. From the time of infancy,

14. Murphree, *Christianity and the Shona*, p. 49.

the family can give a child over (*kurasira*) to an avenging spirit, or to a dead witch's wandering spirit, which may turn the child's spirit into an evil one.

Muzorewa, a Shona theologian, suggests that strife in relationships between humans, and between humans and God or creation, is perceived as the main cause or source of tension in the Shona communities. Chaos and catastrophes may occur when there is violation of the customs, mores, and religious ways of the community. Muzorewa further notes:

> So, we find that African humanity is primarily defined by a sense of belonging, serving one's own folk, and kinship. For the African, it is not enough to be a human being; unless one shares a sense of community, one can easily turn out to be an enemy . . . African theology may derive the criteria for belonging to a community of believers from this traditional concept of humanity in community. Such a definition of the community of believers takes collective survival very seriously. [15]

Here, Muzorewa addresses the importance of community and how African traditional religious culture may influence contemporary African theology. What Muzorewa is saying is in line with what I understand of the significance of communal interpersonal relations in the traditional context. Some of the traditional understandings of communal relations need to be utilized in the Shona pastoral theology of care today.

A pastoral caregiver with an integrative consciousness must understand the importance and primacy of interpersonal relationships in the traditional Shona world-view, e.g. myths, rituals, etc. At times, the traditional Shona understanding of interpersonal relations contradicts that of Christianity in that the Shona understanding may include rituals which call for peace making with creation, for which the Shona Christian rituals now in place do not provide.

GOD AND HUMANITY, AND THE SHONA MYTHS

In the traditional Shona context, humanity was believed to have been created to be in relationship with God. Without a relationship with God, the community and its meaning ceases. In other words, in the Shona traditional society, the community cannot exist wholly or without chaos in the absence of being in relationship with God. In addition, interpersonal

15. Muzorewa, *The Origins*, p. 17.

human relations affect the individual's relationship with God. What an individual does in terms of one's relationship with God affects the family or community just as much as the community's actions affect the individual's relationship with God. For example, according to the traditional Shona beliefs, when an individual murders someone, it will not only affect the individual's relationship with God, but will also affect the entire family's relationship with the family of the deceased and with God for generations to come, until the time of reconciliation.

The entire family and sometimes the community in the traditional Shona society will need cleansing and forgiveness from God for acts of murder yet to be pardoned. The rituals performed are not just for the sake of the individual involved but include the entire community. Murphree talks about the belief of the Shona people, that acts such as incest or any other act contrary to the laws of *Mwari* (God) are punishable by God, who sends lightning as a punishment to the offenders.[16] Murphree is pointing to the communal responsibility aspect. Mbiti says the following about the African communities' beliefs and understanding of their relationship to God and one another:

> Beliefs are expressed through concepts of God, attitudes towards him, and the various acts of worship. Furthermore, they are collective, communal, or corporate beliefs, held by groups or communities. The individual 'believes' what other members of the corporate society 'believe,' and he 'believes' because others 'believe.'[17]

I also agree with Mbiti on the idea of one's relationship with God, others, and one's beliefs. Collective and communal beliefs have an impact on how one relates to or perceives God. The above statement, "he believes because others believe," may not be as simple as it reads. The statement, "one may believe because others believe," may mean that one knows that if what he/she believes along with the community is wrong, then he/she is not the sole person accountable for the wrong belief. Rather, the whole community is accountable.

Many creation stories and myths in the African context point to the importance of relationships between God, humanity, and creation in general. In the traditional Shona society, myths serve as the traditional interpretations of the universe and all of creation; they were used by the elders

---

16. Murphree, *Christianity and the Shona*, p. 49.

17. Mbiti, *Concepts of God*, p. 218.

to explain the origin of things to the children. Many of the myths explained the Shona people's understanding of their relationships with God and creation. These myths are still significant in the traditional Shona society in so much as they help guide some of the people's behaviors in relating to God. The myths are still told today in more traditional contexts such as the rural areas. The purpose of using the myths in this book is to show how the traditional Shonas view their relationship with God from the time of creation. In losing the African myths, the Shonas also lost grounding in their relational understanding of God, creation, and the Spirit World. The following section presents myths referring to the relationships between God and humanity.

One of the main problems is that the Shona Christian church rejected the adoption of the Shona myths about relationships, since everything from African traditional religion was condemned as heathen and pagan. Banana, a Zimbabwean theologian, defines myth as both sacred history and reality, and sees a relationship between myths and theology:

> Myths explain origins of things. Theology is also concerned with the why, whence, of human and societal life, the basic conditions and goals of history, ultimate reality and ultimate concerns. Theology cannot be pursued simply within the framework of Western scientific language . . . The role of mythology gets particularly significant in African theology, where Christian articulation has to relate to traditional African concepts of life which are preserved and conveyed by means of mythology. [18]

The relationship between God, humans, and creation is explained in myths. In some creation myths, God was not just close to creation, but lived among the original people created. God used to dwell with humans, and everything was peaceful and God provided. The Shonas have a myth about how the separation between God and humanity took place. This myth is told by the Karanga who are also part of the Shona people in Zimbabwe:

> The close God is part of this creation as a father is part of his child . . . And the distant God? He came into existence when men disregarded his commandments . . . .When men no longer obeyed God, he retreated into the sky (or high mountain) and let men know "You did not obey me, I leave you. Your land will be dry and salt, thistles will grow on it, and there will be no rain. You will be

18 Banana, *Come and Share*, p. 34. For a more detailed discussion on what is myth, mythmaking in Africa, myth, and social reality, see Okpewho, *Myth in Africa*.

killed by spears and will be slaves until you return to me." Thus evil came to the world. [19]

Separation from God was caused by humanity's disobedience. Humanity suffered and there was chaos among humans due to the separation. However, most myths conclude by saying that God never abandoned humanity, and/or God's relationship with humanity never ceased to exist.

To maintain the relationship between God and humanity, rituals and worship came into place. What Mbiti says about the way to maintain the relationships is also believed true in the traditional Shona society:

> And so the original direct contact and relationship between God and man was broken. The unfortunate consequences for man include the loss of immortality, resurrection, rejuvenation, and free food in addition to the coming of death and suffering. Yet, through acts of worship, man tries to counteract this separation and to maintain . . . contact with God.[20]

Even though the separation referred to in the myth seems to put God very far away from humanity (One who is transcendent), God is perceived as very immanent in honoring the agreement between God and humanity to maintain the relationship, despite separation. The following myth is generally shared among Shona:

> Thus the Karanga [a Shona subgroup] speak of a God who is distant and close simultaneously. They say: "God is far away in the sky, but he is with us too (*Mwari ari kure kudenga kumusoro-soro asi ari pedo nesu*)." . . . Also everyday names convey the impression that God is near. When God is called grandmother (*ambuya*) or ancestor (*mudzimu*) he is honored by terms which are very meaningful to the Karanga and close to their heart. The reality of God manifests itself also in the defenseless, the orphans and the unborn, as well as the insane- all of whom can bear his name.[21]

The idea of God's transcendence is understood more in terms of God's limitlessness and boundlessness. In this sense the Shonas are saying that God fills and controls the universe and the whole of creation. Even the moon, sun, and stars are under God's control and order. Transcendence does not prevent God from being involved in the affairs of humanity or

19. Aschwanden, *Karanga Mythology*, p. 216.
20. Mbiti, *Concepts of God*, p. 177.
21. Aschwanden, *Karanga Mythology*, p. 210-211.

being in relationship with humanity. The Shonas understand God as immanent and closer to them than their breath. Most African prayers plead for God's protection, not as a remote God, but as a God who is close. God's protection is sought at night while one is sleeping and on long journeys. God is not far removed, but close enough that humanity can easily approach God in prayer or times of need.[22]

The continual relatedness of God to humanity, even after the separation of God and humanity, is also found in the attributes the Shona people associate with God. God is seen as Father, Mother, love, kindness, merciful, provider, just, good, faithful, holy, and righteous, etc. Humanity is also perceived as God's children and relates to God as in the context of family relationships. God is seen as *Mudzimu mukuru*, meaning the "Great Ancestor," or *Tateguru*, "Great Grandmother or the one who gave birth to all the people." As God's children, people can easily approach God through prayer and worship in times of need and crisis.

A mother is to her children what God is to men . . . God is like an *(ambuya)*, it is said. He gives to all good and bad, and like an *ambuya* he welcomes everybody and is as generous as she is. One expression says: God's goodness and mercy are like an *ambuya* who is quick to forgive her grandchildren *(ngoni netsitsi dzaMwari dzakaita sambuya vasingatani kukanganwira vazukuru)*[23]

However, there are also attributes, which point to God as a God of anger and a judge who can avenge. These attributes describe God in anthropomorphic terms, and, even more so, in terms of God's interpersonal relationship with humanity. In times of need, people turn to God because they believe God's nature to be loving, merciful, kind, and just. God's loving mercies and kindness are seen or understood in "concrete terms" of humanity's day-to-day survival. Practical experiences of how God provides food, shelter, rain, etc., are given as concrete examples of how God is in relationship with the Shona people.

Muzorewa echoes the fact that in addition to the communal aspect of salvation for the Africans (which includes the Shonas), salvation is also based upon tangible and visible acts of God, for and/or within the community.

Africans believe that while God is invisible, God's acts are tangible . . . This is why African theology believes both that God is spirit and that God's presence can be felt and experienced physically. African theology needs to

22. Mbiti, *Concepts of God*, p. 171.
23. Aschwanden, *Karanga Mythology*, p. 204.

explicate the doctrine of the Holy Spirit in such a way that believers may feel the tangibleness of the benefits of knowing Christ.[24]

Good harvest, hunting, or fishing seasons are more signs of God's interpersonal involvement in humanity's affairs. God's love is experienced when God intervenes in times of calamities or natural disasters. The idea of God's love is also experienced in God's salvation.

God's salvation is also a communal experience. When God does not send rain, or sends an earthquake to a community because of the sin or act of an individual, it affects the entire community. In the same vein, when God blesses or saves an individual, this salvation or blessing is for the benefit of the community as well. This is contrary to the personal responsibility taught and preached to the Shona by Western Christianity.

Maimela makes the argument, with which this writer totally concurs, that, "It will, therefore, not do to try to understand what sin and salvation are in African Traditional Religions from a purely Christian perspective in which salvation is usually understood to be an individualistic unburdening of personal sin through what happened to Jesus Christ on the cross."[25] At another, level sin and salvation affect the individual psychologically, physically, and spiritually inasmuch as the rituals involved require physical, mental, emotional, and spiritual engagement. Individual sin or salvation affect more than the individual; they also affect the community psychologically and spiritually.

Offending God causes chaos and disharmony. God is perceived as One who can become angry. When humanity commits moral transgressions such as murder, incest, etc., God's anger is stirred, thereby bringing disharmony to the community. The Shonas believe that disobedience, wickedness, and evil-heartedness anger God and cause chaos, bringing meaninglessness and disequilibrium to interpersonal relationships in the lives of the society or the community. There are rules and customs used for purposes of social and religious regulations. Breaking such rules and customs creates disharmony in the relationship between humanity and God. Murphree says about disobeying a custom such as the holy day of *chisi* (a day of rest), "Breaches of these regulations would be punished by Mwari sending . . . calamity to the person and property of the offenders."[26]

---

24. Muzorewa, *The Origins*, p. 11-12.

25. Maimela, "Salvation in African," p. 66.

26. Murphree, *Christianity and the Shona*, p. 49-50.

The relationship with God is both corporate and communal. The Shona understanding of God is realized through relationships with or being related to God. God is not One who is just experienced mentally, but is One who, through relationship to humanity, reveals God's Self. God is transcendent, but at the same time very close to humanity. God's relationship with humanity is not impersonal but is an interpersonal relational reality.

HUMAN RELATIONSHIPS

In the Shona society, that an individual's personal and religious identity is based on one's community of embeddedness is a matter that is viewed as a given. One acquires authenticity or individual identity based on his or her community of embeddedness or communal existence. If one destroys the individual, one destroys an entity of the community. At the same time, if one destroys the community, one destroys the individual or an essential part of the individual. This affects how issues of sin, forgiveness, and salvation are perceived in human relations among the Shonas.

Sin, in the Shona context, is defined in terms of relationships rather than in mental or philosophical ideas. Anything evil which one does to harm the other is sin. In any situation where right relationships are absent, sin has occurred. This is different from the Western Christian understanding of sin in terms of original sin. Sin is normally an act that one commits against the other, and one that brings about chaos among interpersonal relationships with the other. The "other" in the context of the human community may mean a relative or a stranger. Peaden notes:

> . . . adultery, theft, murder, and untruthfulness were wrong [the Shona believed] and had rules about the duty of helpfulness to members of their   family. They also believed that a person had a duty to the stranger, to help him if he was passing through their village while on a journey. These morals did not arise from a belief about pleasing or displeasing Mwari, but rather from a conception · of a just society and from the necessity of keeping harmonious personal relationships within a close-knit community.[27]

While for the traditional Shonas, acts of violence such as murder, incest, thievery, putting a curse on someone, or witchcraft are considered sin, even being inhospitable to a stranger is to be avoided, since this could cause

---

27. Peaden, *Missionary Attitude*, p. 2.

disharmony with the stranger's community. Moyo, a Zimbabwean, suggests the following regarding sin and human relationships:

> Traditional societies understand sin as any action violating the integrity of God's creation, disrupting relationships within the family and community as a whole and bringing suffering or even death. A sinful action may deprive the individual and his or her community of peace, happiness, wellness and prosperity. Repentance must therefore involve the whole community and not just the individual . . . In other words, one actually sins against God by sinning against one's neighbour. The emphasis is on relationships here and now, but those relationships ultimately affect one's relation to God and the living dead, who then cease to offer protection to the sinner and the members of his family. God and the ancestors can never be on the side of the sinner until the sinner comes to deal justly with others in the community.[28]

Christianity came to Africa preaching individual responsibility, sin, and salvation for one's actions. As stated earlier a sin is relational and can also perceived as affecting the whole family or community. Contemporary Shona Christians will make statements such as, *Musha wekwa nhingi une ngozi*, which translates into "the village or family of so and so is being hounded by an avenging spirit." A similar saying, *Ndezve dzinza, kana kuti ndezve chidzinza*, suggests that "someone or a family is being affected by an evil deed committed by someone in the previous generation or by previous generations." People do not place sole responsibility on the individual who committed the crime; rather blame is placed on the whole family or community.

The goal in counseling and pastoral caregiving in these contemporary Shona contexts is to integrate traditional practices with Western Christian rituals. The idea is not to replace them, rather, the objective is to add aspects from the traditional Shona religio-culture that may help address spiritual and psychological aspects now missing in the current rituals. The integration supplants the implicit criteria used by Western Christianity, which promoted the notion that anything from traditional Shona religio-culture is pagan. ma Mpolo argues that in providing pastoral care to the African Christian today, the pastoral caregiver must be ready to explore the how and why issues of illness, death, misfortunes, and so forth, including determining which ritual is needed to address each of these situations.[29] Most

---

28. Moyo, *Zimbabwe*, p. 40-41.

29. ma Mpolo and Kalu, *The Risk of Growth*, p. 5ff.

of the Shona Christian rituals adopted from Western Christianity do not answer these questions. On the other hand, traditional Shona rituals (not contrary to Western Christianity) do help answer these questions raised by both the counselees and careseekers.

A specific example is that of the ritual to resolve the problem of a *ngozi* spirit. The Western Christian ritual does not address the "how, why, and what" questions. The prescribed Shona Christian ritual adopted from Western Christianity is to exorcize the *ngozi* spirit, since the ngozi's actions of avenging itself are considered unchristian and evil. Exorcizing the ngozi does not give psychological and spiritual comfort to the Shona Christian, since he/she knows the *ngozi* spirit can move from one family member to another. In addition, the Shona Christian is aware that the processes to bring about justice, forgiveness, and reconciliation with the victim (*ngozi spirit*) and his/her family have not been followed. The traditional aspects of the ritual to resolve a *ngozi* situation preceding the exorcism itself answer the "how, why, and what" questions, in that the ritual involves accountability, restitution, and reconciliation processes for the two families.

As a discipline, pastoral care advocates for such processes of accountability, restitution, and reconciliation in situations, which involve injustice and victimization.[30] This process is in agreement with the traditional Shona understanding in the *ngozi* spirit, since the *ngozi* spirit is a spirit of an individual trying to seek justice for an injustice done to him/her. Exorcizing the *ngozi* spirit without the accountability, restitution, and reconciliation ritual is victimizing the victim, which is what the current Shona Christian ritual does; it fails to address the whole problem and jumps to the end process of exorcism as found in traditional Shona religion.

The processes of accountability, restitution, and reconciliation are seen in the Christian teachings exemplified in the story of Zachaeus the tax collector. Jesus ordered him to go face his victims and repay what he owed them before reconciliation could take place (Luke19:1-10).[31] In most (if not all) of the traditional Shona rituals used to address an injustice or to right people's dysfunctional interpersonal relationships in traditional Shona society, the processes advocated as a criteria (accountability, restitution, and reconciliation) are involved; this would include addressing most death situations, illness, misfortunes, and catastrophes. Most of the Shona Christian rituals subvert the means to justice and forgiveness; rather,

30. Fortune, *Is Nothing Sacred?*
31. Luke 19:1-10 *NRSV.*

they advocate for forgiveness without the fully restorative process. I am suggesting incorporating some aspects of rituals from the traditional Shona religion to strengthen the Western Christian rituals in place and thus to be able to provide comprehensive psychological and spiritual peace for the Shona Christian.

WESTERN CHRISTIANITY VERSUS SHONA TRADITIONAL BELIEFS

Mr. and Mrs. Dzobo, a Shona couple, live in a large four bedroom suburban home in Harare with their only son Robert. They are very rich having inherited their wealth from their deceased parents. There is a rumor that there is a ngozi spirit[32] hounding the family, because Mr. Dzobo's deceased parents killed someone for "muti" or medicine, in order for their business to prosper. Mr. Dzobo's parents died before anything was done to address the situation, and the Dzobos inherited the business from the parents, who both died in a car accident. The father died at the age of 49 and the mother was 47 years old. The same year Mr. Dzobo's parents died is the year Robert, the Dzobo's now 20 year-old only son, was born. Mr. Dzobo was 28 years of age when his parents died. It is said that Mr. Dzobo's uncle (the deceased father's only brother) did not attend the funeral. The uncle is reported to have said that he did not want to attend a funeral of or be associated with someone who had killed for financial gains. Thus, Mr. Dzobo buried his parents without much help from his extended family. Mr. Dzobo's relationship with his extended family is strained and no one has made an effort from either side to work things out.

It is also said that the "ngozi" (the avenging spirit, or the spirit of the person reported as killed for use as "muti" for the business) had also manifested itself through a dream to Mr. Dzobo's father just before he died in the car accident. The avenging spirit is said to have told the deceased that he, his wife, and son would not live past 51 years of age. In the dream the ngozi also indicated that unless accountability, restitution, and justice took place the grandchild (Robert) would become a "rombe," which means Robert would roam the streets, and sometimes exhibit signs of mental illness. The deceased parents had shared the dream with Mr. Dzobo and his wife.

Mr. and Mrs. Dzobo are members of the Methodist church. Mrs. Dzobo has been accused of being proud and disrespectful by her in-laws and no one of the extended family wants to have much association with her. She prides

32. In the DSM V, (2013), this would be diagnosed as a "culture specific syndrome."

herself as "a warrior in Christ," and says that "nothing will harm her family no matter what." Mrs. Dzobo says that anything evil that happens in her nuclear family is just "a test of her faith." She has openly verbally attacked those who have alluded to her family as one being hounded by an avenging spirit. Her family, she declares, "is covered by the blood of Christ, and no powers of darkness can overcome her family." She has called people from both sides of the extended families "heathens and pagans," and those whose minds are run and have been ruined by the devil. People say she also has a sharp tongue and that the husband is under a "petticoat government."

Robert, their son, sometimes acts as if he is mentally ill, but doctors have not been able to diagnose him. He calls himself "Tupac incarnate," abuses marijuana and alcohol, and mostly uses English to communicate. He has beaten the father twice to the extent that the father had to go to the hospital. He has confronted his parents about the issues of ngozi, and wants them to address this before they die (they are both close to 50 years of age). He says he is not well vested in the Shona culture himself and would not know what to do if they die without reconciling with the ngozi. Robert has accused his parents of not being true Christians. How could true Christians inherit riches they know are tainted with human blood? If they were true Christians why do they not even speak to their close relatives? What type of God or Jesus do they believe in who allows them to hold grudges for life? One day, Robert locked himself in his room and talked in the third person, saying something had to be done to make things right. The Dzobos invited friends from church to help, to no avail, and now have turned to their pastor for help.

SOCIO-CULTURAL ISSUES

The Dzobos are an economically prosperous family from the inheritance. They live as a nuclear family in a suburban home, with their only son, Robert. Their interpersonal relationships with their extended family are very poor. The Dzobos appear to live a family life, which depends on the Western cultural values based on economic success rather than relying on their extended family relations. Even though they have not put it into words, the Dzobos appear to have come to the realization that economic success does not equal healthy interpersonal relations.

The Dzobos are caught between a Western culture, which emphasizes individual success based on material possessions and competition, and the traditional Shona culture, which gives priority to one's communal interpersonal relations and cooperation. The Dzobos acknowledge the centrality of communal interpersonal and extended family relations, but choose not to give priority to those relationships. In addition, their friends from church have not provided them with the cultural support system the Dzobos need inasmuch as these church friends also focus personal energy on their own economic success.

The Dzobos are caught between cultures, appear to have lost much of their Shona cultural heritage, and have apparently isolated themselves from participating in the Shona traditional religio-culture. The extended family appears to have also lost respect for Mr. Dzobo, whom they perceive to be "under a petticoat government." The lack of a clear culture of identity on the part of the parents has also affected Robert.

Robert has been left with no culture in which to feel "at home." Cultur-ally, Robert is a "half-breed"; he does not have a specific cultural founda-tion. He has openly told his parents that he does not know much about the Shona culture. Robert grew up isolated from those places in which he could have learned some traditional culture. He does not know how to speak the Shona language well, nor does he understand the traditional cultural issues of respect as pertaining to one's elders. On the other hand, the problem may be due to Robert's lack of awareness of the culture, indicating this conflict may need to be resolved through counseling and pastoral care which fo-cuses on his relationship with his father.

Robert has immersed himself in the Western "rap" culture to the extent of calling himself "Tupac incarnate." On the other hand, Robert is instigating issues addressing the importance of communal interpersonal relations for the family. He complained that his family isolated him from his extended family while he was growing up, cutting him off from develop-ing healthy communal relationships with the extended family. Exploring how economic (socio-cultural) realities play a part in placing them in the position in which they find themselves may help the Dzobos become less defensive (psychologically) and more willing to explore the realities of the problems they face.

ANXIETY, ITS SOURCES, AND PSYCHOLOGICAL ISSUES

There are at least two identifiable sources of the Dzobo family's anxiety on which the pastoral caregiver could focus, as a starting point. First, they do not have a communal support system since they have severed their relationships with their extended family. Their support system from church is more akin to that of business people who invest most of their time in economic success, and who have a lifestyle similar to that of the Dzobos.

Second, the Dzobos are experiencing religious anxiety by trying to reconcile the early deaths of Mr. Dzobo's parents (before the age fifty one) and the behavior of Robert (already as announced by the *ngozi* spirit in the dream) with their Christian religious beliefs. They have publicly denounced the power of the *ngozi* spirit (a Shona traditional belief) but resolving their problems appears to indicate a need for integrating some traditional Shona religious beliefs as well. Choosing the Shona traditional ways to address the situation will mean going against their Christian belief systems. This has created religious dissonance for the Dzobos.

Robert is experiencing an individual identity crisis, based on a lack of a culture of embeddedness. He does not know who he is—Shona or Western? He has assimilated many Western values. However, he has come to believe in the powers of *ngozi* through the little knowledge he gained from studying the Shona traditional religion at the university. The parents have not helped decrease Robert's anxiety because they do not want to explore traditional religious remedies as a possible solution to the problem. Robert is anxiously struggling with the fact that his parents are now approaching the age of fifty-one (the deadline given by the *ngozi* as their life span). If nothing is done, and if the parents cannot take care of the *ngozi* situation and subsequently happen to die, Robert is left without a support system, since the parents cut him off from extended family relations. One way Robert has been coping with his anxiety is by abusing drugs and alcohol. Robert is an embodiment of the anxiety experienced by most of the culturally under-socialized children of the Shona urban context. He feels isolated and lost, and thus is experiencing psychological trauma.

Mr. and Mrs. Dzobo are dealing with their anxiety by denying the power of the *ngozi* spirit. Mrs. Dzobo uses her religious beliefs as a way to defend herself against those who allude to the avenging spirit. She appears to have "blind faith," faith which does not allow the voice of reason to help solve problems. In addition, both parents appear to be experiencing cultural dissonance. They have not put much effort into creating healthy interpersonal relationships with the extended family. They view the extended family members as "heathens and pagans" with whom they do not wish to associate.

Robert's mental state, and the fact that the Dzobos are both close to fifty years of age, may be forcing them to reconsider their situation, which has placed them in a state of anxiety. Their experience of broken communal interpersonal relations is also resulting in anxiety.

THEOLOGICAL OR RELIGIOUS ISSUES

The Dzobos' interpersonal relationships comprise the main theological or religious issue that the counselor or pastoral caregiver would find worthy of pursuit. The Dzobos' interpersonal relations are not only a concern as they pertain to other family and church members, but are also impaired in connection with God and the Spirit World. Based on a Shona relational pastoral theology, the examination of their relationship with others, God, Spirit World, and creation will aid in bringing to the surface most of the issues they need to address. They face the challenge of having to answer Robert's question: how can they call themselves true Christians while holding life-long grudges against other extended family members? Mr. and Mrs. Dzobo refuse to face the issue of their interpersonal relations by projection—they ignore facing the problem raised by Robert, and focus instead on Robert's drinking problems. From both religious perspectives, the Dzobos need to consider re-establishing many communal interpersonal relationships in order to make things right.

Even though the father may not believe in the traditional view that Robert's beating him is a traditional religio-cultural taboo, which will involve a ritual process of accountability and reconciliation, the relationship between the father and son is not right. From a Christian perspective, Robert is not following the Christian values of "honor thy father and thy mother." There is also a need to explore the interpersonal relationships between Robert and the father.

Much work is needed to resolve issues of interpersonal relations between the Dzobo family and their extended families. The Dzobos seem to have intentionally severed these relationships, and only in hindsight have they come to realize the importance of these extended family ties. The fact that they are considered to have a "holier than thou" attitude toward others seems to get in the way of their family relationships. Their pastor is the person best equipped to help them realize how their attitude toward others has damaged their relationships.

The counselor or pastoral caregiver must encourage the Dzobos to explore issues of their conflicting interpersonal relations, and help them identify how evil and good operate in their lives. Questions such as the following must be raised: What is the meaning and quality of community for the Dzobos? What is their interpersonal relationship with God and what is their image of God? How can forgiveness be achieved with others and with God? How is God's power perceived in their life story? Who or what is held responsible for their faulty communal interpersonal relations? What do they perceive as their part in the disruption of these faulty communal relations? With which Bible stories do they personally identify? How do the Dzobos use the Bible stories—negatively or positively—to justify their behaviors? In the final analysis, what issues of estrangement (from God and others), brokenness, forgiveness, accountability, justice, and restitution need to take place before the Dzobo family can feel whole again?

The pastoral caregiver can also help identify the Dzobos' experience of religious dissonance. A pastor working with the Dzobos, using the above questions would allow and encourage the Dzobos to identify and name their experiences of the religious dissonance. The events taking place through Robert appear to be pointing to the *ngozi* spirit's predictions. However, as Christians, the Dzobos are refusing to explore the possibility of facing this evil, as illustrated by the wife's statement that they are "covered by the blood of Christ." Exploring the possibility of this evil would mean the Dzobos may have to involve traditional Shona rituals condemned by the church. In addition, it would mean the Dzobos would have to "swallow" their self-righteous pride and openly admit the possibility that their relationships with God and the Spirit World are not right either. The Dzobos need to be challenged in their belief that their family's "being covered by the power of the blood of Jesus" does not alter the fact that a possible evil committed by the deceased parents may need resolution.

The counselor or pastoral caregiver must explore with the Dzobos their understanding of the *ngozi* spirit. Is the *ngozi* spirit evil or good? Have they considered accepting as possible reality the idea of the presence of a *ngozi* spirit hounding their family? If it becomes a reality, what difference does it make, and what changes would they, as Christians, have to make in their lives? If the evil was committed, what would be right or wrong in engaging in a reconciliation process with the *ngozi* spirit and its family?

SUGGESTED PASTORAL RESPONSE

A counselor or pastoral caregiver with an integrative consciousness could employ different methods and approaches in helping this family. The counselor or pastoral caregiver could provide intensive individual caregiving with Robert, focusing on issues of identity confusion and his fear about parents dying, before they perform the ritual to resolve the *ngozi* problem. Robert also needs individual counseling and care in terms of drug abuse issues, as well as how that might be affecting his perceptions and his relationship with his family.

Another level involves the counselor or pastoral caregiver employing a communal approach in focusing on their communal interpersonal relations when exploring the issues affecting the entire family. With the counselor or pastoral caregiver's exploration of the socio-cultural influences, family members' anxiety and its source, and religious issues, it is the hope of this writer that the Dzobos will be willing to look from a different perspective at what is happening in their lives. The aforementioned process allows the Dzobo family to revisit their Christian beliefs and the Shona traditional values from which they have become estranged. The counselor or pastoral caregiver's comfortable willingness to explore issues such as these gives the Dzobos an invitation, as well as a "green light," to go ahead and be open to discussing issues they formerly had considered "untouchable." It encourages the Dzobos to revisit the Shona traditional rituals and reconsider how to resolve the issues. At the same time, what is important for the counselor or pastor is to understand the ritual to resolve the *ngozi* spirit problem, to be able to explain the process involved.

One of the main problems and core issues in the requirement for incorporating aspects of a traditional Shona ritual into the current Shona Christian rituals in place is the need to address the lack of relevancy and completeness in the latter. The Dzobo family needs to involve inclusion of aspects of traditional Shona ritual to resolve the *ngozi*. Why the suggestion of employing the ritual to resolve the *ngozi* in this case of the Dzobos? One of the main reasons to pursue the suggested ritual to resolve the *ngozi* situation is based on the traditional Shona religio-cultural beliefs in relationship to the occurrences in the Dzobo family. The *ngozi* spirit's announcement that Robert's grandparents would not live past the age of fifty-one (and they subsequently did die before fifty-one), and Robert's behaving as a *rombe*—someone who roams the streets exhibiting signs of mental illness- (which had also been announced by the *ngozi* spirit) are issues which defy an explanation of "coincidence" insofar as most Shonas with traditional Shona religio-cultural values (including the upper middle-class Shona Christians) are concerned.

The Western Christian ritual in use today (which recognizes the existence of a *ngozi* spirit as one which is evil) calls for an exorcism of the *ngozi* spirit, but does not incorporate the traditional methods used to address the avenging spirit via use of the Shona ritual components of accountability, restitution, and reconciliation. The Shona Christian church views the avenging spirit and its actions as evil because Western Christianity condemned it as evil and taught that humans (including spirits of dead persons) are not to avenge themselves; rather, the deceased human being or spirit is to leave the situation which it views as an injustice so that God can render justice. "Beloved, never avenge yourselves, but leave room for the wrath of God; for it is written, 'Vengeance is mine, I will repay, says the Lord.'" (Romans 12:19)[33] For the Shona Christian, however, the influences of the traditional world-view do not free him or her from the psychological impact of relational theological understanding: that justice not only involves God's avenging on behalf of the victim, but involves reconciliation and justice-making rituals which involve the extended family, God, Spirit World (including the avenging spirit), and creation.

The pastoral caregiver playing the role of the traditional medicine person has to inquire from the *ngozi* spirit who he/she is, and to relate the story about how he/she was killed and what happened after he/she was killed. The pastoral caregiver may ask the whereabouts of the bodily remains of the spirit, and whether they are buried. Included in this process are questions about the demands of the *ngozi* and how the *ngozi* feels about accountability, restitution, so reconciliation can be justly meted. The pastoral care-giver would also have to act as mediator between the families of the deceased and the murderer throughout the entire process, which involves bringing the two families together with the *ngozi* retelling its story and stating its demands. The family of the *ngozi* can add further demands, over and above those made by the *ngozi* spirit. Having done all that is required, the final phase involves forgiveness and reconciliation between the extended families. The closing ritual involves a meal shared by the families, as a sign of reconciliation. The payments of restitution are essential; otherwise the avenging spirit will not rest. At the closing of the reconciliation, the pastor must address the *ngozi* spirit, exorcize it, and ask it to leave the murderer's family in peace, since they professed accountability, paid restitution, and asked for forgiveness, and the families shared a reconciliation meal. If the deceased was not given proper burial, its family will need to find the bodily

33. Romans 12:19, *NRSV*.

remains and accord it a proper burial. The church did not want to have anything to do with this ritual with the use of a medicine person, and in part because the process was/is too long and involving.

As mentioned before, I argue that an exorcism alone, which does not involve the full processes of justice-making observed from the traditional Shona religious understanding involving accountability, restitution and reconciliation, is a "solution" which victimizes the victim (the *ngozi* or avenging spirit). Simply employing the method of exorcism does not give any urban Shona Christian whose family is related to an offender (murderer) any psychological and spiritual comfort inasmuch as those related to the offender are aware that the *ngozi* spirit can attack their families through illness or other means, despite their Christian status, until the ritual is performed. The exorcism merely removes the *ngozi* spirit from one person to another within that extended family system, but does not stop the avenging spirit's justice-seeking activities by causing illness and sometimes even death to the family of the murderer. Hence, the way to stop the *ngozi* from avenging is to incorporate some of the traditional problem-resolving steps (as already mentioned) forbidden by Western Christianity in pastoral caregiving situations.

The church is also opposed to the involvement of the traditional medicine person in rituals such as that of an avenging spirit, since the church views the activities of the medicine person as influenced by the paganistic worldview. It is, however, not necessary to use a medicine person in this ritual; since the spirit is ostensibly already speaking through Robert, the pastoral caregiver can play the traditional role of the medicine person in the presence of the Dzobo family, with some of the church members as witnesses.

In spite of their Christianity, those Christians whose families have relatives who have committed crimes of murder live in fear and anxiety because they believe that the avenging spirit can hound them. This belief calls for them to be involved in traditionally known rituals as a way to right their relationship with God, the deceased, and with the family/ community of the deceased. The church, however, forbids Christians, to participate in these traditional rituals. Western Christianity teaches that whoever committed the crime is the one who needs to be forgiven by God and reconciled to the person he/she sinned against. More specifically, Christianity's stance is that reconciliation is between the sinner and God, and sometimes the one sinned against. For those urban Shona Christians, who believe there is need for the rituals of accountability and reconciliation with the deceased and the deceased's family, this creates anxiety, because the ritual of exorcism sanctioned by the church for this process is only one part of the entire ritual.

Forgiveness, then, is not just for the individual but also for the whole community. Rituals of forgiveness in the traditional society involve the entire family or community. A community's perceived guilt stems from the perception that they should have intervened on behalf of the guilty person before he /she committed the evil act. In some cases, forgiveness may end up involving more than the individual and the human community and may also include nature and the Spirit World. Moyo says about the act of incest in traditional Zimbabwean society, "It is so grave that it affects all of God's creation. Rains are withheld as punishment, leading to severe drought, with all the consequences this has for a people who depend on cattle and farming for livelihood."[34] Thus in the traditional society, for example, the sin of incest committed by an individual can affect the entire community including creation.

RELATIONSHIP BETWEEN NATURE AND HUMANITY

In the African world, one is raised with the consciousness that nature and all of creation are interdependent. I concur with Banana's notion that Africans understand God in "ontological terms," meaning there is no doubt in the minds or beliefs of the Africans that God's existence is a given and that, "Traditionally, Zimbabweans experience God's revelation also in natural phenomena such as trees, rocks, caves, rivers, and also mountains . . . in African traditional religions there were no atheists; all members of a particular society belonged to the religion of that society."[35] Creation reveals God's works and continuous creativity. All of creation exists for reciprocal benefit and is to be respected.

Among the Shonas, and most other African traditions and cultures, humanity is believed to have been created out of the soil. I remember, when still young, asking my late grandmother why there were different colors of people. My grandmother took me outside to different places in the yard and the field surrounding the home. My grandmother instructed me to touch and feel the different types and textures of the soil, and asked me to tell her what different colors the soils were. Some of the soil was red clay, black, greyish, brown etc. She related to me how the Shona people believe

34. Ibid., p. 40-41.
35. Banana, *Come and Share*, p. 40.

that humans were created from the soil and as soil has different color and texture so too do human beings differ in color. She went further to say that not only were we created out of the soil, but that the earth is our Mother, and that all of life comes out of, or is connected to, the earth. This story she instructed me to pass to my children.

The Shonas strongly believe that what hurts the earth hurts all of creation, including humanity. Anything, which may upset the balance of nature (including trees, animals, etc.) will hurt humanity. The forces of nature such as earthquakes, drought, storms, etc. are real; however, nature is to be used for human survival but must be used with respect, not abused. The Western idea of humanity "dominating" the earth is foreign to the African context. We were created to be in relationship and harmony with the earth. There are traditional festivals and rituals held before ploughing or planting crops. The purpose of the ritual is at two levels: the first is to ask God and the ancestors to bless the seeds and send the rains in time. Aschwanden, who researched among the Karanga (Shona subgroup) about their mythologies and wrote a book about religious myths, says of the sowing ritual among the Shona:

> Before sowing starts, the chief collects seed of all sorts in a basket and takes it to the tribe's leading medium. He offers a handful of seed to the medium—palm up: he shows it to those in the "sky" and prays to the ancestors especially to the most important one of the tribe (*mudzimu mukuru*), also called *shumba yomudzimu* . . . as well as to God. The prayer says: "The time of sowing has arrived. We ask for your blessing for a good harvest. God, give us rain and keep the insects off the plants, also the grasshoppers. And you, ancestors, look after our fields so the sun does not shine on them too brightly." . . . The people then all return home with a handful of the blessed seed and mix it with their own seed. In this way a good crop is to be secured.[36]

A second purpose of the planting ritual is to announce to Mother Earth that humans are going to be cutting wounds into her and that no harm is intended. This is to make certain that all the relationships are right with God/ Spirit World, and with the land. The important aspect of the rituals had to do with relationships to the Spirits of the area, as well as the maintenance of right relationships with "Mother Earth." Humans are taught to maintain good relationships with their environment and with nature and

---

36. Aschwanden, *Karanga Mythology*, p. 225.

the Spirit world. Bourdilion notes about the need for maintenance of these relationships:

> Any projects of significance, such as building of dams or a school, should have the approval of the spirits of the area. These spirits are usually the ancestors of the chief who is their living representative: in such a case, they are approached through the chief who is their appointee. The chief is closely associated with the land precisely because as the senior descendant of the original owners . . . but this ownership is restricted to very limited rights over the land and certain duties towards it.[37]

The idea of owning land was also foreign to the Africans. No one had a "title deed" over a piece of land. Contrary to the Shona culture and tradition, the Westerners introduced the idea of land ownership. Peaden says, "On the other hand there were the hereditary Shona chiefs to whom the occupation of land was a sacred trust inherited from their forefathers and to whom the question of selling or otherwise permanently alienating land could not arise."[38] The Shona was to take care of the land; he or she ploughed it, and eventually it would be left to rejuvenate after a period of time. Land belonged to the Creator, not to humanity, and humanity is to live in interdependence with it.

I believe many Westerners misunderstood the fact that Africans can address a tree as if it had a soul, and the Westerners believed that action to be animism. However, for a traditional Shona, a spirit can be believed to be dwelling in a tree yet the spirit is not part of the make-up of the tree. As a person can live in a home and move on to another, leaving the first one vacant, it is in the same sense that a spirit can claim residence in a tree and be territorial but can also move on; it is not the make-up of the tree. If one destroys the dwelling place for a Spirit without a ritual, that is when misfortune may occur. In addition, there are certain trees considered sacred due to rituals performed by the community under those trees or just because the community deems the surrounding places and trees sacred (well know in Zimbabwe is a sacred treeknown as *Muti usinazita – meaning the tree without a name)*. Again, the main purposes of the traditional Shona rituals are to maintain healthy interpersonal communal existence with that which surrounds humans.

---

37. Bourdillon, *The Shona Peoples*, p. 68-69.
38. Peaden, *Missionary Attitude*, p. 5.

THE SHONA PASTORAL CAREGIVER AND PROHIBITION OF TRADITIONAL RELIGIOUS PRACTICES

The advent of Christianity meant the Shona had to shift from their involvement from Shona traditional religio-cultural communal activities to ones that were individualistic and ones that, in many ways, were contrary to those with which the Shona were familiar. A shift from the traditional Shona understanding of relationships to a Western Christian understanding was forced upon those Shonas who converted to Christianity.

The prohibition by the Shona Christian church of the utilization of some aspects of traditional religious practices and rituals by pastoral caregivers proves to be a handicap. In order for relational pastoral theology of care to be relevant in addressing the contemporary urban Shona pastoral care needs, the pastoral caregiver must be familiar with the suppressed history of Shona traditional relational theology. As aforementioned, relational theology is a theology whose primary focus is on the dynamics and understanding of relationships between humans, humanity and God, God humanity, and nature or creation.[39] The community relations extend beyond the human community to include God, the Spirit World, and all of creation. This would allow the caregiver to understand the struggles of the urban Shona Christians.

Even though there was a shift in religious doctrine and ideology, the urban Shona Christians are still aware of the traditional beliefs of being responsible for a family member's actions. The ceremonies and rituals such as *chenura* (cleansing ritual), *kupira mudzimu* (veneration of ancestors), consultation of the *n'anga* (medicine person) and polygamy -used in this chapter, illustrate issues of interpersonal relationships lost through the advent of Christianity. The prohibition of these ceremonies and rituals impacts both the urban and rural Shona Christians. In the urban context, however, the impact is readily recognizable in that for most Shona Christians the church provides them with a primary sense of a community of embeddedness, as opposed to the rural context in which the village community along with the church gives the sense of embeddedness.

Moyo notes about the experience of the Zimbabwean Christians today:

> While many Christians today manifest respect for the departed ancestors and take part in ceremonies relating to them, openly, many others do so only privately. They live a Christian life during

39. Russell, *The Earth, Humanity and God.*

the day and live the real African life during the night, resulting in what Desmond Tutu and others have described as a kind of schizophrenia . . . [40]

Some Shona Christians may not fully trust the solutions prescribed by Christianity; hence, they become anxious and feel guilty when they try to solve the problems by utilizing traditional methods condemned by Western Christianity. My argument is that the Shona Christian church needs to revisit its rules and rituals as pertaining to integration of some traditional practices which are not necessarily contrary to Christian teachings, so as to give both the Shona Christian and the pastoral caregiver more freedom in how they practice Christianity in this context.

Despite the time, which has passed, and even with the present United Methodist indigenous-led church in Zimbabwe, the Shona United Methodists still follow most of the beliefs established by the early missionaries. This has perpetuated the problem of bi-religiousness and results in creating anxiety as some of these Christians try to pay respect to their traditional religion, which in the eyes of the church is in conflict with true Western Christianity.

Anxiety arises as a result of Shona Christians mixing the traditional beliefs, not sanctioned by the church, with the ones prescribed by the church. This writer also agrees with Kapenzi, believing that one of the major sources of the bi-religiousness and bi-culturalism in the contemporary Shona context results from the church's failure to revisit traditional practices condemned by Western Christianity, yet deemed necessary to the faith of the Shona Christian today. Kapenzi summarizes this well:

> For conversion to the Christian faith to be more than superficial, the Christian church must come to grips with traditional beliefs and practices and with the world view that these beliefs and practices imply. It would be unreal not to recognize the fact that many church members are influenced in their conduct by traditional beliefs and practices and by the traditional interpretation of the universe. The new convert is poised between two worlds: the old traditions and customs of his culture which he is striving to leave behind, and the new beliefs and practices to which he is still a stranger.[41]

The church today is similarly not preserving or integrating some of the traditional rituals, even those not contrary to the Christian teachings. Mental, psychological, and religious conflict occurs when a Shona

40. Moyo, *Zimbabwe*, p. 19-20.
41. Kapenzi, *The Clash of Cultures*, p. 35.

Christian tries to live a Christian life and at the same time engages in some of the Shona traditional religious practices which involve relationships with the family or community. Does one supplant one's relationships with the family one loves in order to respect one's religious beliefs? Christians are forbidden to engage in such rituals as *chenura* (a cleansing or purification ritual); this is a peace and justice-making ritual, performed by the family for the dead person. Since everything from traditional Shona religion was considered heathen or pagan, it was banned with the advent of the Christian church. In the traditional Shona theological world-view, a dead person is still believed to be part of, and in relationship with, the community. Tension, guilt, and anxiety befalls people in situations where Shona Christians try to engage in traditional rituals or ignore such sayings as, *MaKristo haiti zvinhu zwechivanhu* (Christians are not to involve themselves in Shona traditional religious ways). However, the traditional Shonas, and some of the contemporary urban people, believe that one must always honor and respect one's elders or ancestors. Since life continues after death, honor, respect, and one's relationship with the deceased (ancestors) are not concluded by the burial ceremony.

Conflict arises within families as some members adhere to the Shona traditional practices while others try to adhere to the Christianity prescribed by the church. Furthermore, others in the same family might be comfortable with mixing the two religious practices and beliefs. Peaden notes:

> Christians also came under heavy pressure by non-Christian relatives to conform to traditional patterns, especially in times of trouble and sickness . . . It is more often recorded that Christians in time of trouble themselves consulted *nganga*. They could scarcely do this unless they believed that the cause of the trouble lay with the spirit of their ancestors, or that the trouble would end if the proper ceremonies were carried out.[42]

Tension results because bi-religiousness within family systems is common among the Shonas today. For some, the conflict is within themselves, not knowing which beliefs to follow. In situations where, due to the lack of substitute Christian rituals, the Shona is forced to choose involvement in or performance of the traditional religio-cultural rituals, which have been condemned as heathen, anxiety is the result.

The ritual to resolve a situation of a *ngozi* (avenging spirit) is another example of how one can be caught between religions in the attempt to

42. Ibid., p. 34-35.

resolve interpersonal relational problems. The ritual to resolve the problem of a *ngozi* was never adopted by the church because it had its roots in the African traditional religion and culture. In the United Methodist hymnal there is a song, *Nengozi dzingapere dzose pamuchinjikwa,* which translates to, "the avenging spirits are destroyed at the cross." By singing this song, the Shona Christians are claiming their belief in the existence and powers of the *ngozi* spirit. However, the church did not accept the traditional ritual to solve interpersonal relations of this kind, since the ritual is from the Shona traditional religion. Western Christianity stated that the only religious requirement for the person who committed an act of murder was to believe in and to be forgiven by Christ, and to have an exorcism of the avenging spirit performed.

The avenging spirit (the deceased victim) hounds the family because it seeks the reasons why it was murdered, an accountability for the murder, acts of restitution, and the recreation of harmony within the families involved. The deceased's family seeks justice for the murder of its relative, but there is no Christian ritual for this to occur. The traditional ritual to resolve the problem of *ngozi* is, in my perspective, a theologically sound ritual, which addresses the issues of interpersonal relationships between humans, God, and the Spirit World.[43]

Because traditional rituals are prohibited by the church, again, tension arises in some families or individuals regarding the ritual of *chenura* (cleansing ritual). The church has not done much to change or to integrate some of the aspects of this ritual from the traditional religion which may not necessarily be contrary to Christianity. The *chenura* ritual is a reconciling ritual between the living and the deceased which is performed sometime after burial. This is a ritual at which the spirit of the deceased is sent off to join the spirit world.

Yet another example of interpersonal relationships creating anxiety in mainline churches is polygamy. Christianity banned polygamy for all who converted, although it is not contrary to the Bible, especially the Old Testament. In the United Methodist church, those polygamous men who convert to mainline denominations and who want to participate fully as members are forced to divorce all their wives except the first one.[44] ,

43. Mucherera, *Pastoral Care and Counseling.* In this thesis, the author uses mostly inculturation theological material. In this book this writer does not directly utilize the inculturation material, but makes reference to it by the way of the M.A. thesis.

44. Patterson, ed., *The Book of Discipline,* p. 53.

Western Christianity demands that, in order to qualify as a true Christian, a man abandon secondary and subsequent wives and their children, whom he loves, and remain only with the first wife and her children. A polygamous man cannot be a true Christian and therefore cannot receive baptism or be accorded a full Christian burial ritual. Muzorewa also writes on this issue and notes that polygamy is not contradictory to the Christian teaching based on the Old Testament. Instead, Western ideals defined polygamy as a moral wrong. It was a practice in which Westerners did not believe; hence, the missionaries condemned it.[45]

When misfortune, calamities, or illness repeatedly strike a family or a community in the Shona traditional community, it is usually concluded that aspects of interpersonal relationships are out of balance. The logical traditional solution is to go to the medicine person (*N'ganga*) or the seer (*mushoperi*) to get information about the source of the problem *(kooshopera)*. The seer advises the family or community regarding the causes of illnesses or calamities and about the possible rituals to be performed in order to solve the problem. Moyo notes about the struggles of the Shona Christians in addressing such situations:

> It is common among Zimbabwean Christians of all denominations, including pastors, to participate, in times of prolonged illness or other misfortunes in the family, in the traditional rituals relating to the departed elders. Some Christians stop going to church or away from the Lord's Supper or active participation in church life for a while in order to give themselves time to perform the traditional rites and make the required sacrifices to bring about healing in the family. When they have completed what the traditional diviners have prescribed in relation to the departed elders and spirits, they return to the church authorities to request absolution. African pastors who are close to their people know that these things are happening in both the rural and urban settings.[46]

Anything involving an African medicine person was perceived by the missionary as evil since the medicine person was believed to be using "powers of darkness." This remains the church's stance today, so one cannot consult the seer or medicine person.

As much as most Shona Christians believe in modern medicine, there are some diseases still believed to be curable only by the medicine person.

---

45. Muzorewa, *The Origins*, p. 31-32.
46. Moyo, *Zimbabwe*, p. 20.

Illnesses referred to as *zwechivanhu,* (diseases only curable using traditional medicine) cause considerable psychological conflict for the Shona Christians. Peaden gives an example of such a situation:

> European medicines, although in many ways superior to the drugs that the *nganga* gave, were not infallible and there were many illnesses, which they were not able to cure. On the other hand the *nganga* were able to cure some that the Europeans could not . . . On one occasion, for example, an African teacher was admitted to hospital for observation after suffering for several weeks . . . After a week the European doctor told the writer that nothing physically wrong could be found with the teacher who was then discharged. He thereupon went to an *nganga* and after doing what the *nganga* prescribed, the pain disappeared; and a year later there had been no recurrence of the pain . . . the Shona distinguish between the physical working of an illness and its spiritual cause.[47]

Those Shona Christians who might perceive it necessary to go to a medicine person or seer for the solution to their problems do not have such freedom or permission from the church. Engaging in such behavior is an "evil" which could warrant one's placement on probationary membership in the church (United Methodist) and sometimes results in excommunication from the Holy Communion table. Peaden says, "Many of the rules conflicted with the Shona traditions, and those who broke them were censured by their church. There was a tendency for churches to administer discipline in a rigid and legalistic way, to the exclusion of charity and forgiveness."[48] Some of the same legalistic and rigid tendencies referred to by Peaden, and established by the missionaries, are still part of the Shona Christian churches today.

AN ALTERNATIVE APPROACH FOR SHONA PASTORAL CAREGIVERS

One of the main reasons Christianity fails to meet the emotional and spiritual needs of the Shona is the removal of some of the rituals ingrained psychologically in the minds of the Shona; they were thrown out by the church when they were deemed heathen. In this book I am not arguing that the church must embrace everything from the Shona traditional religion.

47. Peaden, *Missionary Attitude,* p. 18.
48. Ibid., p. 4-5.

However, if the church is going to train pastors to have an integrative consciousness, it must train Shona pastors with a relevant relational pastoral theology, that is: (a) a pastoral theology conversant with both world-views, with African pastoral theology as a starting point; and (b) a pastoral theology which re-evaluates the relationship between Christian rituals and the Shona traditional rituals, creating integrated rituals.

In training of the Shona pastoral caregivers, I concur with the pastoral theological approach used by Wimberly and Smith in pastoral theology of care.[49] Both Wimberly and Smith advocate for a pastoral theological approach, which gives priority to people's narratives and stories when one tries to understand their theological view point. One of the reasons is that story telling in sharing one's struggles and hurts is very common and comes very natural to most Shona people. I believe that, out of the narratives presented to the pastoral theologian and/or caregiver, the caregiver can then identify the problems in faulty interpersonal relationships. These narratives provide the pastoral caregiver with images and a sense of the individual's or individuals' discernment through elucidating interpersonal relationships in which God or others are or are not at work in their lives. Out of the narration of the stories, the faulty interpersonal relationships are presented, revealing the points at which the anxiety arises, causing the care receiver to seek help from the pastoral caregiver.

To illustrate the use of narrative in the Shona context, I will relate another incident that happened with my grandmother. When I was between the ages of seven and eight years old, I struggled with low self-esteem. I was very small in stature and it seemed everyone could easily bully me. I started school at seven years of age and was not doing well. One day as I sat with my grandmother I questioned her about my little cousin's hands. I had noticed that when my cousin came home from the hospital after birth her hands were clasped into a fist, and after about three or so weeks the hands had started unfolding. I asked my grandmother why it was that when my cousin was born the hands were folded into a fist, and now they were unfolded. My grandmother again narrated that, we the Shona people believe that when infants are born they have their hands clamped into a fist because they are holding all the gifts, graces, talents, and uniqueness given to them by God at their creation. After a few weeks their hands start to unfold. This is a sign to the world that they are willing to share with the world the gifts and graces God gave them. She went on

49. Wimberly, *Recalling Our Own Stories*; Smith, *Navigating*.

to say that this was the same way I came into the world. She said she had noticed and heard me talk negatively about myself and how I felt I could never amount to much. God did not create me for rubbish nor failure, she said. There was something that God gave me at the time I was created that no one else in this world possessed. That which God had given me, no one else could give to the world as I could. She instructed me that every time I look at my hands to remember the story of a baby's hands and that I am unique. She went further to tell me that I was better in many ways at some things than the Europeans who were oppressing us and telling us that we Africans were backward and behaved as animals. God had created us as human beings and we were not any less than anyone else. You can imagine what this narrative counseling session did to my self-esteem, my relationship with God, and others.

In addition, asking the following theological questions will help in the theological assessment of the careseeker's relationship with God and others. What is the careseeker's relationship with God and others? Based on the careseeker's communal interpersonal relations, what is the fundamental human predicament in terms of sin, salvation, and forgiveness? What ecologies of culture, nature, and interpersonal relationships are evident? What multiple communities are operative for good or ill? Based on the interpersonal relations narratives presented by the careseeker, what are the theological and spiritual outlooks? Are the spiritual and theological outlooks conflictual, inconsistent, or integrated? What is the meaning and quality of community for the careseeker? Where are the issues of brokenness, estrangement, abuse, forgiveness, justice, and reconciliation? What is the careseeker's source of hopelessness, anxiety and apathy, and how are these aspects connected to his or her communal interpersonal relations?[50] I am arguing that what brings people to the pastoral caregiver in the urban Shona context is anxiety, as a result of broken communal interpersonal relationships.

One of the main reasons for understanding traditional Shona relational theology is to note its continuing impact on the lives of contemporary urban Shona Christians. I am challenging the church to re-evaluate the rituals, theology, and practice of ministry in order to assure their relevance to the contemporary Shona Christian. In order to equip Shona pastors with a relevant pastoral theology of care, pastors are to be trained with a consciousness that is conversant with both world-views, to facilitate

50. Graham, *Care of Persons.*

integration of traditional Shonas with the Western world-view. The next chapter presents case studies and analysis to illustrate this need.

Chapter Five

Marriage and Family in the Contemporary Shona African Context

MARRIAGE IN AN AFRICAN context is rooted in tradition, yet has evolved over time with the Western influence. With the transformation of culture comes change in ideas, practices and worldviews. However, when culture evolves, not everything is eradicated or lost. As much as this chapter uses illustrations from the Shona context, the cultural dynamics described apply to most of the African contexts at large and to many other indigenous contexts. In today's African contexts, both the traditional and the Western cultural practices influence the people and their marriage customs. A Christian marriage today has both the African and Western flavors. When a pastor marries a couple today, the pastor has to be cognizant of the fact that some of the traditional Shona customs (lobola or roora – bride wealth) have been agreed upon by both families before the pastor can announce them husband and wife in the church ceremony. This chapter attempts to address the issue of marriage in modern day Africa, especially among the Shona.

A case study will be used to address an issue that most mainline churches struggle today, the issue of church members in polygamous marriages. The traditional response of just saying "no" to polygamous marriages does not suffice anymore. In light of the fact that the Western church has embraced divorce (which results in serial polygamy in the eyes of Indigenous peoples) and that Christ directly addresses divorce and appears opposed to it, the non-Western church struggles with the fact that polygamy is not condemned in the Scriptures. Using a case study approach, this chapter will try to address the challenges of polygamy in a culture and a governmental system that allows it as customary marriage.

MARRIAGE IS GOD'S IDEA

Most African (including the Shona) people believe in three major life mile-stones/markers for humans that may call for cause for celebration, honor and/or a ritual to be offered. God set these life makers from the time of creation and they are: birth, marriage and death. These life markers are not taken lightly since they are seen as God given events human beings have to participate. Do bear in mind that even in the occurrence of death, the Shona people believe it is still part of God's plan *(Kufa mutemo waMwari)*, even though the Shona believe that some deaths may be untimely (especially when a child or young adult dies or when people die by accident). Such deaths are always painful for those who remain and usually the sorrow is openly expressed. In *the cycle of life,* the Shona believe that life starts with God (in the Spirit world); we then are born into this world (live in physical form) and then after death return to God (Spirit World).[1] Marriage as part of *the cycle of life* is God's original idea not humanity's. This does not mean however, that everyone gets married but that the way *Mwari* (God) intended for humanity was for marriage to be part of the human life cycle. In other words, marriage (which in most Afri-can contexts is the union between a man and a woman) is believed to have originated with God. This makes one of the life markers, -marriage, sacred since God is the one who created humanity and then established marriage from the beginning. The missionaries brought Christianity and the Bible to Africa. There are so many similar stories contained in the Hebrew Scriptures with which the Shona can easily identify. When the Shona read the Scriptures about creation and how marriage came about, it resonates with their beliefs. In Genesis 1:26-27, it states that God created humanity in God's image, mak-ing the creation of humanity a scared event. Humanity is vested with the honor of being created in the image of his/her creator and no other creature is created in God's image. Further, in the second creation story, it says, "Then the Lord God said, 'It is not good that the man should be alone, I will make him a helper, as his partner" (Genesis 2:18). Out of the man's rib (Adam) God created the woman. The man and the woman are then given to each other as companions. "Therefore, a man leaves his father and his mother and clings to his wife, and they shall become one flesh, (Genesis 2:24). In short, God

1. Mucherera, *Meet Me at the Palaver*, p. 78.

created humanity in God's image *(imago dei),* for a relationship with each other, and for humanity be in relationship with God. God also saw that it was not good for a man to be alone thereby created a partner for him. Humanity was also created to worship and honor God. I have therefore, heard a very fitting saying, "A couple that prays together, stays together." Those couples that have a good spiritual, physical and emotional connection do well together. In addition, having created humanity, God blessed humanity and said: "Be fruitful and multiply and fill the earth . . ." (Gen 1:28). Procreation as part of marriage was therefore, God's intent for a marriage partnership. This is very much inline with the worldview of most African as it pertains to marriage and humanity's relationship with God. It does not always mean that every marriage will result in children being born, and the Shona understand these circumstances. For those who adhere to the African Shona practices (just as in Old Testament times), if the problem is/was with the man, in the conception of children, then one of the brothers secretly entered the wife to bear children for the brother. This was done so discreetly that the brother never found out the children were not biologically his own.

In the Shona's understanding of marriage, its source is God, both culturally and Scripturally. Marriage therefore is not to be taken lightly since its sacredness must be honored and revered. Hence marriage becomes a partnership between the two people plus the uniting of two families (which for the Shona family means extended family). Over and above the uniting of the two families, marriage is seen as a covenantal act between the two people, the family, the community and God. Thus, the community, blesses and honors the marriage covenantal act that the two make before God and humanity.

Cultural Considerations

There are cultural norms that guide how a married man and/or woman are supposed to act. As much as the culture permits polygamy, (for those who practice it), it must be done in a way that respects first wife *(vahosi).* Similar to the Old Testament (eg, Abraham, Sarai and Hagar) readings many of the Shona people (especially some of the Indigenous churches) who practice polygamy, see a likeness in the Jewish marriage practices of polygamy and that of the Shona people, hence they see no contradiction in the practicing of polygamy as part of their faith. Mainline churches, such as the United Methodist church of which I am a member) tend to be against the practice of polygamy even though one will find members who are polygamous in these churches. A case example will be used to illustrate the issue of polygamy in this chapter. As a way to demonstrate the clash in cultures, and that the Shona are living in between the Shona and Western cultures; the traditional chiefs or customary laws recognize and allow for polygamous practices, but in the court of law, mostly based in the cities, a Western based worldview, bigamy (being legally married to two wives) is against the law. This is not in any way supporting of polygamous marriages, but to state the cultural clashes that are taking place in the Shona culture, if not in most African cultures today. This author recognizes the complication of the cultural practices of polygamy and the Scriptures, I believe and always emphasize monogamous marriages as standard to Christian teachings in my pre-marital sessions. I usually addressed the man to beware of *(ruz-isoziso)* which is married man looking at other women lustfully, since this would easily lead to the breakage of a marriage covenant or to polygamy. This counsel I give of monogamy is the standard and is an important part of the United Methodist church's teaching in pre-marital counseling sessions. However, I am one who believe that all people from polygamous marriages must be offered communion and must not be denied this means of grace that is available to both the sinner and the righteous.

Having stated how the Shona believe that marriage is a sacred act and God's idea, I will proceed to now highlight some of the important things I have learned over the years, and taught in pre-marital counseling, about what I see as foundational to a successful marriage. The very fact that the act of marriage is sacred and that it originated from God was and/or is the basis to everything else that happens in a marriage relationship. That marriage is a sacred act is one of the major starting points to preparing those offered pre-marital and marital counseling sessions. The following pages will highlight this author's understanding of the types of marriages and then later flesh out the ingredients of a happy marriage.

There are many kinds of marriages, but in this chapter we will only address three different types of marriages: 1) an awesome –a happy marriage, where the couple have learned to resolve problems when they arise; 2) a marriage that needs resuscitation or re-fueling; 3) and then marriage 999 911 or 10111. As the old Shona adage goes, *"Hakuna imba isina makonzo,"* and in Swahili it is, *"hakuna nyumba isiyo na panya,"* translating, there is no house or home without rats or mice. The gist of this saying is that there is no home or marriage that does not have its own problems or fights. In all, the three types of marriages I have mentioned there are still problems experienced. However, some homes are ill prepared to handle conflict and/or others to handle those fights in a civil way, through love and understanding.

An awesome marriage is one in which the couple has learned to "fight fairly." Each person in the marriage relationship realizes that they have "blind spots" and once in a while they are in the wrong. There is no perfect human being and the same goes with all marriages of "non-perfect human beings." Couples in this type of marriage have learned to choose their battles and to let go of the non-essentials. They have learned that in arguments, "you may win the battle but loose the war." These are couples who have no hidden agenda in trying to change their spouse but respect and "agree to disagree" in certain issues. As the common saying goes, "In a marriage if a couple is always in agreement on *everything*, it means one of them is not using his or her mind or is following blindly." The couple in an awesome marriage does not keep lists and know when not to pick arguments. In summation, this is a couple that has their relationship based out of mutual respect and love for one another, including children if part of the marriage. Again, they have grown to fight fairly, and to keep the fires burning.

Then there is the type of marriage that is in need of *resuscitation or refueling*. This is a marriage where you have a great couple, but for some reason they are no longer clicking, little things/arguments seem to push them apart or create some static in the marriage. The couple loves each other, but there is some "tune-up" that needs to happen. They no longer enjoy spending time together. An example to this marriage is one of a person who has fainted or is out of it. That person will need an EMT or paramedic to come and help resuscitate, do some CPR, or provide some oxygen. This is a marriage that needs outside help; the couple needs oxygen provided, or CPR done to their marriage. Let's use another imagery of a car that is still looking good and has a great engine but no longer has enough fuel to keep it going. The car is now running on *fumes*, the fuel gauge is now on E. Some have joked that the E on a fuel gauge does not mean you have *Enough* fuel, but that the engine is telling you there is not *Enough* fuel in the tank to burn, to push the engine. It's on empty. There is nothing wrong with the car per se, other than the fact that its now sputtering for power to drive the car. There are marriages such as these that need just a little bit of fuel or oxygen added to help them come alive again. One will hear statements such as "we hit it off from the beginning but the spark is no longer there, but I still love her though."

Then there is that marriage all couples dread to be in _marriage 999_ _or 10111 or 911 or Exit D_. In most Southern African countries, 999 is the emergency number one calls for help or when one's life is in danger. In the USA, Canada, Mexico and other countries, 911 is the number to call. Unstable and abusive marriages are the ones I am calling _Marriage 999 or 911_. These are marriages that _thrive on conflict_. There is abuse—sexually, physically and/or emotionally. The couple is staying together for convenience. In other cases, this is where couples stay together for the sake of the children finishing school or until the kids can be on their own. In this type of marriage some couples are sleeping in different bedrooms and they are no longer intimate. This is a _chaotic marriage_, with no peace. The children run into hiding in their bedrooms when mom or dad come home. Abuse happens publicly and in the presence of children. Spouses can stay away from home to avoid the other for a week without the other bothering to find out where the other spouse is. Some of these marriages have "small houses or mistresses" as part of the marriage. This is a marriage of couples who are still married but either one or both have "checked out of the marriage." The only way to save such a marriage is to find where the "exit" is and make sure its locked or sealed. The exits of abuse, avoiding each other, small houses, etc, need to be sealed. One of the major exits is the use of and threatening by using the "D word." Divorce is the major exit and so couples that are still wanting to be in this marriage have to avoid "Exit D." Couples in Marriage 999 or 911 have little or not much respect for the other spouse.

God never intended for marriages to be a nightmare, but for it to be a dream come true, and the two to be companions for life. And yet some marriages are as if one is having a nightmare with one's eyes fully open. These are the types of marriages where the expression of "dead-on-arrival," would be used. There is no joy and/or a sense of companionship in the marriage. They are as if someone was forced to be in the marriage, and sometimes these marriages would fit the expression, "a marriage of convenience." This chapter will also explore some of the factors that build stronger marriages and while also exploring others things that are a threat to a healthy marriage.

How was the Marriage Founded?

A major two prong question that I ask, which I also believe is key and foundational to a successful marriage is: _"How did the two of you meet and_ *how long have you known each other as boyfriend and girlfriend?"* In other words, how long have you known about and/or of each other and as two people interested in a marriage partnership. How people met and where they met has an influence on the marriage partnership or covenant. Even to those who have been married for a long time, how people initially met still has an impact on the marital relationship.

People meet in many different places such as at someone else's wedding, funeral, at school, church or grew up in the same neighborhood. When the response is at a beer drinking party (Shabeen), at a pub or beer hall, this must automatically throw some red flags to the person asking or responding to the question and ultimately to the marriage itself. If the two people who meet under these circumstances of drinking parties are serious about marriage, there is much work to be done for this marriage to be successful. In addition, how long the people have known each other plays a big part in how well they know each other. People who meet each other for the first time and decide to get married within, for example, six (6) or less months of that first encounter of each other, are building their marriage on a shaky ground. I am not arguing that such marriages won't survive, but the two will have much more to learn about each other after they are married. Sometimes, what the two will discover about each other may be quite the opposite of what they assumed of each other in the short six months of dating, thereby the marriage might be rocky and not a happy one or ending in divorce. You can hear people make statements such as; "It was love at first sight, but we are discovering that we are opposites as it pertains to real life issues, interests and beliefs." It is general knowledge by most marriage counselors that a minimum period of a year of dating before someone seriously considered to get married is recommended.

Another important factor to consider for couples is the question of *mapoto,* couples that live together or cohabiting couples before marriage. Starting a marriage as co-habiting couples is not usually a good foundation for a marriage. If couples had their marriage begin this way, they have to address the issues that caused them to cohabitate and try to resolve such issues before making a covenantal commitment to marriage. It is general knowledge that one of the reasons why couples cohabitate before marriage is because of lack of commitment to the marriage. In short, they are afraid of to make a commitment and say "I do," and cohabitating gives one the way out anytime they feel it is not what they expected and can easily walk out of the marriage since nothing is official or has been signed. One of the main purposes of pre-marital counseling is to eliminate as much surprises as possible in the marriage. As much as these statistics are based on Western research, it also been found that in 80% of the couples who cohabitate (*mapoto*), the marriage end in divorce if they decided to get married.[2] There are some who cohabitate for financial reasons and this is neither a good reason to get married. Besides cohabitating there are also issues of the couples that marry because of pregnancy or due to the fact that they eloped. Other couples have been known to marry because of the circumstances in their families of origin such as trying to escape from an unhappy family of origin home and/or sometimes out of rebellion. Again, if such couples are serious about staying married and want to have a successful marriage, much marital counseling work has to be done to address the issues that led to the untimely marriage.

Today, with the high rate of death due to HIV/AIDS in the African (Shona Context) another consideration to be given attention is the issue of "rebound." Rebound generally occurs when someone looses a spouse usually to divorce or death and tries to soothe the pain of that loss through too quickly entering into another relationship. Instead of the person dealing with the pain or the loss of their spouse, s/he tries to relieve the pain through the new relationship. A marriage based on re-bound is not laid on a solid foundation and the two will have to work hard especially on the unresolved grief issues of the individual experiencing grief and entering into the relationship.

Successful Marriage: Consider These Things

In most marriages it is common knowledge that couples that are successful have some of the following common factors embedded in their marriage or early in their relationship. If these factors were and/or are not part of the grounding of their marriage, it is necessary that a couple try to explore together these aspects or factors through marital counseling. These are: 1) the marriage was/is built on friendship, meaning the two were friends or had a good dating relationship before they decided to get married; (as stated above, usually long court-ships survive the test of time versus short court-ships which are associated with higher risk of divorce). 2) The couple expresses love for one another, common interests, especially similar

2. Wright, *Before You Say I Do.*

religious practices and/or beliefs, show respect to one another and generally have a good relationship with the in-laws. 3) The couple generally communicates openly about issues of concern in their marriage. All the above factors will be discussed under subtopics of: Power, Money, Sex and the Gun (Communication): with the acronym (PMS and a Gun). Every time I have presented at workshops (including the presentation on June 11, 2011 at Old Mutare Mission, (to about 100 couples married by Bishop Muzorewa and other family members and friends), I was told this acronym (PMS & a Gun), will always help them remember some of the issues that help formulate a solid foundation to a marriage. As we turn to the first word "power," I will quote the common saying attributed to Lord Acton in a letter to Bishop Mandell Creighton in (1887) that goes, "Power corrupts and absolute power corrupts absolutely." This saying can easily be applied to a marriage partnership leading to a divorce and will be the first point discussed below. In a marriage relationship, couples that feel "in control," and not "being controlled,"[3] feel more satisfaction in the marriage since these couples have an experience of "power with" as opposed to "power over them or the other."

Power in a Marriage

Power in and of itself is not an evil thing or force, rather it can be used to preserve life. Power can be used to empower or for disempowering a person or a people group. What sustains and preserves us in the things we do in life in general, is based on power and feelings of being in control. Just as we know that in order to cook, destroy or to create anything, we need power. In our bodies we need power in order to live, do work or to move from one place to another. Power can be used positively to build or it can negatively be used to destroy. Fire as a form of power is good, but out of control, fire can easily destroy acres of land, and property. We need the power of water, wind, and electricity but at the same time these same forces or power can be destructive.

The same applies to *power in a marriage*; it can be used positively to build the marriage or negatively to oppress and dehumanize a spouse in a marriage relationship. The question is then, is power and control in your marriage relationship, *making* or *breaking* your marriage? What is the

3. Markman, *Fighting for Your Marriage*, 2010.

history of the issues of power and control in your marriage? How do you define your relationship as marriage partners? Do you feel *in control* or do you feel as *being controlled*? Being in control does not mean that you have power over your spouse. All it means is that one feels s/he is able to do things or even make decisions for the benefit of the marriage without the fear of being reprimanded by the other spouse in a parent-child manner. Yes, there are decisions that require a joint voice of the spouse in the marriage as well as agreement. At the same time, there are some issues that a spouse can independently decide without fear.

When we read in Genesis, in the first creation story, both Adam and Eve were created in the image of God. "Let us make humankind in our image, according to our likeness, . . . So God created humankind in his image, in the image of God he created them; male and female he created them (Gen. 1:26- 27). Reading this passage is an indication that God did not create human beings (men and women) one as being of less value than the other. Even when we read the second creation story where Eve is created from the rib, (Gen. 2:21-22), there is symbolism of a partnership. Eve is not created from Adam's foot but from the rib. The ribs protect the vital organs of the body, such as the heart and lungs, etc., so essential are these parts of the human body without which a person can live. The heart, for example, has also been taken as a symbol of love. Interestingly, the rib is also on the *side* of the human body, symbolizing that a man a woman are to walk in life *side by side*, not behind, under or in front of each other. This is a call for an equal partnership between husband and wife. They are supposed to honor and respect one another. People have a tendency to confuse the role a spouse plays in a marriage and God given abilities, with the issues of power and control in a marriage. Marriage is a shared partnership and responsibilities. Happy marriages that have survived the test of time have agreed upon functions through mutual understanding on the roles each spouse plays in the marriage.

We need to always remember that Scriptures have been misused for many centuries to destroy nations and oppress others. Many of the systems of slavery around the world, colonial oppressive structures and apartheid in South Africa were all based on the misinterpretation of scriptures. It is always amazing that Scriptures have been used to both oppress and free people. Similarly many men especially, have also misused (Eph. 5: 21-33) as a way to oppress their wives. They usually do not read the whole chapter of what Paul is driving, but only focus on part of verse 22; "Wives be submissive to your husbands." The opening to this whole argument that Paul is making begins with: "Be subject to one another out of reverence for Christ." (Eph. 5:21). In addition, he further says, "Husbands love your wives just as Christ loved the church and gave himself up for her . . . .. In the same way husband should love their wives as they do their own bodies. He who loves his wife loves himself . . . . Each of you, however should love his wife as *himself* (italics are mine for emphasis) and wives should respect their husband" (Eph. 5:25, 28, 33). How then can one abuse a person he so loves as himself? A closer look at the emphasis of this passage shows that what Paul is driving at is love and respect of each other in a marriage more than the issue of submissiveness. I still believe Paul is calling for a mutual partnership type of marriage that is centered on love and respect.

The issues of power and control in a marriage can easily destroy the marriage relationship. Interestingly, any marriage relationship where there is abuse of power especially physical, emotional and sexual abuse, most times started during the dating relationship. The one abused thought that once they got married the abuse would stop and/or that, they would be able to change the other person. This is a very wrong assumption since the abuse usually escalates once people get married because the abuser knows that there is now a commitment and covenantal relationship. It is my conclusion that once there starts to be any form of abuse, especially physical, verbal, sexual, and emotional in a marriage relationship, the original marriage covenant now has big cracks in it and has started loosing its quality of what God intended. When abuse occurs, it is the point at which the couple is to re-assess the issues causing the abuse in the relationship, since early intervention to problematic issues in a marriage is the best solution. When physical force (beating or hitting the other spouse) is used in a marriage to try to control or change the other person, this marriage is no longer based on mutual love. The best change comes out of a mutual relationship and understanding. If changes are to be made in a marriage, both partners need to change either in the approach, perspectives or in understanding of each other. It is good to remember that one does not marry someone with a goal to change him or her; it usually does not work.

In the Shona culture, there are terms used to describe a husband and wife that symbolize mutuality in power and equal need for each other. Generally, the understanding is that in a marriage one cannot function without the other or the marriage becomes paralyzed or dysfunctional. The man is referred to as the head (*musoro wemba*), (similar to the Ephesians quoted above text); and the woman is referred to as the backbone (similar to Eve being created from the rib or protective cage of the vital organs) of the family, or *mukadzi ndiye musana wemba*. (Literally, the woman carries the baby in her womb and on her back). It is so important in the Shona marriage customs that the son-in-law "to be" has to pay a cow *(mombe yemusana or yehumai)*. This is a sign of appreciation to the mother-in-law's *backbone* for having spent nine month carrying (the fetus, plus the baby on her back as an infant) the daughter, which the son-in-law is intending to marry. There is great symbolism to be derived from this imagery of *head* and *backbone* that is applied to a good marriage partnership in the Shona context. The head cannot properly function without the backbone (meaning vertebrates, spinal codes, etc.), just as the backbone without a head is also useless. Each one of these parts has power over the other; however, they have to mutually function with each other to give fullness to life in the body. The brain *(head)* and the nervous system (all connected through the spinal cord, *backbone*), cannot function without the other if the body is to work properly. In other words, the head (man) and the backbone (wife) in a marriage are equally important if allowed to play their role well in a marriage relationship. I have used this symbolism and imagery in my pre-marital and marital counseling with Shona couples and for those who apply it, it has created strong happy marriages.

In the Shona patriarchal society there is yet another saying: *musha mukadzi*, translating; a home is because of the wife. In other words, without the wife a home cannot stand since the woman is the *backbone* of the home. This is quite contrary to where a home might have a strong "willed woman" and one hears negative comments usually from men that such and such a home is "under a petticoat government." A strong willed woman is just symbolic of a strong backbone. Again, the husband and wife in a marriage have to be careful of such comments since they can be very divisive of their marriage partnership. No one home is the same as the next one and thereby couples don't always have to do things as their next-door neighbors.

We make marriage covenants in the presence of and with the witness of humanity and God. There is however, much danger in allowing the witnesses, especially humanity, be in charge of what goes on in one's marriage partnership. In any marriage, there are those who will stand by the married couple in thick or thin and will try to help the marriage to succeed. Then, there are those who are there to make the marriage a miserable experience. These are those who believe that the two were not to be married in the first place. This is worse in many of the African cultures, especially if one marries from a family, which the extended family does not approve. It is a hard marriage to start if one's family of origin had an ideal partner in mind and then one marries one that does not fit their approval. Therefore, be aware of the *true "in-laws and friends"* who want to help, and the *"out-laws and foes"* who mostly out of jealousy and disapproval of who the person has chosen to marry, would have the marriage fail. The "out-laws and foes" will not rest until the marriage has fallen apart. In other words, do not give power to outsiders to control your marriage. Listen to others for advise, but put on your thinking caps before going by everyone else suggestions for your marriage. Yes, we marry into a family and marriage is a community event, but don't forget that you are the one married to your spouse and you have to live with him/her. It is amazing that many people have "great" ideas on how your marriage "should be" or "could be better," and how marital problems or issues need to be resolved. However, remember that at the end of the day you are the one who is going to be facing the consequences of the decisions you make 24/7, and 365 days.

As mentioned earlier, *"Hakuna imba isina makonzo,"* and in Swahili it is, *"hakuna nyumba isiyo na panya,"* translating, there is no house or home without rats or mice. Each home has its own "rats" or simply speaking, "problems" but it is the people who live in the home who decide how they are going to kill the "rats." Some use poison, other traps, others ignore, and others may chase after the rats until they kill them. In other words, what works for one home may not work for another; therefore, use the power and abilities accorded each other in your relationship to face the problems in your marriage. In short, don't give full control of your marriage over to outsiders. Listen and use whatever advice you deem helpful, but don't relinquish power and control to those outside of the home. Solidify your marriage boundaries so as to decrease unwarranted intrusions etc., or let others take-over.

Money, Money Money!!!

Money can make a marriage merrier or it can make it miserable. It is not necessarily having too much of it or having less that will break marriages. Usually it is how the couple agrees or disagrees on how to spend the money that makes the finances *build or break* the marriage. The old saying holds true that "money can't buy love." A marriage based on money or a relationship that was founded on one spouse being attracted to the possessions of the other rather than falling in-love with the person will most likely fail.

Possessions come and go and if someone was to make a marriage commitment to another based on wealth, the day the wealth is lost is the day that marriage ends. Paul makes an argument with which I agree about money when he says: "For the love of money is the root of all evil,"(1 Tim. 6:10). Paul's argument is that the *love* of money is the root of all evil, but not that money in and of itself is evil. It therefore, holds that if one was to fall in love with someone's money, not the person, s/he has trapped him/herself in loving "the root of evil." Where someone falls in love with the wealth, the commitment is not to the person but the person's wealth. People who are married to someone's wealth lie when they make the marriage vow that they will love the person "in richer or poorer," since the day when the money is gone, they are also gone out of the marriage. In this sense, the person was married to the status, possessions and luxuries, but not really committed to the marital relationship.

Some of the questions to ask about money in your marriage are: Have we agreed on how we are spending what we are making? Are we open about our finances to each other? Who controls the money or the bank book(s)? Are the bills being paid on time? Did we know much about each other's indebtedness before getting married or is this an issue that came up as a surprise and still needs to be resolved? Secrets about finances are not healthy for any marriage. When one of the spouses discovers that the other has a secret banking account, this can also write disaster on the marriage. In short, couples have to be open to each other about their finances.

Who makes the most money? If the wife is the one working and the husband is out of work, how does this affect the marriage relationship? In a patriarchal society such as Zimbabwe, this has many implications to the man's status in the community plus to his ego. The men, in most African communities are expected to be the breadwinners. Having no work or something that the husband is doing to bring income to the family has a great negative impact on the marriage. *Rovha,* a Shona word meaning "a loafer," is quite a damaging term emotionally to be used on any man. It implies that one is a loser, failure and/or dropout. In short, the implication is that one has become a failure in life and for his family. When the Shona read the Scriptures in Genesis, this confirms that one of the roles of man in his family is as a breadwinner. As much as this comes as a punishment God tells the man: "cursed is the ground because of you (man) . . . in toll you shall eat of it all the days of your life; thorns and thistles it shall bring forth for you; . . . By the sweat of your face you shall eat bread until you return to the ground" (Gen. 3:17-19). In other words, men are expected to work hard and sweat in raising or bringing food for his family.

Money, if not handled properly in a marriage can be the wedge that will drive couples apart. How money is spent on buying for the children or relatives and friends can also be critical. If the children in the marriage realize that if they go to the mother she usually buys whatever they ask, and the father usually says no, that spells c-o-n-f-l-i-c-t for the marriage and the children will create triangles between the couple. Children know well how to play this game of getting parents into triangulated relationships, arguments and/or fights over money. It is usually a good idea when one's child(ren) come to ask for some money, to check what the other spouse might have said to the child before coming to you. In other words, do not allow your children to control your marriage over money and/or material things. There are things that children have a right to, such as basic necessities as food clothing, shelter, etc., but electronic gadgets or the latest toy or fashion, are not a right but a privilege if they can be afforded. You can give your child all the toys in the world, but that will never be good enough in building a strong relationship with them. The greatest gift you can give to your children is not a lot of money or the latest thing in fashion or toys, but your love, care, a good relationship and meeting their basic material needs.

Couples who know much about each other spending habits help each other. There are people who are not afraid of credit cards or borrowing money from other people and/or from the bank. They will not shy away from keeping on borrowing even when they have so much debt. Then, there are people who are always thinking about saving money for "the rainy day" even when the money needs to be used for something tangible, they are always too frugal about spending the money they have. A marriage that has "a miser and a spender," needs much help on how the couple can reconcile on how they use their money. The miser is the: "Get all you can, put it in a can and then sit on the can," type person. On the other hand, "the spender" is one that wants to use whatever penny, is earned at any time or chance given. In any marriage the couple will need to agree or sit down and discuss about their spending and saving habits. Other questions to consider are: How are you communicating about bills and how are they being paid? Has the couple given each other limits of how much a spouse can spend without consulting the other? Some couples will agree, for example; that a spouse can spend a certain amount per month without having to consult, however, any sum above the agreed amount, the couple will first have to check with each other. Does the couple have separate accounts and if so, are the bills being paid? When it comes to money, there is nothing so damaging to a marital relationship than finding out that you are in debt because your spouse has not been paying the bills s/he is responsible. Out of trust of the other spouse, one spouse expected the bills to be paid, and may only find months later that the money was used for something and the couple is behind in bills.

You can earn all the money you think you need in life, have all the luxuries and yet still be very unhappy in a marriage. In other words, it is good to have money in a marriage, but at the same time money is not the sole answer to a happy marriage. It is how the couple communicates about money, is transparent and/or agrees on how to use their finances together, that makes for a happier marriage. Some of the happiest couples I have encountered are people living below the poverty level, and other married couples with all the money they need, plus a surplus, are some of the most miserable ones I have met. Being content with what the two have, transparency, being responsible, respect and a loving marital relationship makes of a rich couple, living within their means. There are couples who are rich in material things but have no relationship.

In the African context, the saying goes that "I take care of you so you take care of me tomorrow." This is usually used to mean that parents take care of their children so that the children will take care of them in the parent's old age. This can be damaging to a couple's marriage if not handled properly. How much to spend each month on the in-laws can be a bone of contention in marriage. Has the couple agreed how much support is given to each pair of in-laws, especially if both sides of the in-laws are still alive? Is support given based on the in-laws needs or just equally? If one set of in-laws needs more support than the other, is this based on an understanding, or could this be a potential for conflict? When support is given, is it announced that it is coming from the couple or from the daughter or son? It is always a good marriage decision to announce support as coming from the couple rather than from the son or daughter.

Sex (Intimacy)

Before there was sex or sexual intercourse, there was a relationship between God and humanity. In the beginning, God created humanity first to be in relationship with Him and each other. In the second creation story (Gen. 2:ff) God created Adam and noticed that the man was lonely and so God created a partner for him. This is not to say that sex (in this section, the word sex is being used to connote sexual intercourse not gender), is not a great part of a marriage, but if it becomes the main focal point for a marriage, that marital relationship is built on shaky ground. Sex is a gift, blessed from God and a very important part of the marriage, but for sex to be fulfilling in a marriage, it has to be part of the loving relationship. Having sex does not translate into intimacy. People can have sex for money, benefits etc., based on a relationship that has no commitment or love for the other. Intimacy has in it, love, respect, commitment, and a close and understanding relationship. Therefore, intimacy is the foundation for a good marriage. Intimacy includes couples playing and/or doing fun activities together. In general, couples that have similar interests tend to do things together and enjoy each other's company. When couples no longer enjoy each other's company except for sex, it is an indication that the marriage is in trouble. It is normal that during the "honeymoon period" or the first few months, sex or sexual activity is high in most new marriages. As time goes on, and when children are born to the marriage, the rate of sexual activity may go down, but the love and intimate relationship does not fade. The decrease in sexual activity is because, anytime there is an addition to any relationship, the people involved have to adjust to whatever has been added to the relationship. Meaning, if a child has been added, the love and time that used to be shared between the couple has now to include the child. All the activities (including the time they used to have sex) or the couple used to be by themselves now has to include the child or children born to the relationship. This does not however, limit the intimate activities, only that the couple have to factor in what to do with the child(ren) at those times. In addition, this is where intimacy now becomes something that is beyond having sex. Couples can be "intimate" with each other without having sex. In other words, the couple has to be creative to "keep the fire burning," by creating space for themselves to be with each other. Medical conditions may limit sexual activities but that must not kill the intimacy between the couple. Sometimes a couple may be separated by geographic distance, yet they can still keep in an intimate relationship through other means, phone, skype, chat, e-mail, and etc.

It is a shame that there are individuals who are living "being single in a marriage." This means that these individuals though married are never happy in their marriage. They are in the marriage to make others (husband or wife, children, extended family happy) but happiness in the marriage is not meant for them. You hear especially women, who will make such statements as "I am staying in the marriage for the sake of my children, and my church does not condone divorce." In other African cultures, a woman may not leave an abusive marriage because her family of origin cannot pay back the *lobola (bride wealth)* if she was to leave. In such marriages the woman will take all the abuse to keep the extended family happy, but never for her. Woman in these types of marriages will define "being raped" by their husband as the way they experience "intimacy" and still cannot leave the marriage. I have heard horror stories of a wife "being raped" by her drunken husband in the presence of their little or small children. A happy marriage has boundaries, respect, love and understanding. There is a sense of sacredness to sex between humans that must be maintained. When we see animals mate we do not react the same way as we would, if we were to see two people having sexual intercourse in public. The sense of shame we feel when we accidentally see two people having sex has to do with how sex between spouses has a high degree sacredness, privacy and sanctity to it.

Some of the following questions are good for couples to ask to make an assessment about the strength of their marriage: Is the relationship free of abuse (verbal, sexual or physical)? Are they open with each other about their sexual relationship, needs or ideas of intimacy? Have they talked about their feelings such as what turns the other on or off sexually? Do they pray together about their sexual relations as they do other needs? Has either one been into pornography – (how deep and have they sought help)? Is one a "morning person" and the other a "night owl" and so how does this interfere with time to be intimate or have enjoyable sex? What plans do they have to keep the fire burning (date nights, times apart just be with each other, movies, etc)? Among the Shona we have a saying *"Rudo imoto runoto kuchidyirwa,"* meaning love is like a fire, one will have to keep putting the wood logs onto the fire to keep it burning. In other words, continue to do some of the things you were doing when you were dating and re-visit some of the places you used to go to have fun. Are small gifts, flowers and spending a night at the hotel important for the growth of intimacy for either one of the couple and how does the other view these times apart from others as a couple? Is there still romance in the marriage? Does the couple buy little things for each other as surprises to show they still care for the other? Do not allow your house-maid give more attention to you spouse (especially husbands) while you watch. Marriages have been know to break, especially with working couples, where the wife leaves "everything" as it pertains to the home to the maid. The danger is the temptation that may ensue, which may drive a wedge in the spouse's relationship. When some of the best meals the husband enjoys are made by the maid, and the wife does not pay notice, the maid may take the better attention of the husband, and this is made worse if the maid is more attractive than the wife.

It is so important to keep the "fires burning" in the marriage relationship by making sure that couples continue to do those things that they loved to do for each other while they were still dating. In addition, there are things that one couple may like/love to do, which the other couple doesn't, such as share the love of types of food. I love minnows, and my wife does not like cooking or eating minnows. Many times my wife has cooked me minnows, a food she does not eat, just to show that she loves me or cares. I love to see flowers out on the yard but don't care much about flowers on a table in our house. I am one who likes the beauty of flowers outside, not in a vase. Why would someone cut flowers from their bush, stick them in a vase to watch them slowly die? I, however, buy flowers for my wife because she loves them and she believes its romantic. I do it happily since it brings joy to her heart and makes her feel cared for and loved. These are good examples of intimacy that is not always sexual.

Infidelity

Infidelity is one of the biggest marriage killers in cultures such as that of the Shona where polygamy is acceptable. It creates jealousy and the spouse (usually the wife) does not focus on the husband giving into temptation, issues of lust, etc; rather the wife self- blames and feels guilty for not having done something right to keep her husband from wandering. Infidelity is usually about one partner submitting to the temptation of seeking sexual pleasure or gratification outside of one's marriage. The dangers of infidelity are such that it can cause someone to give in, to the point of committing murder (2 Sam 11 & 12). King David after having lusted after Bathsheba, had Uriah killed in the battlefront so he could have his (Uriah's) wife. Nowadays, there are many ways a person can commit murder and one way would be that of knowingly infecting someone with HIV, which for me has become, "a secret weapon of mass destruction,"[4] When a husband or wife cheats, contracts

---

4. Mucherera, *Meet Me at the Palaver*, p. 43.

HIV, knowingly infects the spouse and/or children, one has physically, spiritually, emotionally, etc., committed a form of murder to his/her family.

Infidelity is usually a sign that there are problems in the marital relationship or that one of the spouses has just given into temptation and lust. People tend to run away from problems in their home and look elsewhere thinking they will find comfort and empathy outside. Sadly, running away from the problems does not resolve the problems, because when the person walks back into their home, the problems are "still looking at him or her," waiting to be resolved. Before one decides to cheat on one's spouse, one has to ask oneself questions such as: "What is going on in my marital relationship that is driving me out of my marriage? How have I contributed to the problem? What are some of the solutions we could work out to resolve the problems? What is likely to happen if I am found out that I have cheated on my spouse? What does that say about me as an individual and/or as a Christian?

Infidelity also happens when sex is *used as a weapon* in the marital relationship. This is when one of the couples gets into the habit of refusing sexual intercourse every time there is disagreement. Sex then, is used to manipulate the other person to submit to whatever disagreement might be there. Paul says about sexual relations in a marriage (not as a command but as a concession):

> Because of the temptation to immorality, each man should have his own wife and each woman her own husband. The husband should give his wife her conjugal rights and likewise the wife to her husband. For the wife does not rule over her own body, but the husband does; likewise the husband does not rule over his body but the wife does. Do not refuse one another except perhaps by agreement for a season that you may devote yourselves to prayer; but then come together again, lest Satan tempt you through lack of self-control (1 Cor. 7:2-5).

As much as it is sad to say, there are some spouses that might not be as strong in controlling his or her sexual urge ending looking for a willing partner outside of the marriage if sex is constantly used as a weapon in the relationship. Paul knew about this temptation, thereby his urging of couples not to refuse each other of conjugal rights.

It is important as well to note that women and men's bodies are wired differently as it pertains to sexual arousal. I have heard the saying that women are like (crock pots – slow cookers and men are like microwaves) when it comes to sexual arousal and response. Which means, it takes much more time for a woman to reach orgasm as compared to a man. Growing up I used to hear older men say, "Do not act like a rooster that just bites on the head of the hen ejaculate and walks away," when training the young men about sex. This all to say that foreplay is an important part of the sexual relationship between a husband and wife. Sex is not about pro-creation only; it is a gift from God uniting the two in intimacy, to be enjoyed in a marital relationship. The husband and wife have to establish a pattern of communicate during foreplay, in most cases with the wife giving hits of when she is ready. I have counseled couples where the wife has complained that the husband is always reaching ejaculation before she has even started being in the mood. There are cases where this might be a medical condition, however, most of the times this is something a man can train his mind and body to be able to wait for his wife to reach orgasm, so they can enjoy "the moment" together. There is, however, nothing that reduces a man's self-esteem or self-image sexually more than hearing the spouse say she is never satisfied. This is where a husband and wife have to discuss openly why is it so? Is it a medical problem or is it something the man would need to train himself in controlling his body and mind? Some couples make the mistake of comparing their spouse to what they might have read or seen on TV, and if the spouse does not act as such then one claims dissatisfaction. The person you read about or saw on TV is not the same as the one in your bed. Control your mind to focus on your spouse during intimacy not on other memories or fantasies you may hold outside of the sexual activity.

Being angry with one another in a marriage is common, expected and is a natural process. Anger is an inbuilt emotion, however, it has to be kept in check. Paul in his writings says: "Be angry but do not sin; do not let the sun go down on your anger, and give no opportunity to the devil" (Eph. 4:26-27). Anger that goes on week-in week-out, ruins a marriage relationship. Couples have to learn to forgive each other on issues rather than keeping a list of what the other has done wrong. It does not mean you just rush to forgiveness without facing the issues and discussing them, but the goal is not to let problems pile or stretch out. As couples, when you are starting to feel you can no longer stand the anger in your spouse, it is time to look for outside help from a neutral person who might be able to help. Try praying together for your problems, even in those moments you are hardly making eye contact with each other. Anger can easily create a wedge between a couple's relationship. Couples have to be aware of the temptation that comes in when they start growing apart. Old love relationships re-kindle on Facebook, Whatsapp, emails, sexting, pornography, etc. Technology is good, but has also been know to be destroying marriages. Many marriages suffer through couples being involved in pornography and this includes both men and women. Couples are to guard their marriage from these types of temptations.

The Gun (Mouth or Communication)

In the letter of James, in writing about the tongue the author says: "And the tongue is a fire. The tongue is an unrighteous world among our member, staining the whole body, setting on fire the cycle of nature, and set on fire by hell. For every kind of beast and bird or reptile and sea creature, can be tamed and has been tamed by humankind, but no human being can tame the tongue – a restless evil, full of deadly poison. With it we bless the Lord and Father, and with it we curse men who are made in the likeness of God" (James 3:6-9). We communicate what we feel most of the times with our words. One of the things that will serve a marriage is to carefully choose the words we say to our spouse. There is a saying that God gave us two ears and one mouth for a purpose. The purpose is for us to listen more and talk less, in other words, listen twice before you speak out that one word. Definitely, words that come out of a person's mouth have been the most dangerous gun bullets that kill marriages. The problem with words is that once we say them out loud we can't take them back. Couples have to be careful on how they use words, and by all means try to avoid some of the two dangerous words in their heated conversations, "always and never." Try to avoid such statements as, "You are *always* lying to me, or you *never* help me around the house." If, for example, a spouse does not frequently help around the house as much as the other spouse expects, and the other makes the statement "you *never* help around the house," that statement is not accurate since the other does, help once in a while. This can create a passive-aggressive be-havior out of the one being told they *never* help around the house since s/he may feel the times s/he helped were never appreciated or acknowledged. The alternative way to communicate would be to make a statement such as, "I appreciate so much when you help around the house and I would appreciate it today if you could help me with this particular chore."

Lies, lies and lies are some of the greatest marriage killers! The old adage is true that, when one tells a lies, they have to create another lie to cover up for the first one until the lie does not make any sense or does not add up. Couples who communicate and are transparent with each other have nothing to hide from each other. Strong marriages are set on trust, honesty and open communication. Couples who lie to each other never will gain trust of each other, are always second-guessing, and suspicious of each other's actions and intentions.

One of the worst ways for a couple is to communicate through their children or other people rather than face-to-face with one's spouse. Why is it that one has to use their children or others to communicate with their spouse? Whenever there is fear to face each other in a marital relationship it spells danger for the marriage. Similarly, couples have to avoid communicating through people who are outside of their marriage. What one will miss in this style of communication are the actual feelings and emotions attached to whatever is being expressed by the other spouse since s/he will receive it second hand. In this day and age of technology, there those couples that avoid using face-to-face verbal communication with their spouse, but choose communicate through text messaging while they are in the same house. Technology is good, but we were created for relationships, since God gave us words, gestures, mouths, and eyes, so that we can communicate. What does open communication mean for each one of them? Have they experienced conflict and how did they resolve it? When there is conflict does one tend to want to resolve the issue there and then and the other withdraws, (that is asking for space and time to think through issues)? What styles of communication do they bring to the marriage that they learned from their families of origin? Does the couple's marriage thrive on conflict and who puts in the last word? What are their stories about how their parents fought, communicated or had arguments? Do voices get raised at any sign of disagreement? Are there secrets from the past being brought to the marriage that either one has not shared? Many marriages are known to have failed due to poor communication and conflict management skills. If one spouse has a complaint, in what way does the other respond? Couples who tend to take each other for granted do not listen to each other and make very big assumptions in the way they respond to one another. When couples stop listening to one another, it "deadens" the relationship, in other words, it is an indication that the "fire driving the relationship is dying out." It is my experience that no one wants to be embarrassed in public. When couples start arguments on private issues publicly and no longer care how the other feels, it is an indication of a marriage in trouble. Respect, a loving relationship and avoiding as many relational triangles help in gluing the marriage together.

In this chapter I have covered issues that I believe are foundational to a happy marital relationship. I have used some ideas from the Shona contest, integrated other ideas from the West and others are Biblical. One of the primary layers is the idea that marriage is God's idea and that God created a man and woman both in His image, to be equal partner in a marriage. Marriage is both sacred and is a sacred act, and couples that pray together tend to stay together. Those couples that start their marriage as a covenant between them and God are more likely to have a long lasting and happy marital relationship. It is important that couples pay attention to the matters of power, money, sex and communication in building a strong marriage. Couples also have to pay attention the changes in the Shona culture that is, how heavily influenced they are by some of the Western values.

Marriage in the African context is neither fully traditional nor is it fully Western, rather it is a mixture of both. In the African (Shona) context today, the church struggles with how to handle issues of polygamy as mentioned earlier. The following section will address the issue of polygamy using a case study of a polygamous marriage.

A CASE OF POLYGAMY

Mr. and Mrs Moyo are in their mid to late sixties. Mrs. Moyo is in poor health; she is asthmatic and has heart problems. Mr and Mrs Moyo used to attend the Zion Apostolic church that allowed polygamy. In their middle ages they started to attend a mainline church. Mrs. Moyo first brought up the idea of polygamy into the marriage. She suggested that her husband get another wife: her niece, Rudo. After menopause, due to a cultural belief she holds, Mrs. Moyo stopped engaging in sexual intercourse with Mr. Moyo. She argued that Rudo would be of good help to them, and Mr. Moyo would also have a stable wife. Mrs. Moyo is afraid that her husband could be tempted by an indecent woman and could perhaps contract AIDS or other sexually transmitted diseases. Rudo is a 35-year-old teacher.

Mr. Moyo tried to convince his wife that her beliefs involving sex after menopause were cultural and had no scientific basis. He took her to a white male young medical doctor to discuss the disease. This made Mrs Moyo more adamant, saying the doctor was young, she (Mrs. Moyo) was not White, and that White doctors did not understand or know about some of the African diseases. Mrs. Moyo did not waver from her beliefs.

Two months after the visit to the doctor, Mrs. Moyo's niece, Rudo moved in with them. Mrs. Moyo talked to Mr. Moyo and to Rudo separately, wondering whether the two would be interested in each other. Rudo has always had a "crush" on Mr. Moyo, and has indicated she would be interested in the marriage, if she had her aunt's blessing. Initially, Mr. Moyo was opposed to the idea, since this is contrary to the mainline Christian church standards that they belong. There is no sexual relationship between Mr. Moyo and Rudo, but the issue of a customary marriage between Mr. Moyo and Rudo has been raised. The extended family members on both sides approve; however, the Moyos' church does not allow polygamy. The Moyos are perceived by the church members as role models. They have come to you as a counselor or pastor for help about their situation.

SOCIO-CULTURAL ISSUES

The Moyos are an affluent couple who live in a suburban home. Mrs. Moyo converted to Christianity in her thirties, after having been raised by parents who were African traditionalists. When they converted to Christianity, they attended a church that had no problems with polygamous practices even though theirs was a monogamous marriage. Now they are members of a mainline denomination that does not allow polygamy, even though for Mrs. Moyo being polygamous is not a problem. While Mrs. Moyo is a very strong Christian, she also has high respect for Shona traditional values, as evidenced by her beliefs about sexual intercourse past menopause. In addition, she does not seem to have any problem with her husband marrying another wife, which she says she does not see anywhere in the Bible where Jesus Christ condemned polygamous marriage practices and for her its also culturally acceptable.

The Moyos honor their extended family ties. Before going to consult with the pastor, they consulted with both sides of their respective extended families, to seek their blessings. Neither family had any problems accepting a second marriage, and left the final decision to be made by Mr. and Mrs. Moyo. In addition, the couple also consulted with their children, who voiced support for a second marriage, but realizing their parents' Christian values, asked Mr. and Mrs. Moyo to make the final decision themselves. The Moyos' communal interpersonal relationships appear to be healthy.

Regarding the issue of polygamy, the main issues raised today by most African women theologians and other writers primarily involve men's desire for power, control, and oppression of women. The Moyos' case does not clearly bring those particular issues to the surface. Mrs. Moyo initiated the idea of Mr. Moyo marrying a second wife; Mr. Moyo himself initially opposed the marriage.

Because of her health problems, Mrs. Moyo realizes she needs Rudo's help, as well as procuring someone who can fulfill her husband's sexual needs, which Mrs. Moyo feels she can no longer meet. Rudo is a 35-year-old educated woman and a self-supporting primary school teacher. She is not being forced into the marriage, but rather sees it as an opportunity to help her aunt, and at the same time become married to someone she loves. In short, the general issue of man's need of power and control, common in most polygamous marriages, is not apparent in this case. It appears the idea of a second marriage was reached with the full and voluntary involvement of the three people who would be the major figures in the marriage. In this case, Mrs. Moyo took the leading role, choosing to initiate the second marriage.

ANXIETY, ITS SOURCES, AND PSYCHOLOGICAL ISSUES

The main source of anxiety for the Moyos is the prospect of participating in a polygamous marriage, a lifestyle contrary to Western Christian teachings. The Moyos are considered role models in the church they helped start, and becoming polygamous would have a detrimental effect on the life of the church. This would mean Mr. Moyo would have to relinquish his leadership position in the church and forfeit the right to bring forth for baptism any children born (if any) to his second, polygamous marriage. Even though it is culturally acceptable, religiously and theologically this is something perceived as contrary to the Christian teachings of the Moyos' church, hence, the anxiety.

Mrs. Moyo appears to be psychologically accepting of the entire situation. Some of her feelings may be based on her level of comfort with issues involving the Shona traditional culture. When she converted, she did not try to do away with most of the Shona traditional cultural beliefs. On the other hand, Mr. Moyo is caught between Shona religio-cultural beliefs and the Western Christian beliefs. His Western Christian beliefs have posed a psychological conflict for him. He has been a role model for the church, and engaging in polygamy sets a bad example. Yet, when Mr Moyo reads the Scriptures, he does not experience conflict in that he is not a Bishop or Deacon in the church, he is a member. The Scriptures specifically state that a Bishop or a Deacon "are to be husbands of one wife."[5] He struggles with understanding why his marriage to Rudo will be in conflict with Scriptures since in Paul's writing to Timothy it seems to imply that it was simply saying that those people who were polygamous could not hold positions such as Bishops and Deacons. Mr. Moyo is not interested in being a Bishop or Deacon, only a faithful Christian member. What gives Mr. Moyo anxieties are the questions such as: How is he going to fit into the congregation with two wives? Will it mean changing churches? And what would the act of changing churches say about his Christianity? The fact that Mr. Moyo has agreed to take the step to consult the pastor about this issue appears to indicate that he is beginning to question the religious beliefs involving polygamy and is anxious about engaging in it without the pastor's counsel or blessing.

Rudo does not appear to have any problems with the prospective marriage. One could also argue that the fact that she already had a "crush" on Mr. Moyo has clouded her critical judgment about marrying Mr. Moyo. She does not appear to be caught in the psychological dilemma of whether this is Christian or unchristian. She appears to have a clear conscience about her decision, and awaits her aunt's blessing.

RELIGIOUS OR THEOLOGICAL ISSUES

I recognize that I am not the first one to attempt to address the general issue of polygamy in Africa. With this awareness, I will utilize other people's views in the analysis of this case. There are several aspects of polygamy this author may not pursue in greater detail, such as the analysis of polygamy as a system oppressive to women, and the socio-economic basis of polygamy in the Shona traditional society.[6] These are all important issues, which need to be addressed when discussing polygamy. However, as stated earlier, in the Moyos' case the focus of this analysis does not appear to bring these issues to the surface.

At another level, I argue that some polygamous marriages are better than monogamous ones. There are some Shona Christians who are involved in monogamous marriages in which the husbands are very abusive,

---

5. *The Bible*, p. 1025 NRSV.
6. Hastings, *Christian Marriage*, p. 135-149.

oppressive and behave in ways as unchristian-like as can be imagined. If the church's stance contends that polygamous marriages are oppressive, why does the church fail to discipline such abusive and oppressive monogamous men in the same manner as the polygamous men?

One could also argue that the appearance of apparent peace in these polygamous marriages is due to the submissive nature of the women involved; in short, they are not truly happy. Still, this author is convinced that there are some Shona polygamous marriages, which would meet all the Christian standards of being a Christian family. Those involved in the polygamous marriages cannot be considered fully Christian simply because of the type marriage in which they live? The argument for or against polygamy in the Shona Christian church can go either way. I however, also argue that justice and issues of equality in a marriage are not automatic simply because the marriage is monogamous.

I find myself in a dilemma; having observed some of the injustices and oppression within some polygamous marriages, I also struggle with advocating for polygamy in the Shona context. However, cases such as that of the Moyos or cases in which a polygamous man converts to Christianity and is forced to divorce all but one wife, and cases involving peaceful responsible polygamous men who participate in the life of the church but who are not given all the rights and privileges awarded other church members, force this writer to challenge the church to re-visit this issue.

In addition, in the West, as much as polygamy is legally prohibited, it is common knowledge that it still exists in States such as Utah.[7] The other irony in the West is that polygamy is prohibited but, what has been commonly termed *serial polygamy or serial monogamy* is flourishing. Serial polygamy is where a man marries and divorces as many times as they want. Hammond Cheney and Pearsey say this about USA serial polygamy or monogamy:

> What if a person marries, divorces, marries, divorces, etc.? Serial Monogamy or Serial Polygamy is the process of establishing an intimate marriage or cohabiting relationship that eventually dissolves and is followed by another intimate marriage or cohabiting relationship that eventually dissolves, etc., in a series. So, polygamists have simultaneous multiple spouses while serial monogamists or serial polygamists have multiple spouses in a sequence of relationships. Millions of U.S adults will experience serial marriages and divorces.

7. http://scholarship.law.duke.edu/cgi/viewcontent.cgi?article=1288&context=djglp

It often amazes me how much we love marriage in the United States. Many marry then divorce yet still want to be married again.[8]

The question of who is more Christian a *serial polygamist* who marries and divorces more than five wives or a responsible polygamist who is committed and happily married to his two wives. From my opinion, serial polygamy encourages lack of commitment in marriages. Many will go into the marriages with the mind set that if the marriage does not work they will divorce and marry someone else. Wonder why the divorce rate in the USA has always been higher than most countries? I believe this is one of the reasons in my opinion. Examples of Christian prohibitions involving polygamous men include: denial of full membership in the church, no freedom to hold a church office (all polygamous United Methodist men have probationary membership in the church), forbidding polygamists to bring their children forth for baptism, and denying them the right to be accorded a full Christian burial ritual.

The theological and religious issues this author would focus on in the analysis of this case are related to the question of whether polygamy is wrong for all Christians. Are polygamous people less Christian and less valuable in the eyes of God? Why can polygamous people not be accorded the full membership rights of other Christians? The focus will be primarily on the theological and religious issues precipitated by polygamous marriages in the African context, and more specifically in the Shona context.

Most polygamous Christian converts were ordered to divorce all their second and subsequent wives, and to remain only with the first wife in order to participate fully in the life of the church. The coming of Christianity, in that respect, created many broken homes, with newly divorced and disenfranchised women and their children forming many new single parent homes. One could ask, what is more sinful—breaking up a home or letting someone remain polygamous, take care of his family, and raise all his children together with all his wives, and living within the dictates of Christian morals?

Muzorewa, a Shona theologian, sees the change taking place in matters of polygamy as more economically based, and of course, due to Christian influence on the Africans. He notes:

> Over a few decades, the African breadwinner began to feel that a large family was not an asset but a financial burden in a cash economy. This new attitude was a clear departure from the traditional

8. http://freesociologybooks.com/Sociology_Of_The_Family/09_Marriage_and_Other_Long-Term_Relationships.php.

view that cherished a large family. Thus, the institution of the family was immediately affected by the presence of Christianity as it was presented in Western garb. Polygamy was despised by the missionaries so much that African converts began to condemn it too. In fact, present-day missionaries like Aylward Shorter still insist that monogamy, and not polygamy, is the Christian ideal . . . But such a claim is classified as backward; worse still, it is labeled unchristian. [9]

The opposition to polygamy by missionaries was contrary to what Africans found in the Bible. When they read about the God-fearing men and famous leaders such as David, Solomon, and many others, it led to the breaking away and founding of so-called "Independent" or "Indigenous" churches in many countries on the continent. Why did the missionaries label polygamy a sin or wrong when great and faithful men such as David were not condemned for it? Even our forefather Abraham had two wives. The Old Testament is very close to the culture and religious beliefs of the African people; it therefore would support the African understanding of polygamy. The Western interpretation of Jesus' teaching about marriage is understood differently by many Africans.

There are many arguments posed regarding what Jesus meant in the gospels about marriage, especially Mark 10:6.[10] First, after Jesus quoted Genesis, he did not conclude by saying "therefore polygamy is a sin." Second, "the two shall become one flesh" is a phrase used even by Paul in reference to being united in sexual intimacy. Paul uses the same verse to warn man against prostitution. He says, "Do you not know that he who joins himself to a prostitute becomes one body with her? For it is written, 'The two shall become one flesh'" (1 Corinthians 6:16-17).[11] The phrase "the two shall become one flesh" has been used to justify monogamy. However, based on this biblical language, it does not translate to a simple mathematical problem (such as 1x1=1), as most Westerners interpret this verse. The "one flesh" is understood by most Africans (especially those who advocate polygamy) to mean the unity that takes place between a man and a woman in the intimate and sexual relationship.

A third argument, which could be posed, is that the verse Jesus quotes is out of the book of Genesis, at the beginning of creation. Interestingly,

9. Muzorewa, *The Origins*, p. 31-32.

10. Mark 10:6 *NRSV.*

11. 1 Cor. 6:16-17 *NRSV.*

after God said, "A man leaves his father and his mother and cleaves to his wife, and they become one flesh" (Genesis 2:24), many men, including Abraham, went ahead and married more than one wife, and were not rebuked, condemned, nor punished for it.[12] No prophet in the Bible preaches against polygamy as a sin. Why has it become a sin today for one to be polygamous? Is this not something adapted by the Western community to fit their cultural and social beliefs, and then baptized into Christianity? One could also say there were definitely polygamous people during Christ's time; instead, Jesus did not address the issue of polygamy but of marriage, as aforementioned.

Augsburger, a Western pastoral theologian, makes a good point when he notes:

> Since marriage and family are such varied human structures, any theology of marriage and the family must address a world of institutions . . . Polygamous societies in Africa and polyandrous societies in the Himalayas have their own ethics; extended families in the East have their own traditions and values . . . Such marriages are not loose multiple associations but stable parallel unions contracted under communal law, recognized as marriage by the society, entered with lifelong intentions, and providing a permanent context for offspring.[13]

This aforementioned point by Augsburger makes a good theological argument for any type of a marriage contract, as long as it is sanctioned, approved, and blessed by the society. Many times there is a tendency for people to judge others' behaviors and culture as out of norm, based on their own.

Polygamy has been said by many Christian churches, including the Shona United Methodist church, to be a sinful and inferior type of marriage. This is not biblically based, yet is the Western norm Christians are expected to follow. Augsburger again notes the following about what he thinks most Christians around the world have been lead to believe about polygamy:

1. Polygamy is unacceptable. It is simply a sin comparable to adultery.

2. Polygamy is an inferior form of marriage, not sinful where it is the custom but always unacceptable for Christians.

3. Polygamy is a form of marriage less satisfactory than monogamy and one that cannot do justice to the full spirit of Christian marriage but

---

12. Genesis 2:24, *NRSV.*

13. Augsburger, *Pastoral Counseling*, p. 206-207.

one can still put up with it, as they put up with slavery, dictatorial government, and much else. Existing multiple marriages can be accepted while monogamous change is invited.[14]

What the missionaries thought, and what the present Shona Christian church still thinks is best for the Shona Christian people, involves doing away with polygamy, breaking families, and causing significant psychological burdens to those Christians who found (or find themselves today) in such relationships.

To turn back to the Moyos' case, there is no biblical basis for arguing theologically against Mr. Moyo marrying a second wife. If Mr. Moyo was to be posed this question, the answer for Mr. Moyo would be to respond that monogamy is a religious belief which has been followed by the Christian church and which has been standardized into a Christian tradition. Within the Shona context, where Independent churches welcome polygamy, Mr. Moyo could also ask the question of whether those Independent Christian church members are less Christian for marrying more than one wife. Mr. Moyo could ask whether polygamy would make him less Christian, and if he remained strong in his Christian beliefs and practices, would God not accept him as God's child? Mr. Moyo needs to be openly told that Independent Christian church members are not less Christian, and that Mr. Moyo would not become less Christian, nor would God reject him for marrying a second wife. He is not planning to enter into a loose relationship with his new wife but a committed one. It is sanctioned by the culture and there seems to be nothing in Scripture arguably against polygamy.

Again, monogamy is a Christian practice established by the church for the purposes of order and conduct of its members, but polygamy is not biblically condemned as a sin. Augsburger argues that there is no clear biblical basis upon which to condemn polygamy. Bearing this point in mind, he raises the question: "Does the pastoral counselor facilitate persons acting in a more loving way within the accepted structures of the particular society? Or does effective pastoral care require a critique or rejection of some structure and the innovation of others?"[15] The answer to the questions raised by Augsburger about the work of the pastoral counselor (in this case, the pastoral caregiver) is to facilitate relationships within acceptable structures of the Shona society. In places where the structures are oppressive and un-

14. Ibid., p. 209.
15. Ibid., p. 194.

just, it is the work of the counselor or pastoral caregiver to critique or reject such oppressive structures. Augsburger goes further, making a strong point against undoing some family structures using a single theological and biblical model:

> Biblical and theological studies that seek to offer a single model for families violate the rich diversity present in two thousand years of biblical history. A theology of the family that seeks to deal inclusively with the biblical diversity is best expressed in paradoxical truth rather than in propositional truth.[16]

The Shona counselor or pastoral caregiver must struggle with theological justification versus the problems inherent in condemning polygamy theologically, even as the church adamantly promotes monogamy. Mr. Moyo must be informed of the consequences, and be made aware that his subsequent loss of the right to participate in Christian church sacraments is not based on the scriptures but rather is based on precepts designed to bolster and confirm the order of the church.

Dickson, an African theologian from Ghana, cites the case of a similar situation in Ghana, stating how polygamous man are not accorded full burial rights and their bodies are not allowed to enter the sanctuary. However, the ritual read at the graveside recognizes the deceased polygamous man as one who "had faithfully lived, and faithfully died."[17]

A similar circumstance would happen to Mr. Moyo if he chose to marry a second wife. Would Mr. Moyo's polygamy make him less Christian, and therefore warrant that his body, upon death, be denied interment from the church he helped create? The irony of the situation is that, before death, such people are allowed to enter the sanctuary, but as soon as they are dead their (dead) bodies cannot enter that same sanctuary.

SUGGESTED PASTORAL RESPONSE

There are at least two probable ways in which to approach this case. First the counselor or pastoral caregiver could provide intensive pastoral counseling or care, focused on the Moyos' maintaining their present marriage. This would mean working with Mrs. Moyo to change her cultural beliefs about sexual intercourse after menopause. One prospect would involve

---

16. Ibid., 210-211.
17. Dickson, *Theology in Africa*, p. 105.

bringing in a married Shona female nurse or perhaps a woman pastor, of the same age as Mrs. Moyo, who is still engaging in sexual intercourse with her husband, to counsel Mrs. Moyo. The reason Mrs. Moyo may have ignored the white male doctor's advice to continue sexual intimacy could be her suspicion that he was not well invested in women's issues, let alone Shona cultural matters. However, if Mrs. Moyo is firmly entrenched in this cultural belief, change to this belief system might not be an option. One has to observe great caution in trying to change cultural beliefs since this has significant and far reaching psychological effects if the beliefs are changed without a solid base upon which to fall back.

The suggested inclusion of a nurse is based on the nurse's knowledge of feminine physical, emotional, and medical issues. Impact would be maximized if the nurse was someone Mrs. Moyo knew, and was also a member of her own church. It could be someone Mrs. Moyo already trusted, who could talk to with her openly about her fears, and would at least facilitate valid and beneficial communication.

Mr. and Mrs. Moyo have been able to live for the past ten years without having sexual intercourse with each other. How have they been handling the situation of sexual abstinence? Are there other preferred alternatives, which might be satisfying for Mr. and Mrs. Moyo, in the absence of traditional sexual intercourse? It is also necessary to explore whether cultural beliefs are the sole reason for the cessation of sexual intercourse between the Mr. and Mrs. Moyo. How has the issue of Mrs. Moyo's health played a role in the relationship? The Moyos are an affluent family and can afford to hire help to do the housework and so forth, if her health is the key issue.

Another alternative (not available in the Shona urban church) is to honor the views of the Moyos. If polygamy becomes their primary alternative, then there are several areas to be addressed. As much as both Mr. and Mrs. Moyo appear to be leaning toward the second marriage, the counselor or pastoral caregiver has to explore the following with the Moyos: What is the main reason which brought them to the counselor or pastor for care? Is it Mrs. Moyo's failing health, or the impaired sexual relationship, or perhaps another reason—alone or in combination with the other possibilities? Have their current beliefs about polygamy changed compared to the past? If so, how—and why? In addition, how is the idea of a second marriage affecting their present marriage relationship? How do the Moyos foresee their relationship with other church members? Might other church members begin to treat Mr. Moyo as a weak Christian? Even though he is endeavoring to be open about his feelings, the reaction from most of the congregation could be to point fingers of blame rather than extend help and understanding to him.

In addition, how do the Moyos see their relationship with God, and with their extended family, in the event of a second marriage? What are some of the biblical stories with which they identify? How are these biblical stories construed or perhaps used positively by the Moyos? Are there issues of guilt as to how they perceive God's love, following the second marriage?

Issues surrounding the impact of the second marriage on the Moyos' primary relationship need to be considered. What is the role of a second wife? What about issues of jealousy? In the Shona culture, the first wife is treated as the "host" wife, which literally means she has more power than the second wife. The issue of power and control between the two women needs special attention. In short, what are the pros and cons of having a second wife in the marriage? A positive factor that is to the advantage of the Moyos in this situation is the fact that both know Rudo well and seem to respect and accept her.

In addition to the relationship between the two women, Mr. Moyo's relationship with both women must be explored. How is Mr. Moyo going to treat the two wives equally? If Rudo is going to provide that which Mrs. Moyo is currently unable to provide (sexual intercourse), what does that mean for Mrs. Moyo senior? Is Rudo's job mainly to provide sexual intimacy or does Mr. Moyo truly love her? These questions would help the Moyos explore ideas and feelings about their future relationship.

This aforementioned alternative is one, which helps those exploring the possibilities of a polygamous marriage to reach their decision, informed of the pros and cons. This option is not available in the contemporary urban Shona Christian context. The church's stance is: no polygamy, period. I am proposing that, with cases such as this one involving the Moyos, the Shona church could provide such an option.

The counselor or pastoral caregiver is according respect to cultural beliefs, and working from the counselee or careseeker's context, to include whatever new information may become available to the careseeker or counselee. Western knowledge (new information) is useful, but must not be forced on the careseeker or counselee, since this may counter the progress in counseling or pastoral care. The urban Shona Christians need a new pastoral care approach in helping counselees or parishioners resolve their crisis experiences.

CHAPTER SIX

Integrative Counseling and Pastoral Care
Implications for Theory and Practice

> "*The beauty of a quilt is in the merging of colors and the interweaving of the different cotton strings. The intertwining strings give the quilt strength and the different colors benefit from the blending reflection of each other, presenting beauty to the eye.*" *(Tapiwa Mucherera, PhD)*

> "*To the Jews I became as a Jew, in order to win Jews. To those under the law I became as one under the law (though not being myself under the law) that I might win those under the law*" *(1 Cor. 9:20).*

THIS BOOK HAS ARGUED that for counseling and pastoral care to be relevant in the contemporary urban Shona Christian context, counselors and/or pastoral caregivers serving in this context must be equipped with a pastoral theological and psychodynamic understanding of integrative consciousness. Integrative consciousness means that a counselor or pastoral caregiver must possess knowledge of, or easily comprehend, both African Shona and Western world-views, as well as the blending and integration of aspects of Shona and Western world-views in personal or religious identity formation and/or in providing counseling and care. The following case illustrates how a counselor or pastoral caregiver could easily blend western and traditional Shona practices into helping a woman faced with a crisis that had developed over her lifetime.

DESIRE FOR ANOTHER CHILD

Tsitsi is a married woman, who came to a pastor requesting prayers so she could conceive a child. The couple already had a ten-year-old together, and had been trying to have another child since the weaning of the first. Tsitsi related to her pastor the story of her growing up with both a mother and grandmother who believed she was supposed to be a nun. Tsitsi was told by the mother never to get married (the mother said she had seen a vision of Tsitsi as a nun) but to dedicate her life to Christ, become a nun, and be used as God's instrument. When she was growing up, the mother used to examine Tsitsi to make sure she was still a virgin. Tsitsi's mother died of a heart attack at the age of 40. At age 13, she went to live with her grandmother in another village. The grandmother was stricter with Tsitsi as pertaining to religion compared to the deceased mother.

The grandmother repeated the story of the vision told by the mother. In addition, she told Tsitsi since she was "a chosen one," to be a nun, and if she ever had any sexual intercourse with a man she would never be able to stand the pain. Any intercourse would be as if a man was drilling with a hot iron through her vagina. Sex was dirty, and if Tsitsi was ever to have sex it would be painful as a punishment for disobeying. Tsitsi personally did not want to be a nun but developed a fear of having any relationships with boys. Tsitsi also had a dream in which she was a nun, and in the dream a voice told her she was a chosen one to serve Christ.

After the deaths of both the mother and the grandmother, Tsitsi moved to live with one of her aunts in the city. The aunt allowed Tsitsi to do all the things that the mother and grandmother had forbidden. Tsitsi's aunt allowed her to wear trousers and go to birthday parties and the boyfriend whom she was seriously dating when she was 19 years old was allowed to take Tsitsi to the movies as long as they got back home by 8:00 p.m. Tsitsi was surprised by all this freedom but always felt guilty whenever she went out with her boyfriend. She did not tell her aunt about the story the mother and grandmother had told her about becoming a nun.

When Tsitsi was 21 years old, the boyfriend asked that they take a drive to the mountains. Both Tsitsi and the aunt agreed that she could go. While out in the mountains, just before getting back home, the boyfriend insisted that they have sex. Tsitsi refused, saying she was not ready. The boyfriend being physically big, easily overpowered Tsitsi and raped her. Tsitsi said she cried and screamed, but since they were in the car and in the middle of nowhere, she knew there was no one who could hear her. She was bleeding and terrified.

The boyfriend tried to comfort her after the act, but all she wanted was to go home. She reported, "It happened just the way grandmother and mother had told me." She felt as if someone was drilling a hot iron through her vagina. She said when the boyfriend was raping her, she could hear the voices of both the mother and the grandmother repeating how she had committed an unforgivable sin, that she was defiled, and that she would pay for it the rest of her life. When she arrived home, no one was there, and she went straight to her room and cried all night. When she tried to sleep, she would have a re-occurrence of her mother and grandmother's voices. She could not bear the pain. She kept a cold towel on her genitals that night to numb the pain. Tsitsi said she prayed that night like she had never before, asking God's forgiveness. She finally fell asleep for two hours and when she awoke she felt better, but was not herself most of that following day. The boyfriend came by to see her and she refused to go out of her room to see him.

After about a month Tsitsi found out she was pregnant. She told the boyfriend and the aunt, and she consented to getting married. Within six months the two got married. Tsitsi said their wedding night was another "horror night." It was a re-play of the day she was raped. The husband could not understand this, and Tsitsi could not gather enough courage to tell him her life story growing up with the mother and grandmother. She said every time for the past ten years, the only way the husband had sex with her was by forcing himself on her. Tsitsi said it is painful, but now she found out one way to deal with the pain was to leave her body and she could watch her husband having sex with her from above. She said she loves her husband, and wants another child, but just cannot bear the pain of having sex with her husband. Tsitsi said it is just like the grandmother said, "she would pay for the rest of her life," and she is now paying. She says she is even ashamed to see her husband naked. They never take baths together and the husband always forces himself on her in the dark. After saying all this, Tsitsi looked tired but there was a lot of relief from her face.

Tsitsi also told of how they had been to different doctors to be checked and that nothing came out of these visits. She mentioned to one of the doctors about the initial rape encounter with the husband, to which the doctor encouraged her to see a counselor, psychiatrist, or pastor.

THE SOCIO-CULTURAL ISSUES

The importance of examining the socio-cultural issues in this case is to aid a counselor or pastoral caregiver with an approach, which would be relevant in giving voice to Tsitsi and space to vent her pain. It helps the counselor or pastoral caregiver explore, at a cultural level, the degree to which Tsitsi might be comfortable exploring her issues as an individual without immediately involving the extended family system. The socio-cultural analysis also aids the counselor or pastoral caregiver in assessing how Tsitsi's cultural world-view affects her perspective on her interpersonal relations.

Tsitsi and her husband are an economically lower middle class family. The husband is familiar with both the African traditional religio-culture and Christianity. Given Tsitsi's relationship with her mother and grandmother, it can be easily assumed that she did not have as much exposure to African traditional religion and culture, but might have some familiarity with it. The couple appears to be comfortable operating in both cultures. They visited Western doctors who could not diagnose any medical reasons why Tsitsi failed to conceive a second time. The saving grace is that, one of the doctors encouraged her to see a counselor or pastor. Since she had been brought up by a religiously strict Catholic mother and grandmother, Tsitsi's issues are not directly related to Shona traditional religio-cultural practices and beliefs in her inability to have another child. However, the issues of reconciliation in her relationship with her deceased mother and grandmother are something both worlds (Christian and Traditional Shona) would deem necessary for her to undertake. Tsitsi needs some work to resolve her relationship with her deceased mother and grandmother whom she feels she disobeyed. This could be done with the help of a counselor or pastoral caregiver. She also has not disclosed to her husband the history of her upbringing, or the impact of the rape on their relationship.

ANXIETY, ITS SOURCES, AND PSYCHOLOGICAL ISSUES

One of the main tasks of a counselor or pastoral caregiver is to help Tsitsi become aware of the fact that much of her anxiety stems significantly from her sense of guilt about being married when she had been taught most of her life that she was supposed to have been a nun. She believes that her experience of pain during sexual intercourse with her husband is a result of disobeying her mother, grandmother, and God's desire. Tsitsi feels anxiety for having disobeyed God, and believes that God will never forgive her. She has prayed for all these years for another child, and she sees the fact that she has not been able to conceive as a sign from God that God hates her sin of disobedience. The experience of the initial rape itself put Tsitsi in a state of anxiety for all subsequent contact in which her husband initiates sexual intercourse with her. Tsitsi has to "make love" to someone who raped her, and now has to do this in "a loving marriage relationship" for the rest of her life.

In addition, a counselor or pastoral caregiver must work with Tsitsi on her feelings of anger toward God, the mother, the grandmother, and her husband. Tsitsi has anger against her husband mixed with her guilty feelings and is therefore unable to confront the husband about the rape. Questioning why she feels God is "punishing her" could reveal the source of her anger toward God. Tsitsi could be angry at her mother and grandmother for raising her the way they did, as well.

Psychologically, Tsitsi feels as though she is a misfit and rejected by God. She functions well in everyday life, but her marital relationship, and the guilt placed on her by her mother and grandmother, are emotionally and psychologically a constant burden. Tsitsi had lived, and continues to live, her mother and grandmother's prescription for her "contact." Due to the teachings from the mother and grandmother, in addition to the rape incident, Tsitsi has developed a poor self-image and a guilty conscience.

The problem of *vaginismus* is a major one for Tsitsi.[1] The explanation of vaginismus to Tsitsi, even though based on a Western perspective, will help relieve Tsitsi of some of her psychological burden and anxiety. Her understanding of vaginismus will help with the process of pursuing counseling, care and resolution. Tsitsi might gain additional insight from a female nurse who can explain vaginismus[2] to Tsitsi and discuss how the rape impacted her physically, psychologically, and in her marital relationship.

1. Carson, ed., *Abnormal Psychology*. These authors say about vaginismus: " . . . women who suffer from vaginismus also have arousal insufficiency, possibly as a result of conditional fears associated with a traumatic rape experience . . . " p. 416.

2. Perez, *"Gone,"* p.1. (In DSM-5, the spasm-based definition of vaginismus was dropped, and vaginismus was combined with dyspareunia, the other "sexual pain disorder," which resulted in *genito-pelvic* pain/penetration disorder . . . the new DSM-5 diagnosis of GPPPD reflects this spectrum conceptualization and allows for a diagnosis if the woman has recurrent and distressing difficulty with one (or more) of the following for at least 6 months: vaginal penetration during intercourse; marked vulvovaginal or pelvic pain during intercourse or attempted intercourse; marked fear or anxiety about the experience of vaginal or pelvic pain as related to vaginal penetration; marked tensing of the pelvic floor muscles during attempted vaginal penetration).

THEOLOGICAL OR RELIGIOUS ISSUES

A pastoral caregiver with an integrative consciousness must be willing to explore with Tsitsi her religious world-view and work with her, starting from what she understands. Tsitsi expressed that she believes spirits can prevent conception (African traditional religious belief); however, she does not believe that there is any spirit preventing her from having another child. Tsitsi knows there is nothing which was ritually placed on her in childhood, to prevent her from conceiving. On the other hand, in the process of seeking reconciliation for Tsitsi with her deceased mother and grandmother, there is a need to explore whether Tsitsi might also think the spirits of her angry deceased mother and grandmother might be responsible for her inability to conceive. Every time she tried to sleep during the night of the initial rape, she reports having heard her mother and grandmother's voices telling her she had sinned. As much as one might try to reduce this phenomenon as a psychological trauma, it is also closely tied to the African traditional belief that the spirit of a dead person (living dead) can still influence or communicate with the living.

Tsitsi does not believe that God will forgive her, and believes that God is punishing her—a false idea she picked up from the misguided Christianity of her mother and grandmother. Tsitsi also quoted the Christian teaching of honoring one's parents, adding that she had failed to do so. There are questions of disobedience and punishment from the Christian point of view. Coming from a Catholic background, Tsitsi needs absolution from someone in authority who is in a priestly or pastoral office. Reassuring her that she did nothing wrong in not becoming a nun, that she is not living in sin with her husband, and that she is not under any punishment from God will give Tsitsi a sense of peace, a positive self-image, and a new sense of self-esteem.

SUGGESTED PASTORAL RESPONSE

This is a case in which a pastor with an integrative consciousness can employ or utilize the Western approach to pastoral care while paying particular attention to the African traditional religious themes that may arise. There are many psychological issues that need to be addressed. Here the Western approach of first engaging individual pastoral care will be more plausible than the Shona traditional group or community oriented approach.

Tsitsi's individual experiences have shaped her life and can be approached from her unique and specific point of view. The issues with which she is dealing require addressing Tsitsi as an individual before involving others with her in pastoral care. Before Tsitsi can expose her experiences to others, she must confront them and deal with them in the presence of someone she trusts. She has never opened her life story to anyone other than the counselor or pastor. In short, Tsitsi needs to do the bulk of the work with a counselor or pastor before other people are introduced to the other general relational counseling and pastoral care issues. However, before the process of counseling or care is completed with a counselor or pastor, her husband and possibly the aunt will need to be introduced and involved. The husband has to hear Tsitsi's story, and there is a need for reconciliation between the two of them in terms of the issues of date rape. Her suffering stems from the fact that her husband raped her and continues to do so in the marriage.

A counselor or pastoral caregiver might also want to encourage Tsitsi to relate her life story to her aunt, so she can have another female hear her pain and receive reassurance of the fact that her pain is not imagined. As mentioned above, a female doctor or nurse can also help explain the vaginismus to her, and continue to work with Tsitsi on how to desensitize her body to that pain. The counselor or pastor has to bring to Tsitsi's awareness that she is depersonalizing while having sexual intercourse with her husband, and must be taught that this phenomenon is one way her mind is dealing with the pain emotionally, psychologically, and physically.

> Depersonalizing can be defined as a sense of being cut off or detached from oneself. The feeling may be experienced as viewing one's own mental processes or behavior, some patients feel as though they are in a dream. When a patient is repeatedly distressed by the episodes of depersonalization, and there is no other disorder that better accounts for the symptoms, you can diagnose depersonalization/de-realization disorder (DDD). [3]

A counselor or pastoral caregiver must work diligently to persuade Tsitsi that she did not sin against God by not becoming a nun. In addition, she needs to understand the source of the pain (vaginismus), which she experiences while having intercourse with her husband. In the final analysis, the question of prioritizing the issues of interpersonal relationships or estrangement (from God and others), brokenness, forgiveness,

---

3. Morrison, DSM-5 Made Easy, p. 237.

accountability, justice, and restitution need to be resolved before Tsitsi can feel whole again.

Having illustrated how a Western approach/knowledge can also benefit the African Shona context today, this concluding part of the book has two subsections focusing on the theory and practice of counseling and pastoral care in the urban Shona context. The first part addresses the implications for education and training of counselors and pastoral caregivers serving in the urban Shona context. The second section focuses on the implications for practice of counseling and care in this context.

IMPLICATIONS FOR EDUCATION AND TRAINING OF COUNSELORS AND PASTORAL CAREGIVERS

What are the implications for counseling education and training in pastoral methodological approach to counseling and pastoral care in the urban Shona context? I suggest the following five implications for the Shona context in counseling and pastoral methodological approach.

1. First and foremost, the church needs to create rituals pastors can be trained to use in serving in the contemporary urban Shona context. These are rituals, which integrate both traditional Shona religious rituals and Western Christian rituals and are intended to replace those currently in use. The integrative rituals then can be sanctioned by the church for use in the training of and utilization by the urban Shona counselors and pastoral caregivers.

   What this implies for counseling and pastoral care methods in the urban Shona context is similar to the proposal by Patton in pastoral theological method in pastoral care. He notes:

   > The second-order language of theology is distinguished by critique and comparison. It examines the essential religious meanings growing out of the first-order language and experience (. . . in story, hymn, or ritual express the way an individual or community affirms its relationship with God) and compares them with the beliefs of particular community of faith. In that process, theology further explicates and reinterprets the doctrines of the community in relation to ongoing religious experience of the first order.[4]

---

4. Patton, *Pastoral Care*, p. 237-238.

The urban Shona context needs Patton's type of approach. The currently used rituals and theology, operative in the urban Shona context, are first-order and need to be reinterpreted in order for them to be relevant. Most of the rituals and doctrines in place do not always address the issues of the urban Shona bi-religious experiences, so there is a need for critique and reinterpretation of these rituals.

In addition, curriculum for training counselors and pastoral caregivers needs to incorporate the use of the proposed new rituals. Raising the issues regarding the need for integration of rituals in the urban Shona context, and analyzing the old rituals, helps raise trainees' consciousness to the ways rituals are inadequate and sometimes non-liberating. As Patton says: "Awareness of the tension between oppression and liberation in the institutions and ideologies of the communities that shape human lives and of which one is a part . . . " is one of the goals of pastoral theology and care.[5]

2. The training and education of counselors and pastoral caregivers serving in the urban Shona context calls for counselors and caregivers to be conscientious about the need for methodological flexibility in those providing counseling and care. Sole use of Western methods in approaching counseling and care issues is inadequate since most Western theories of counseling and pastoral care are individualistic in approach and are sometimes contrary to the urban Shona context in which many people are still in flux within their individual or communal orientation. At the same time, employing traditional Shona approaches to counseling and pastoral care alone does not suffice, due to the influence of Christianity and Westernization. Hence, the need exists for a counseling and pastoral approach, which is flexible and takes into account the aspects, which influence the counselee and pastoral careseeker's world-view and values.

Van Beek, a Western pastoral counselor and theologian, notes the following about the importance of world-view:

> Worldview entails the way people judge the world around them, including what is beautiful or despicable, what is moral and wrong, what is wise and foolish, what our rights, as well as our responsibilities, are. The list goes on. But worldview also determines how people view themselves and the community of which they are a

---

5. Ibid., p. 241.

part. Conversely the family community, and society in which we belong to a large extent determine our worldview.[6]

Starting with what is known by the careseeker (in terms of world-view and religious and cultural values) helps in terms of establishing rapport, and creates common ground upon which the pastoral caregiver and careseeker can connect.

All the case studies presented indicated the need for flexibility in the method of the caregivers' approaches. Only Tsitsi's case could utilize much of the Western individual approach in pastoral care, yet it still requires integration of aspects from the traditional methods. The other three cases require an integration of methods, especially in the rituals.

The lack of communal interpersonal relationships for the upper middle class urban Shona calls for training of counselors and pastoral caregivers which can tap into the traditional approach in care (group or communal oriented care). This requires pastors to be trained and to acquire some expertise in reorganizing their congregations into support groups for those experiencing similar problems in personal or religious identity confusion. The same applies to counselors; they need to have skills to do effective group work. In this way the counselees or parishioners can share their stories with others, giving them a sense that they are not alone in their struggles.

3. A counselor or pastoral caregiver in the urban Shona context needs to be trained and educated in a method of analysis, which utilizes a critical consciousness. This is an ability to analyze situations beyond the presenting problem. It requires hermeneutical skills with which to analyze situations that are influenced by two cultures and two religious world-views, and to avoid naive value judgments, which can impede providing adequate care.

Since the urban Shona experiences conflict in religion and culture, it is also necessary that the counselor or pastoral caregiver be able to identify the particular sources of anxiety inasmuch as there might be more than one source of anxiety resulting from the tension within and between the cultures and religions. Identifying the sources of anxiety will in turn help identify the anxiety itself. The ability to detect a counselee or careseekers' experiences with cultural and

6. Van Beek, *Cross-Cultural Counseling*, p. 43-44.

religious dissonance, aids in assessing the anxiety and its sources. The goal is to help the counselees or careseekers learn to identify multiple world-views and manage their anxiety so it does not stifle their self-understanding.

4. The urban Shona counselors or pastoral caregivers need education and training which make them aware of the experiences of identity confusion within the urban upper middle class, resulting from colonization and the persistent influence of Western culture versus the influence of the traditional Shona cultures. A counselors or pastoral caregiver needs education and training that will help him/her point out factors (such as lack of communal support and economic pressures) which contribute toward personal identity confusion in the urban Shona society.

Cultural and religious dissonance creates identity confusion. The work of the counselor or pastoral caregiver is not to re-create a "traditional Shona identity" in the counselee or careseekers, but is rather to help minimize the level of anxiety resulting from the identity confusion. The counselor or pastoral caregiver may recommend the need for the counselee or careseeker to explore communal interpersonal relations as a way to correct his or her (counselee or careseeker's) identity confusion. van Beek also notes about individual identity:

> Knowing that identity does not develop on its own, we could say that identity is a plant that can flourish only in the soil of belonging. The idea of being able to "find oneself" by separating from the belonging group may be popular in contemporary North American society, but it may be largely a fallacy. How can we know who we are if we do not belong anywhere? [7]

This calls for a counselors or pastoral caregivers to be equipped through appropriate training in conscientizing (without being judgmental) or socializing those struggling with issues of personal identity who come seeking counseling or care. Furniss calls this task of pastoral care, "adult socialization":

> Pastoral care, understood sociologically, is a type of adult socialization. We often think of socialization only as the process by which children are changed from human animals to social beings. Yet learning and developing new skills are life long processes.

7. Ibid., p. 57.

Socialization is any structured social relationship for purposes of enhancing learning, coping, and developing new attitudes and perspectives . . . When pastoral care does a good job of helping careseekers understand their choices, it facilitates people's learning in a striking way.[8]

In this case, those struggling with personal and religious identity matters can be socialized by helping them understand their choices, in terms of personal and religious identity confusion issues.

5. The urban Shona context requires that counselors or pastors be trained or equipped with the ability to utilize relational pastoral theological methods of counseling and care. As stated in earlier chapters, relational pastoral theology is one which pays attention to individuals' narratives in connection to their communal interpersonal relationships with other individuals, God and creation. In the traditional Shona context, broken relationships cause much anxiety. The traditional world-view, condemned as heathen by some of the early missionaries, still influences the urban Shona people. Dismissing the Shona traditional religious world-view, or simply labeling traditional rituals as heathen or pagan practices, may overlook some of the issues of communal interpersonal relations, which might be a cause of breakdown in relations.

IMPLICATIONS FOR THE PRACTICE OF COUNSELING AND PASTORAL CARE

The practice of counseling and pastoral care in the urban Shona context, as already alluded to in the above section on training, requires that counselors and pastoral caregivers utilize a diversity of methods. This, therefore, requires flexibility in the modalities of providing counseling and care. In providing counseling and care in the urban Shona context, the counselor or pastoral caregiver must be attuned to the following five issues in order for care to be effective.

1. Narratives (stories) come naturally to most Africans. Even many of the upper middle class urban Shonas still use narratives to relate their problems to the caregiver. In some cases, the narratives may be

8. Furniss, *The Social Context*, p. 56.

presented in the form of a traditional fairytale, story, or sometimes using Shona proverbs or sayings. A counselor or pastoral caregiver has to probe to get beyond the surface meaning of these stories, or needs to be able to analyze the story, so as to understand what the counselee or careseeker derives from the story or proverb.

Directly connected to the narratives are Biblical stories with which counselees and careseekers identify. It is the work of the counselor or caregiver to explore how the counselee or careseeker is using these stories. Are the biblical stories being used for ill or for good? Are there ways in which to give positive meaning to the stories if they are being applied negatively in the counselee or careseeker's life?

2. The counselor or pastoral caregiver must be attuned to issues of communal interpersonal relations, or the lack of them, in the narratives. How are the counselee or careseeker's interpersonal relationships? Are the interpersonal relations, or lack thereof, the source and cause of the anxiety he/she might be experiencing? The analysis of the interpersonal relations involves the family, church, the community at large, God, and creation.

3. The counselors and pastoral caregivers must be attuned to both the cultural and the religious world-views of the counselee or careseeker. Has the counselee or careseeker assimilated many of the Western cultural values at the expense of the traditional Shona values? Does the counselee or careseeker feel culturally connected or lost? Is the counselee or careseeker feeling a sense of cultural dissonance or confusion? How is the culture, with which he or she does or does not identify, related to his/her identity confusion? Does the counselee or careseeker move between world-views (Western and traditional Shona), or feel caught between cultural world-views? Or is he or she grounded in one but borrows from the other?

The same analysis applied to the cultural world-view is important in addressing the religious world-view of the careseeker. Some counselees or careseekers move back and forth between the practices of Western Christianity and traditional Shona religion. Are the religious world-views and values mainly influenced by Western Christianity or by the traditional Shona religion and/or by both? The counselor or pastoral caregiver must be attuned to issues of bi-culturalism, bi-religiousness, or religious and cultural dissonance.

4. The counselor or pastoral caregiver must be attuned to the type of diagnosis given by the careseekers in any situation, especially where illness, death, or spirits are involved. Even after being given a Western diagnosis as to the cause of an illness, some upper middle class Shona Christians, as in the traditional Shona context, will still seek answers which involve traditional explanations for an illness. ma Mpolo notes:

> Etiology and diagnosis in the context of traditional African thought poses the following basic questions: "Who is the cause of my illness?" In this context, organically manifested symptoms are always the result of some external aggression. What is essentially sought in every illness, either somatic or emotional, is significant of such disease.
>
> Therefore, diagnosis was always synthetic in that it searched for, and announced, the cause of illness by providing its socio-psychological and spiritual significance. The consequences of such illness for the individual and the community were also indicated. [9]

The counselor or pastoral caregiver must be attuned to the world-view held by a counselee or careseeker and not too readily dismiss it as heathen. In other words, the counselor or caregiver must start from the counselee or careseeker's point of view and explore with him/her the meaning of the diagnosis and other alternative explanations.

5. The counselors or pastoral caregivers must be attuned to the counsel-ee/careseeker's sense of community of embeddedness or lack thereof. Is the counselee/careseeker's community of embeddedness based out of the church community, or in a community geared toward economic success, or within their extended family or their nuclear family? It is important to understand the counselee/careseeker's community of embeddedness because that community provides him/her with values, culture, and a sense of personal and religious identity. Furniss notes, regarding the value and function of one's reference group, which is similar to the community of embeddedness:

> The group whose definition of the situation constitutes a plausibil-ity structure for the person's worldview is called her or his *refer-ence group*. There are many possible reference groups available in the pluralistic society, and the one we choose as ours has major implications for our self identity.

9. ma Mpolo ed., *The Risk of Growth*, p. 9-10.

Pastoral care, as the exploration with careseekers of the possibility and implications of religious definitions of their situation, is crucially involved with the dynamics of reference group behavior and resulting social identity.[10]

Similar to what Furniss describes above about a reference group, the community of embeddedness provides the basis and values for one's religious and cultural context during times of crisis.

CONCLUSION

In conclusion, this book has argued that colonization, Western Christianity, and the continual influence of urbanization and Westernization have created a context of personal and religious identity confusion in the urban Shona context. As a result of this bi-culturalism and bi-religiousness, a different type of counselors or pastoral caregiver is needed to relevantly serve the needs of the urban Shona population, which is caught in the experience of religious and cultural dissonance. The lack of communal interpersonal relations creates identity confusion and anxiety for most Christians who live in the urban Shona context. As demonstrated in the analyses of these cases, it is this writer's argument and conclusion that those counselors/pastoral caregivers serving the contemporary urban Shona context need to possess an integrative consciousness, which includes an awareness of both the Shona and Western world-views and which integrates both.

I agree with Sullivan's theory, which postulates that what brings wholeness to one's personal identity, is right interpersonal relations. In the Shona context, right relationships involve right communal interpersonal relationships with others, including the Spirit World. Within the Shona context, acts such as murder bring disharmony to the whole community. In such circumstances, rituals and ceremonies play a central role in bringing about healing to the entire community.

Alienation and estrangement, whether in relationships or with regard to one's culture of embeddedness, create anxiety and the need for pastoral care for those living in this urban Shona context. When individuals' interpersonal relationships feel disjointed, and they develop a sense of alienation and estrangement from the community, from God, and from others, rituals

---

10. Furniss, *The Social Context*, p. 37.

are needed to recapture the necessary sense of wholeness, as demonstrated in the case studies.

Counseling and pastoral care processes in the Shona Christian churches need to integrate some of the Shona traditional religious methods or rituals in order to be appropriate. The church and some of the counseling approaches used today fail to initiate good credible progressive work in integrating some of the Shona traditional rituals which would minimize the anxiety arising from the bi-religiousness in which the urban Shona Christians find themselves. Finally, the counselor/pastoral caregiver in the urban Shona urban context must possess an integrative consciousness, a consciousness able to comprehend both the Western and the traditional Shona religion and culture and the integration thereof.

Bibliography

Acton, R. "A Colonial Childhood: Coming of Age in Rhodesia." *The North American Review* 272 (June 1990): 9-14.

Ajani-ya-Azibo, D. "Towards a Metatheory of the African Personality: Incorporating an African World View into Psychology." (Special Issue) *Journal of Black Psychology* 17 (Spr. 1991): 37-45.

Akbar, Na'im. *Chains and Images of Psychological Slavery.* New Jersey: New Mind Productions, 1984.

Akin-Ogundeji, O. "Some Thoughts on the Relevance of Applied Psychology in Africa." *International Journal of Psychology.* 22 (1987): 483-491.

Allport, Gordon. *Personality: A Psychological Interpretation.* New York: Henry Holt, 1937.

Anchin, J. C. & Kiesler, D. J. Eds. *Handbook of Interpersonal Psychotherapy.* New York, NY: Pergamon, 1982.

APA, Diagnostic and Statistical Manual of Mental Disorders (DSM-V) 5th ed, 2013.

Appiah, Anthony. *In My Father's House.* New York: Oxford Press, 1992.

Appiah-Kubi, K. "Religion and Healing in an African Community: the Akan of Ghana." in L. Sullivan ed. *Healing and Restoring.* (1989): 203-224.

————. *African Theology En Route.* N.Y.: Mayknoll Orbis Books, 1977.

Aschwanden, H. *Karanga Mythology: An Analysis of the Consciousness of the Karanga in Zimbabwe.* Gweru: Mambo, 1989.

Augsburger, D. W. *Pastoral Counseling Across Cultures.* Philadelphia: Westminster, 1986.

Banana, C. S. *Come and Share: An Introduction to Christian Theology.* Gweru, Zimbabwe: Mambo, 1991.

Baumeister, R. F., *Identity: Cultural Change and the Struggle for Self.* New York: Oxford University Press, 1986.

Beach, D. N. "The Initial Impact of Christianity on the Shona: The Protestants and the Southern Shona." In Dachs, A., (Ed.), *Christianity South of the Zambezi.* Gweru: Mambo, 1973.

Bediako, K. "The Roots of African Theology." *International Bulletin of Missionary Research* 13 (Apr. 1989): 58-62.

Bell, C. *Ritual Theory and Ritual Practice.* New York: Oxford University Press, 1992.

Berends, W. "African Traditional Healing Practices and the Christian Community." *Missiology* 21 (Jul. 1993): 275-288.

Berinyuu, A. A. *Towards Theory and Practice of Pastoral Counseling in Africa.* N.Y.: Peter Lang, 1989.

————. "Change, Ritual and Grief: Continuity and Discontinuity of Pastoral Theology in Ghana." *Journal of Pastoral Care* 46 (Sum 1992): 141-152.

Bhila, Hoyini. "Trade and the Early Missionaries in Southern Zambezi." M. F. C. Bourdilion, ed. *Christianity South of the Zambezi.* Vol 2. Gweru: Mambo. 1977.

Bodian, Stephan. "Is Psychotherapy a Waste of Time." in *The Yoga Journal*. (May/June, 1992): 50.

Boulaga, E. *Christianity Without Fetish*. N.Y.: Maryknoll, Orbis, 1984.

Bourdillon, M. F. C. *The Shona Peoples: An Ethnography of the Contemporary Shona With Special Reference to Their Religion*. Gweru: Mambo, 1991.

————. *Where are the Ancestors: Changing Culture in Zimbabwe*. Harare: University of Zimbabwe, 1993.

Boyd-Franklin, N., *Black Families in Therapy: A Multisystems Approach*. New York: The Guilford, 1989.

Brakensiek, L. S. "Cognitive Dissonance Theory." in Rodney J. Hunter, ed. *The Dictionary of Pastoral Care and Counseling*. Nashville: Abingdon. 1990. 188.

Brokenleg, Martin. Reclaiming Children and Youth. Fall 2012 volume 21, number 3.

Buecher, H. *Spirits and Power: An Analysis of Shona Cosmology*. Cape Town, South Africa. Oxford University Press, 1980.

Capps, D. *Pastoral Care: A Thematic Approach*. Philadelphia: The Westminister, 1979.

Carson, R., and J. N. Butcher, Coleman, J. (Eds.) *Abnormal Psychology*. Illinois: Scott Foresman and Co., 1988.

Carter, J. D. & Narramore, B. *The Intergration of Psychology and Theology: An Introduction*. Grand Rapids, MI: Academie Books, 1979.

Cesaire, Aime. *Discourse on Colonialism*. (English edition) New York: Monthly Review, 1972.

Chavhunduka, G. L. "Traditional Medicine and Christian Beliefs." M.F.C. Bourdilion, ed. *Christianity South of the Zambezi*. Vol 2. Gweru: Mambo. 1977.

Chidyausiku, P. *Broken Roots: A Biographical Narrative on the Culture of the Shona People in Zimbabwe*. Gweru: Mambo, 1984.

Chikara, F., and M. R. Manley. "Psychiatry in Zimbabwe." *Hospital and Community Psychiatry* 42 (Sept, 1991): 943-947.

Clinebell, H. *Basic Types of Pastoral Care and Counseling*. Nashville: Abingdon, 1984.

Couture, Pamela D. & Hunter, Rodney, eds. *Pastoral Care and the Social Conflict*. Nashville: Abingdon, 1995.

Csordaa, T. J. "Healthy and the Holy in African, and Afro-American Spirit Possession." *Social Science and Medicine* 24 (1987): 1—11.

Dachs, A. ed. "Traditional Religion in Shona Society." In *Christianity South of the Zambezi*, 11-24. Gweru: Mambo, 1973.

Dale, J. R., and D. I. Ben-Tovim. "Modern or Traditional? A study of Treatment Preference for Neuropsychiatric Disorders in Botswana." *British Journal of Psychiatry* 145 (1984): 187-192.

Daneel, M. L. "The Encounter Between Christianity and Traditional African Culture: Accommodation or Transformation?" *Theological Evangelica* 12.3 (Sept. 1989): 36-51.

————. *Old and New in Southern Shona Independent Churches Vol. 1*. The Hague: Mouton, 1971.

————. "The Growth and Significance of Shona Independent Churches." M. F. C. Bourdillon ed. *Christianity South of the Zambezi*. Vol. 2. Gweru: Mambo. 1977.

David, Sue and Sue Derald. Counseling the culturally diverse: theory and practice. New Jersey, John Wiley & Sons. 2013.

Deng, F. M. "Identity in Africa's Internal Conflicts." *American Behavioral Scientists*: 40 (Sept/Oct. 1996): 46-66.

Dershimer, R. A. *Counseling the Bereaved.* New York, NY: Pergamon, 1990.

Dickson, A. Mungazi. *Colonial Policy and Conflict in Zimbabwe: A Study of Cultures in Collision.* New York: Crane Russak, Taylor and Francis Group, 1992.

Dickson, K. A. *Theology in Africa.* London: Doarton, Longman and Todd, 1984.

———. "African Theology: Origin, Methodology and Content." *Journal of Religious Thought* 32 (Fall/Win. 1975): 34-45.

Dillard, J. *Multi-Cultural Counseling.* Chicago: Nelson Hall, 1983.

Dooyeweerd, Herman., *A New Critique of Theoretical Thought. Vol. IV.* Philadelphia: U.S.A. The Presbyterian and Reformed Publishing Co., 1969, 164.

Dubois, W. E. B. *The Souls of Black Folk.* New York: New American Library, 1969.

Dueck, A. "American Psychology in Cross-Cultural Context." *Journal of Psychology and Theology* 11 (1983): 172-180.

Edards, S. D. et. al., "Traditional Zulu Theories of Illness in Psychiatric Patients." *Journal of Social Pscychology:* (121) 1983: 213-221.

Ela, J. *African Cry.* Maryknoll, N.Y.: Orbis Books, 1986.

Erikson, E. H. *Identity and the Life Cycle.* New York: International University Press, 1959.

———. *Childhood and Society.* 2nd ed., New York: W. W. Norton and Company, 1963.

Eugene, U. "Notes on Methodology for an African Theology." *AFER* 19 (Je. 1977): 155-164.

Fanon, F. *The Wretched of the Earth.* New York: Grove, 1963.

———. *Black Skin White Masks.* New York: Grove Press, 1967.

———. "On National Culture." P. Williams, & L. Chrisman, ed. *Colonial Discourse and Post-colonial Theory: A Reader.* New York: Columbia University Press. 1994.

Forde, D. (Ed.) *African Worlds: Studies in the Cosmological Ideas and Social Values of African People.* Great Britain: Oxford University Press, 1991.

Fortes, M. and G. Dieterlen. *African Systems of Thought.* London: Oxford University Press, 1960.

Fortune, Marie. *Is Nothing Sacred?* San Francisco, Harper and Row. 1989.

Freire, P. *The Pedagogy of the Opressed.* Translated by Myra Bergman Ramos, New York: Continuum, 1983.

Freud, S. *The Problem of Anxiety.* Translated from the German by H. A. Bunker. Albany, NY: The Psychoanalytic Quarterly, 1936.

———. *New Introductory Lectures on Psychoanalysis.* Translated by J. H. Sprott. New York: W. W. Norton & Company, Inc., 1933.

———. *The Standard Edition of the Complete Psychological Works of Sigmund Freud.* (Pre-Psycho-Analytic Publications and Unpublished Drafts) Volume I (1886—1899). General Editorship of J. Strachey, Anna Freud. London: The Hogarth, 1966.

———. *A General Introduction to Psychoanalysis.* Authorized English Translation of the Revised Edition by J. Riviere and E. Jones. Garden City, NY: Garden City, 1935.

———. *An Outline of Psychoanalysis.* Authorized translation by James Strachey. New York: W. W. Norton & Company Inc., 1949.

Fry, P. *Spirits of Protest: Spirit-mediums and the Articulation of Consensus Among the Zezuru of Southern Rhodesia (Zimbabwe).* London, England: Cambridge University Press., 1976.

Furniss, G. M. *The Social Context of Pastoral Care: Defining the Life Situation.* Louisville, KY: Westminister John Knox, 1994.

Gelfand, M. *The Spiritual Beliefs of the Shona.* Gweru: Mambo, 1977.

———. *African Background: the Traditional Culture of the Shona-Speaking People.* Cape Town: Juta & Company Limited, 1965.

———. "Psychiatric Disorders as Recognized by the Shona." In *Magic, Faith and Healing: Studies in Primitive Psychiatry Today*, ed. A. Kiev New York: Free Press, 1974: 60-74.

———. "African Perspective on Pastoral Theology: A Contribution to the Quest for more Encompassing Models of Pastoral Care." *The Interdisciplinary Journal of Pastoral Studies* 112 (1993): 3-12.

———. *The Witchdoctor: Traditional Medicine Man of Rhodesia (Zimbabwe).* London: Harvill, 1964.

———. *Growing up in Shona Society: From Birth to Marriage.* Gweru, Zimbabwe: Mambo, 1971.

———. *The Genuine Shona: Survival Values of an African Culture.* Gweru: Mambo, 1973.

———. *The Shona Religion.* Gweru: Mambo, 1962.

Gilkes, C. T. "Colonialism and the Biblical Revolution in Africa." *Journal of Religious Thought* 41 (Fall/Win. 1985): 59-75.

Goba, B. "Toward a Quest for Christian Identity: a Third World Perspective." *Journal of Black Theology in South Africa* 2 (1988): 31-36.

Gombe, J. M., *Tsika dza VaShona.* Harare, Zimbabwe: The College Press (Pvt) Ltd., 1986.

Graham, L. K. "From Psyche to System." *Theology Today.* 49 (Oct 1992): 320-333.

———. *Care of Persons, Care of Worlds: A Psychosystems Approach to Pastoral Care and Counseling.* Nashville: Abingdon, 1992.

Hall, C. S. & Lindzey, G. *Theories of Personality.* New York, NY: John Wiley & Sons, Inc. 1957.

Hamutyinei, M. A., *Tsumo Namadimikira.* Gweru: Mambo, 1984.

Hannan, S J. *Standard Shona Dictionary.* (Rev. ed.) Gweru: Mambo, 1994.

Hastings, Adrian. *Christian Marriage in Africa.* London: SPCK. 1974.

Hatendi, R. P. "Shona Marriage and the Christian Churches." A. J. Dachs, ed., *Christianity South of the Zambezi.* Vol. 1. Gweru: Mambo. 1973.

Haviland, W A. *Cultural Anthropology.* (7th Ed.) Fort Worth, TX: Harcourt Brace College Publishers, 1993.

Heider, F. *The Psychology of Interpersonal Relations.* New York, NY: John Wiley & Sons, Inc., 1958.

Helgesson, A. *Church, State and People in Mozambique.* Uppsala: International Tryck AB., 1994.

Herrnstein J. R., & Murray, C. *The Bell Curve: Intelligence and Class Structure in American life.* New York: Free Press, 1994.

Hesselgrave, D. *Counseling Cross Culturally.* Grand Rapids: Baker House, 1984.

Hiltner, S. *Preface to Pastoral Theology: The Ministry and Theory of Shepherding.* Nashville: Abingdon, 1978.

Hunter, R., ed. *Dictionary of Pastoral Care and Counseling.* Nashville: Abingdon, 1992.

Idowu, B. J. *African Traditional Religion.* Maryknoll, N.Y.: Orbis Books, 1975.

Ikenga-Metuh, E. "Towards an African Theology of Man." *Africa Theological Journal* 11 (1982): 143-150.

Imasogie, Osadolor. *Guidelines for Christian Theology in Africa.* Achimota, Ghana: African Christian, 1983.

Jahn, J. *Muntu: An Outline of the New African Culture.* New York: Grove Press Inc, 1961.

Jennings, T. W. "Pastoral Theological Methodology." Rodney Hunter, ed., *Dictionary of Pastoral Care and Counseling.* Nashville: Abingdon. 1990.

Jones, A. "Psycholgical Functioning in Black Americans: A Conceptual Guide for Use in Psychotherapy." *Psychotherapy* 22 (1985): 363-369.

Jongh van Arkel, J. T. de. "Teaching Pastoral Care and Counseling in an African Context: A Problem of Contexual Relevancy." *Journal of Pastoral Care* 49 (Sum. 1995): 189-199.

Kabore, G. The Importance of Self-Image. *UNESCO Sources* 79 (May 1996): 14.

Kabweza, M. "Teaching Religion to the Shona." *AFER*: 23 (June. 1981): 138-141.

Kahari, G. P. "Missionary Influences in Shona Literature." In *Christianity South of the Zambezi*. ed. M. Bourdillon. 2 (1977): 87-102.

————. *The Search for Zimbabwean Identity*. Gweru: Mambo, 1980.

Kalilombe, P. "The Salvific Value of African Religions." *AFER* 21.3 (June 1979): 143-155.

Kapenzi, G. Z. *The Clash of Cultures: Christian Missionaries and the Shona of Rhodesia*. Washington, D.C.: University Press of America, Inc. 1979.

Kegan, Robert. *The Evolving Self: Problem and Process in Human Development*. Cambridge: MA, Harvard University Press, 1982.

Khoapa, B. A. *The African Personality*. Tokyo Japan: The United Nations University, 1980.

Kiev, A. *Magic, Faith, and Healing: Studies in Primitive Psychiatry*. New York: Free Press, 1966.

Kileff, Peggy and Clive. eds., *Shona Customs: Essays by African Writers*. Gweru: Mambo, 1992.

Lagerwerf, L.*Witchcraft,Sorcery, and Spirit Posession: Pastoral Responses in Africa*. Gweru: Mambo, 1992.

Lambo, T. Adeoye. "Mental Health of Man in Africa." *African Affairs*, vol 80, (319), April, 1981, 278.

Lartey, E. Y. *Pastoral Counseling in Intercultural Persepective*. New York: Peter Lang, 1987.

LeVine, R. A. "Patterns of Personality in Africa." *Ethos* 1 (1973): 123 -152.

Lloyd, P. C. *Africa in Social Change: Changing Traditional Societies in the Modern World*. Baltimore: Penguin Books Inc., 1967.

ma Mpolo, M. & Kalu, W. *The Risk of Growth: Counseling and Pastoral Theology in the African Context*. Nigeria: Daystar, 1985.

ma Mpolo, M. and D. Nwachuku. *Pastoral Care and Counseling in Africa Today*. New York: Peter Lang, 1991.

ma Mpolo, Masamba. "African Pastoral Care Movement." Rodney J. Hunter ed. *Dictionary of Pastoral Care and Counseling*. Nashville: Abingdon. 1990.

Mafuba, Chemist. "Children Risk Losing Mother Tongue, Culture." *The Herald*, Monday June 17, 1996: 22.

Magesa, L. *African Religion: The Moral Traditions of Abundant Life*. NY: Maryknoll, Orbis Books, 1997.

Maimela, S. S. "Salvation in African Traditional Religions." *Missionalia*. Vol 13, No. 2, (Aug, 1985): 67.

Makura, T. *Vatete Vachabvepi*. Gweru, Zimbabwe: Mambo, 1976.

Manyambiri, F. *Akafa Apenyu*. Gweru: Mambo, 1990.

Markman, H., Stanley, S., Blumberg S. Fighting for your Marriage: A Deluxe Revised Edition of the Classic Best-seller for Enhancing Marriage and Preventing Divorce, Jossey-Bass, 2010.

Marsella, A. J., and B.P. Pedersen, eds. *Cross Cultural Counseling and Psychotherapy*. New York: Pergamon, 1981.

Martey, E. *African Theology: Inculturation and Liberation*. N.Y.: Maryknoll, Orbis Books, 1993.

Martin, Denis-Constant. "Out of Africa! Should We be Done with Africanism." In *The Surreptitious Speech Presence Africaine and the Politics of Otherness 1947-1987*, ed. V.Y. Mudimbe. Chicago and London: University of Chicago Press, 1992.

Masasire, Albert. "Kinship and Marriage."

Mbiti John S. *African Religions & Philosophy*. 2nd Ed. Portsmouth, NH: Heinemann. 1997.

————. *Concepts of God in Africa*. New York, NY: Praeger, 1970.

————. *Introduction to African Religion*. 2nd Ed. England: Heinemann International Literature and Textbooks, 1991.

————. *Bible and Theology in African Christianity*. New York, NY: Oxford, 1986.

Mbuy, T. H. "The Need for Pastoral Care of Youth in Africa." *AFER* 38 (1996): 2-10.

McFadyen, A. I. *The Call to Personhood: A Christian Theory of the Individual in Social Relationships*. Cambridge, England: Cambridge University Press, 1990.

McIntosh, I. F. *Pastoral Care and Pastoral Theology*. Philadelphia, PA: Westminister, 1972.

Mead, M. *Growing up in New Guinea*. New York, NY. William Morrow & Co., 1953.

Mead, G. H. *Mind, Self and Society*. Chicago: University of Chicago, 1934.

————. *The Individual and the Social Self*. Edited with an Introduction by D. L. Miller. Chicago, IL: The University of Chicago Press, 1982.

Memmi, Albert. *The Colonizer and the Colonized*. Boston: Beacon, 1991.

Merwe van der, W. J. *The Shona Idea of God*. Fort Victoria (now, Masvingo): Morganister Mission, 1957.

Metuh, D. E. I. *God and Man in African Religion: A Case Study of the Igbo of Nigeria*. London, England: Geoffrey Chapman, 1981.

Meyers, L. Counseling Today (ACA) Vol 59, Num 7, Feb, 2017, p.27

Mitchell, L. L. *The Meaning of Ritual*. Connecticut: Morehouse-Barlow, 1988.

Morrison, J., DSM-5 made easy: a clinician's guide, Guilford, New York, 2014, 237.

Moyo, A. *Zimbabwe: the Risk of Incarnation*. Geneva: W. W. W., 1996.

Mpofu, E. "Counsellor Role Perceptions and Preferences of Zimbabwe Teachers of a Shona Cultural Background." *Counselling Psychology Quarterly* 7 (1994): 311-326

————. "Exploring the Self-Concept in an African Culture." *Journal of GeneticPsychology* 155 (Sept, 1994): 341-354

Mucherera, Tapiwa. N. *Contextualization of Pastoral Care and Counseling: Reclaiming Shona Indigenous Healing Methods*. M.A. Thesis, Denver, Iliff School of Theology, 1994.

————. "A Historical Perspective to Pastoral Care and Counseling in the United Methodist Church in Zimbabwe Context 1890 to Present." Old Mutare Mission Center, Aug, 1997, (unpublished paper).

————. Meet me at the Palaver: A Holistic Approach to Narrative Pastoral Counseling in a Post-Colonial Context Battling Poverty and HIV/AIDS, Eugene Oregon, Cascade, 2010.

Mulemfo, M. M. "Palaver as a Dimension of Communal Solidarity in Zaire: A Missiological Study on Transgression and Reconciliation." *Missionalia* 24 (Aug, 1996):129-147.

Mullahy, P. & Melinek, M. *Interpersonal Psychiatry*. New York: SP Medical & Scientific Books, 1983.

Muller, J. "African Contextual Pastoral Theology." *Scriptura* 39 (1991): 77-88.

Mungadze, J. J. "A Descriptive Study of a Native African Mental Health Problem Known in Zimbabwe as *Zvirwere Zvechivanhu.*" *Disseration Abstracts Internation* 51 (Mar, 1991): 4272.

Mungazi, Dickson A. *The Mind of Black Africa.* London: Praeger, 1996.

———. *Colonial Policy and Conflict in Zimbabwe: A Study of Cultures in Collision, 1890-1979.* New York: Crane Russak, Taylor and Francis Group, 1992.

Murphree, M. W. *Christianity and the Shona.* London: Atholone, 1969.

Musopole, A. C. *Being Human in Africa.* New York, NY: Peter Lang Publishing Inc., 1994.

Mutswairo, S. ed., *Introduction to the Shona Culture.* Kadoma: Juta Zimbabwe Pvt. Ltd., 1996.

Muzorewa, G. H. "A Definition of a Future African Theology." *African Theological Journal* 19 (1990): 168-179.

———. *The Origins and Development of African Theology.* Maryknoll, N.Y.: Orbis Books, 1985.

Mwikamba, C. M. "A search for an African Identity." *AFER -African Ecclesial Review.* (Vol 31, February, 1989): 92.

Myers-James, L., and D. E. Montgomery. "The Development and Validation of an Instrument to Assess an Optimal Afrocentric Worldview." *Journal of Black Psychology* 17 (1990): 37-54.

Namboze, J. L. "Health and Culture in an African Society." *Social Science and Medicine* 17(1983): 2041-2043.

Nandi, Ashis. *The Inimate Enemy: Loss and Recovery of Self Under Colonialism.* Oxford: Oxford University, 1983.

Ngara, E. "Language Influence and Culture: Comments on the Impact of English on Shona." *Diogenes* 161 (1993): 27-34.

Niebuhr, H. R. *Christ and Culture.* New York: Harper & Row, 1956.

Nkurunziza, D. R. K. *Bantu Philosophy of Life in the Light of the Christian Theology.* Frankfurt am Main, Bern, New York: Peter Lang, 1989.

Oduyoye, M. A. *Hearing and Knowing: Theological Reflections on Christianity in Africa.* Maryknoll, N.Y.: Orbis Books, 1986.

———. "The Value of African Religious Beliefs and Practices for Christian Theology." K. Appiah-Kubi and S. Torres, eds. *African Theology En Route.* New York: Maryknoll, Orbis Books. 1979.

Ogbonnaya, A. O. *On Communitarian Divinity: An African Interpretation of the Trinity.* New York, NY: Paragon House, 1994.

Okorqcha, C. C. *The Meaning of Religious Conversion in Africa: The Case of the Igbo of Nigeria.* Aldershot: Avebury, 1987.

Okpewho, I. *Myth in Africa: A Study of its Aesthetic and Cultural Relevance.*Cambridge: Cambridge University Press, 1982.

Olupona, J. K. *African Traditional Religion in Contemporary Society.* New York: Paragon House, 1991.

Partain, J. "Christians and Their Ancestors: A Dilemma of African Theology." *Christian Century* 103 (1986): 1066-1069.

Patel, V. "Spiritual Distress: An Indigenous Model of Nonpsychotic Mental Illness in Primary Care in Harare, Zimbabwe." *Acta Psychiatrica Scandinavica* 92 (Aug. 1995):103-107.

Patterson P. R. ed. *The Book of Discipline of the United Methodist Church: Africa Central Conference Edition.* Nashville: United Methodist, 1990.

Pattison, S. *A Critique of Pastoral Care*. London, England: SCM Press Ltd., 1988.

Patton, J. *Pastoral Care in Context: An Introduction to Pastoral Care*. Louisville, KY: Westminister/ John Knox, 1993.

Paul, Richard and Linda Elder. How to Study and Learn a discipline using critical thinking concepts and tools. Foundation for Critical Thinking, 2011.

Peaden, W. R. *Missionary Attitudes to Shona Culture 1890-1923*. Salisbury (Harare): The Central Africa Historical Association, 1970.

Pedersen, P. B, et al., eds., *Counseling Across Cultures*. (3rd ed). Honolulu: University of Hawaii Press, 1989.

Perez S., and Binik Y. M., Vaginimus: "Gone" But Not Forgotten. Psychiatric Times, July 29, 2016.

Perrin-Jassy, Marie-France. *Basic Community in the African Churches*. Translated by Sister Jeanne Marie Lyons. Maryknolls, NY: Orbis Books, 1973.

Phiri, Millie. "Much has to be Done to Save our Culture." *The Sunday Mail* (August, 25, 1996). C1.

Pobee, J. S. *Towards an African Theology*. Nashville: Abingdon, 1979.

Presler, T. "Missionary Anglicanism Meets an African Religion: A Retrospect of the Centenary of Bishop Knight-Bruce's Entry into Zimbabwe." *Journal of The Southern African Missiological Society* 17.3 (Nov. 1989): 162-175.

Preston, H. *Tsika Dzakanaka*. Gweru: Catholic Mission, 1963.

Radcliffe-Brown, A. R. "Taboo," in William A. Lessa and Evon Z. Vogt, eds. *Reader in Comparative Religion: An Anthroplogical Approach* New York: Harper and Row, 1972.

Radin, P. ed. *African Folktales*. New York: Schocken Books, 1983.

Ranger, T. O., and I. N. Kimamba, eds. *The Historical Study of African Religon*. Los Angeles: University of California Press, 1974.

Rasmussen, L L. *Earth Community Earth Ethics*. Maryknoll, NY: Orbis Books, 1996.

Reagan, C. E. "The Self as Another." *Philosophy Today* 37 (Spr, 1993): 3-20.

Reynolds, P. *Traditional Healers and Childhood in Zimbabwe*. Athens, Ohio: Ohio University Press, 1996.

Roland, A. *In Search of Self in India and Japan: Towards a Cross-Cultural Psychology*. Princeton: Princeton University Press, 1989.

Romme, M.A. J. "Social Psychiatry in Zimbabwe or the Interplay of Culture and Psychosocial Disorders." *International Journal of Social Psychiatry* 33 (Win, 1987): 263-269.

—. "Culture and Psychosocial Disorder in Zimbabwe," In *Clinical Psychology in Africa (South of the Sahara), the Caribbean and Afro-Latin America: A Textbook for Universities and Paramedical Schools*, eds. K. Peltzer and P. O. Ebigbo. Enugu, Nigeria: S. Asekome & Co., 1989

Ruch, E. A. "African Christianity and African Theology." Ministry 11 (1971):116-120.

Ruether, R. R. *Gaia & God: An Ecofeminist Theology of Earth Healing*. New York, NY: Harper Collins, 1992.

Russell, C. A. *The Earth, Humanity and God: The Templeton Lectures Cambridge*. London, England: UCL, 1994.

Safransky, Sy. "Psychotherapy," *The Yoga Journal* (May/June, 1992): 52-53.

Samkange, S. & Samkange, T. M. *Hunhuism or Ubuntuism: A Zimbabwean Indigenous Political Philosophy*. Salisbury (Harare), Zimbabwe: Graham, 1980.

Sarpong, P. K. B. "Everyday Spirituality in Africa." Ecumenical Review, 38 (Jan, 1986): 4-11.

Schuerkens, U. "The African: an Image Created by the Occident Colonization." *Interculture* (English Edition) 25 (Sum, 1992): 15-25.

Schultz, D. P. & Schultz, S. E. *A History of Modern Psychology*. 4th Ed. San Diego: Hatcourt Brace Jovanovich, 1987.

Setiloane, G. M. *African Theology: An Introduction*. Johanesburg, South Africa: Skotaville, 1986.

———. "Where are we in African Theology?" *African Theological Journal* 8 (1979): 7-14.

Shorter, A. *African Culture and the Christian Church*. London: Geoffrey Chapman, 1973.

———. "Urbanization: Today's Missionary Reality in Africa." *AFER* 32.5 (Oct. 1990): 290-300.

Shohat, Ella. "Notes on the "Post-Colonial." in *Social Text* Vol. 31/32, (1992), 101.

Shropshire, W. T. *The Church and the Primitive Peoples*. London: Macmillian, 1938.

Sindima, H. "Community of Life: Western Corruption of African Worldview." *Ecumenical Review* 41 (Oct. 1989): 537-551.

Smith, Archie. *Navigating the Deep River: Spirituality in African-American Families*. Ohio: United Church, 1997.

Some, M. P. *The Healing Wisdom of Africa: Finding Life Purpose Through Nature, Ritual and Community* New York: Penguin Putnam, 1998.

Spiegel, Y. *The Grief Process:Anaylsis and Counseling*.Nashville: Abingdon, 1977.

Spielberger, C. D., Diaz-Guerrero, R. (eds.) *Cross-Cultural Anxiety Vol 3,* Washington, DC: Harper & Row, 1986.

Ssempija, S. "Needed African Pastoral Psychotherapy." *AFER* 32.3 (June 1990): 150-156.

Stone, H. W. "Sojourn in South Africa: Pastoral Care as a Community Endeavor." *Journal of Pastoral Care* 50 (Sum, 1996): 207-213.

———. *Theological Context for Pastoral Caregiving: Word in Deed*. New York, NY: The Haworth Pastoral, 1996.

Stricker, G. ed. *Toward Ethnic Diversification in Psychology Education and Training*. Washington D.C.: American Pyschological Association, 1990.

Sue, D. W. & Sue, D. *Counseling the Cultural Different: Theory & Practice*. (6th Ed.) New York, NY: John Wiley & Sons. Inc., 2013.

Sullivan, H. S. *Personal Psychopathology*. New York: W. W. Norton & Co., 1947.

———. *Concepts of Modern Psychiatry*. New York: W. W. Norton & Co., 1953.

———. *Clinical Studies in Psychiatry*. New York: W.W. Norton & Co., 1956.

———. *Interpersonal Theory of Psychiatry*. New York: W. W. Norton & Co., 1953.

Tessier, R., ed. "Young People in African Towns: Their Pastoral Care." *Missionalia* 13 (Apr: 1985): 45.

Turnbull, C. M. *The Lonely African*. Garden City, N.Y.: Doubleday & Co. Inc., 1962.

van Beek, A. M. *Cross-Cultural Counseling*. Minneapolis, MN: Fortress, 1996.

wa Thiongo, N., *Decolonizing the Mind: The Politics of Language in African* Harare: Zimbabwe (reprint), 1994

Wan-Tatah, V. "In Search of a Relevant African Theology Today." In *Footprints: Theological Essays on Church in Cameroon*. ed. Nyansakao ni Nku, Yauonda, (1992):19-45

Waruta, D. W. ed. *Caring and Sharing: Pastoral Counselling in the African Perspective*. Nairobi Kenya: Act Print Limited, 1995.

Watkins, D., and E. Mpofu. "Some Zimbabwean Evidence of the Internal Structure of the Self Description Questionnaire—1." *Educational and Psychological Measurement* 54 (Win 1994): 967-972.

BIBLIOGRAPHY

Wehrly, B. *Pathways to Multicultural Counseling Competence: A Developmental Journey.* Pacific Grove, CA: Brooks/Cole, 1995.

Weiss, R. S. *Loneliness: The Experience of Emotional and Social Isolation.* Massachusetts, England: The MIT, 1973.

Wessels, W. H. "The Traditional Healer and Psychiatry." *Australian and New-Zealand Journal of Psychiatry* 19 (1985): 283-286.

Whidborne, V. A. "Africanisation of Christianity in Zimbabwe." *Religion in Southern Africa* 4 (Jan, 1983): 31-50.

Wicks, R., and Estadt, B.E. eds. *Pastoral Counseling in the Global Church: Voices From the Field.* N.Y.: Maryknoll, Orbis Book, 1993.

Wideman, J. E. *Reclaiming the African Personality.* London, England: Susquehanna University Press, 1995.

Wilson, D. J., and S. Lavelle. "Loneliness and General Psychological Distress Among Zimbabwean Students." *Journal of Social Psychology:* 130 (Apr. 1990): 273-275.

Williams P., & Chrisman, L. *Colonial Discourse and Post-colonial Theory: A Reader.* New York: Columbia University Press, 1994.

Willowghby, W C. *The Soul of The Bantu.* Garden City, NY: Doubleday, Doran & Co. Inc., 1928.

Wimberly, E. P. *Using Scripture in Pastoral Counseling.* Nashville: Abingdon, 1994.

———. *Recalling Our Own Stories: Spiritual Renewal for Religious Care-givers.* San Francisco, CA: Jossey-Bass, 1997.

———. *Counseling African American Marriage and Families.* Louisville, K.Y.: Westminster John Knox, 1997.

———. *African American Pastoral Care.* Nashville, TN: Abingdon, 1992.

———. *Pastoral Couneling and Spiritual Values: A Black Point of View.* Nashville. TN.: Abingdon, 1982.

Wiredu, K., and K. Gyekye, eds. *Person and Community.* Washington, D.C.: Cultural Heritage and Contemporary Change Series, Africa, Vol II, 1992.

Wright, Norman. *Before You Say I do: A marriage preparation manual for couples.* Eugene Oregon, Harvest House. 1997.

Wulff, D. M. *Psychology of Religion: Classic and Contemporary Views.* New York, NY: John Wiley & Sons, 1991.

Young, R J. C. *Colonial Desire.* London: Routledge, 1995.

Zvobgo, C. J. M. *A History of Christian Missions in Zimbabwe, 1890—1939.* Gweru, Zimbabwe: Mambo, 1996.

———. "Shona and Ndebele Responses to Christianity in Southern Rhodesia, 1897-1914." *Journal of Religion in Africa/Religion en Afrique* 8 (1976): 41-51.

———. "The Influence of the Wesleyan Methodist Missions in Southern Rhodesia 1891-1923." J. A. Dachs, ed. *Christianity South of the Zambezi.* Vol. 1. Gweru: Mambo. 1973.